Highrise Building and Urban Design

Highrise Building and Urban Design

Hans Aregger and Otto Glaus

Frederick A. Praeger, Publishers
New York · Washington

Photographenverzeichnis
List of photographers
Liste des photographes

Ulfert Beckert, Frankfurt am Main 123
Walter Binder, Zürich 133
Brecht-Einzig, London 105

Orlando R. Cabanban, Oak Park, Ill. 89
Casali, Mailand 109, 175
Sala Dino, Mailand 111
Jane Doggett & Malcolm Smith, New Canaan, Conn. 81
Max Dupain, Sydney 99
Roland Feuersänger, Zürich 93
Jean Pierre Flury, Lausanne 145
Marcel Gautherot, Rio de Janeiro 95
Greater London Council, Photographic
Unit Department of Architecture, London 143
Peter Grünert, Zürich 181
Chuji Hirayama, Tokio 101
L. Jimenez, Madrid 113
Phokion Karas, Melrose, Mass. 87
Helmut Kloth, Gelsenkirchen 125
Baltazar Korab, Birmingham, Mich. 85
Fritz Maurer, Zürich 129
Panda Associates Photography and Art Services, Toronto 97
Fernand Perret, La Chaux-de-Fonds 159
Pius Rast, St. Gallen 131
Inge und Arved von der Ropp, Rodenkirchen, Köln 167
Franz Scheper, Bremen 119
Momino Schiess, St. Gallen 183
Malcolm Smith, New Canaan, Conn. 91
Ezra Stoller, Mamaroneck, New York 79
Strüwing, Kopenhagen 117
Hans-Guenther Suderow, Hamburg 121
J. A. Vrijhor, Rotterdam 147
Kurt Wyss, Basel 163

Books that Matter

Published in the United States of America in 1967
by Frederick A. Praeger, Inc., Publishers
111 Fourth Avenue, New York, N.Y. 10003

© in Zurich 1967 by Verlag für Architektur (Artemis), Zurich, Switzerland
Library of Congress Catalog Card Number: 67–18826
Translated from the German by Maria Kroll, London
Traduction française: André Chappex, Zurich
Printed in Switzerland

Contents

The Highrise Building —
Symbol of Our Time

Hans Aregger

Illustrations by Otto Glaus

Introduction

Originally, huts were made of dung, clay, wood or other handy, natural building materials. These simple dwellings offered protection from the world, the weather and the enemy outside. They represented the refuge that each species builds for the preservation of its kind. This primeval achievement on the very threshold of civilization forms the basis of architecture. From there, architecture set out with man on a long, arduous road of development. For a long time, it was the yardstick against which civilizations could be compared. But architecture was not confined to civilizing achievement alone. Early in time, it grew to be a basic cultural force. It would be idle to speculate when and where this significant point was reached. It occurred wherever buildings, transcending their purely utilitarian purpose, expressed the creative and spiritual aspirations of any group of men.

The important position held by architecture in any given cultural environment is due to this twofold significance. Unlike the other arts, architecture is always concerned with the utilitarian; but unlike other achievements of civilization, it always forms part of ideological and artistic development. This holds true not only for buildings of cultural significance, but for ordinary buildings as well.

Of course, not every building represents a cultural achievement in itself. But as it contains definite proportions of shape and size, it is, whether by intention or not, part of a distinct cultural pattern, far more so than even its creators may have realized.

Architecture's importance in the cultural environment and the durability of its products ensure it a constant audience.

Of course, museums and libraries are filled with works of art and intellect that have endured for hundreds of years, but it is peculiar to architecture that each and every architectural work worthy of the name tends to outlast its creator. Even the rural architect, building a simple farmhouse, may easily be producing a house which will survive the next century or two. The little man, having saved up for his modest home, tends to see it filled with grand- and great-grandchildren.

Whenever the buildings of long-established districts are catalogued by age, the number of old and ancient ones is surprising. Usually a district's character is determined by its old buildings and not by those constructed by the contemporary generation. Present-day conditions may of course effect changes in this respect, but that will not minimize the significance of architecture's permanent value.

Naturally, architectural work, work that endures, is approached more seriously than what may be here today and gone tomorrow. The architect designing the house, the owner who has commissioned it, the builder who is to work on it, all form a team and bring to the task a certain humility and a feeling of responsibility beyond the limits of their own sphere. The ceremonial mounting of a wreathed pole when the roofbeam is in position may be symbolic of this state of mind, the visible sign of dedication and celebration. Not only architects, owners and craftsmen are involved in new buildings, but neighbours, relations and friends and anyone else who happens to come along, attracted as if by magic to a house in the making. Wherever deviations of form or proportion are recognized, there follow heated discussions concerning the beauty and character of such innovations. The functional aspect is hardly ever mentioned, but much is heard about the aesthetic content, because at the back of man's mind lurks the fear that the building might not stand the test of time.

Not surprisingly, public buildings meet with even greater interest. This is the field where building tradition has found the continuity which transformed it into an art, into architecture. From ancient times, lords spiritual and temporal have endeavoured to manifest their power and magnificence by monumental building.

'The Free Cities build mightly cathedrals to satisfy above all their municipal pride and also to surpass their neighbours.' (Jakob Burckhardt, *Die Kunst der Renaissance in Italien*.)

Indeed, cathedrals were constructed with a particular feeling for their permanence. Evidence of this are the plans which generally stretch over several generations. Men who assign the completion of a building to later generations do indeed build for the future.

Stronger even than public reaction to public buildings is the interest excited by private buildings which, because of their proportion, prominent siting or unfamiliar shape, attract the attention. Arguments are likely to be all the more heated as such buildings, although private property, assume all the attributes of public buildings. This used to apply, and still does apply, to the highrise building.

The attitude towards buildings has undergone an unmistakable change in our day and age. The volume of houses in production, their frequent uniformity, the relatively short building time and the increase of industrial fabrication all make for utilitarian buildings, at least where domestic and commercial types are concerned. Le Corbusier, recommending the huge multi-family blocks of our day as 'machines for living in', makes this more than plain. Less respect for buildings also puts their permanence in question. In an age when anything and everything is seen from the commercial point of view, buildings too are likely to be regarded primarily from the economic angle. And in an economy built increasingly on turn-over and obsolescence, the notion of permanent goods does not easily gain acceptance.

So modern buildings become increasingly anonymous products, built by anonymous builders and designed by anonymous architects. Even the custom of naming a new house, endowing it, so to speak, with some personality, has become obsolete. Houses today are numbered.

However, two architectural forms have managed to escape from the otherwise growing apathy displayed towards activity in the building world. These are flat-roofed and highrise buildings. It may seem arbitrary to mention these two phenomena in the same breath. But different though they may be in character, they have this in common: each offers a refuge to architecture. 'The flat-roof is more than a mere constructional innovation, it is proof of an architectural achievement, which states the ideological and artistic values of the present in terms of individual one-family houses' (Wright). Highrise building, in the place of representative public buildings, offers one of the rare opportunities for truly expressive architecture.

Architecture's break-away from the forms employed by mass building could not remain unnoticed. Both flat-roof and highrise building, each in its day, attracted immediate public interest. Opposed and defended, welcomed and damned in turn, each had to stand its ground in the face of a fierce barrage of criticism.

Without appreciating the civilizing and cultural background of architecture or considering its significance and position in society, the arguments surrounding highrise buildings, especially residential highrise buildings, would be hard to understand. In contrast to the production of standard housing, which is accepted in much the same way as the manufacture of boots, and unlike the rare cases when a public building still evokes some criticism, highrise buildings clearly touch a sensitive spot in human nature. The arguments, as a result, remain still extremely controversial.

Yet one wonders, even today, whether highrise building, especially the residential type, will remain the architectural exception, or whether it will quietly merge into the general pattern of standard housing.

Highrise building is accepted

After a controversial beginning and a period of reluctant toleration, Europe seems to have accepted highrise building. Objections on aesthetic grounds, warning of its disruptive effect on established townscapes, made no impression. Sociological arguments denouncing it as an undesirable medium for accelerated mass-housing did not prevent its popularity. Nor was much attention paid to the criticism that highrise building was simply not suitable for the housing of large families. Yet these arguments were justified and deserved a hearing.

They were not concealed from the public. Columns in the daily press were dedicated to them. Objections were voiced not only by laymen but by sociologists, planners, architects and urban designers. None, evidently, prevailed against the enthusiasm of the form's supporters. It may be noted that times of rapid technological advance favour experimentation.

For all the eagerness with which the champions of modern architecture supported highrise building (mainly for reasons of

11

city planning
or
Chance

town-planning, as will be shown later), they had qualms when highrise apartment blocks began to mushroom up after the initial resistance had been overcome.

'Massing huge numbers of people in single edifices provided architect-visionaries with an opportunity to treat town-planning as a large-scale, three-dimensional exercise in landscaping. Planning no longer concerned streets and houses but involved mountain-like structures to accommodate thousands of people, as exemplified by Le Corbusier's projects in Paris, Algiers and Rio de Janeiro. Nowadays such dreams, in which people are relegated to an ant-like existence, seem less worth fulfilling, indeed they appear somewhat satanic.' (Ernest F. Burckhardt, *Observations on the question of highrise building*.) Further cause for unease lies in the manner of progress which highrise building has made. Its creators had envisaged it as a focal point; they saw in it a special element, to be used consciously in the planning of towns. The original vision saw highrise building as a special form-giving element, but by now few areas are earmarked for differentiated development. Instead of bringing form and order to the city, highrise buildings appear scattered over the townscape, thus making far less of an impact than their champions intended.

All this happened because highrise buildings succeeded far beyond the expectations of even their own creators. Town-planning authorities, for one thing, did not always handle them in the way originally visualized. Sometimes they were simply not capable of grasping the subtleties of the concept, sometimes they deliberately rejected them. Then it was not always financially possible to commission only architects who were first-class; second-class architects, often more alert commercially, tended to get into their stride more quickly than their abler colleagues. And finally, speculators, not unduly burdened with scruples, began to take an interest in highrise building, scenting there means of considerable profit.

Highrise buildings has made such headway that it is catching up with traditional forms. What was at first the exception is threatening now to become the rule, and there lies the real danger.

To be told reassuringly that the average European highrise building is between 10 and 15% more expensive to build than ordinary housing is cold comfort. It is not beyond the skill of the building industry to cut the extra cost in the foreseeable future. This has already happened to some extent and this is not dangerous in itself, but the possible result is. Highrise building would immediately become even more interesting to speculators, to those who care more for money than the well-being of their fellow-men, already forced by the long-standing housing shortage to put up with inadequate accommodation. Unfortunately, tower-blocks of flats are potential slums when the basic requirements of space, sunshine, light, site layout and privacy are neglected. It is very important that this aspect of the tower-block as a solution to housing is recognized. Anyone familiar with the pseudo-economic arguments employed in urging an unsuitably high population-density of sites, realizes how easy it would be to exploit tower-blocks politically.

The spread of highrise building proves that public controls afford far less protection than would appear from the wording of many a by-law.

The speculator waiting to develop gainfully the still-obtainable open spaces around highrise buildings (just as the internal courts of old districts were once built up), is ready to pounce and provides yet another alarming effect of the unquestioning acceptance of highrise building.

Historic roots of highrise building

Highrise building established itself astonishingly fast if one considers the initial objections and the general indolence with which changes in building, particularly urban building, occur. This can scarcely be traced back to its aesthetic impact alone, still less to its usefulness, nor yet to present-day conditions, favourable though they may be. It is even stranger to think that this new way of building should have been so widely adopted at a time when town-planning tended toward smaller-scale, garden-city-like development. Highrise building seems to have touched something in human nature which responded to it regardless of logical argument.

'The tendency to "rise above the self" by building is a fundamental human urge. Building into the sky satisfies a primeval instinct. Acted-out collectively, it signifies the desire to dominate and for danger. Where such instincts are involved, incommensurables invariably appear'. (Burckhardt *ibid.*) 'Plan' no.1, 1951.

In the Western world, and in Switzerland to a positively extreme degree, power now lies with the people. We have no potentates and Maecenases, building splendid monuments to their power and dignity for the edification of their contemporaries and as lasting reminders to future generations. What we have now is the manifestation of the collective desire to express a well-established democracy.

Formerly, the daring architectural constructions that towered above all else were temples, fortresses, cathedrals and palaces. Today, in a similarly ambitious manner, tower the office blocks and, most surprising of all, residential blocks, buildings that offer accommodation to ordinary people. In this respect at least the modern tower-block has no historical parallel.

But there is a parallel in motive, unavowed but nonetheless contributive. The very forces which prompted the building of the prototype at Babel are at work today and stimulate the construction of the modern residential towers.

'... go to, let us build us a city and a tower, whose top may reach unto heaven; and let us make us a name ...' (Gen., II, 4).

Man's longing for building unto heaven was never founded in

usefulness. Nor did artistic aspiration alone sponsor such building. Art was only the means to an end. What caused buildings to grow taller than trees was man's urge, albeit sublimated, to achieve distinction, dominance, and the manifestation of power.

Up to now, the motive in creating ostentatiously high buildings was threefold:

- architectural emphasis of a certain place in the city: artistic/aesthetic motive
- social distinction of individual, group or nation: sociological motive
- demonstration of an abstract or concrete power: religious motive

The original tower-building of Babel was brought to a strange end by the angry God of the Old Testament. He confounded the languages of the builders who, no longer able to understand one another, scattered abroad on the face of the earth. The tower was never finished, but the idea remained.

The roots of European highrise building are historical. Its character is not, and is more likely to have been inspired by the skyscrapers of America.

Rationally as incomprehensible as any Tower of Babel, the first really high building appeared in the New World around 1860; a time when Europe, regarding itself as the dominant power in the world, spread out its cities in width and breadth.

The origin of the skyscraper is, according to legend, as amusing as the name itself. John Wanamaker, businessman, social reformer and owner of many department-stores, is said to have had the idea of dealing a blow to his competitors by building a store to tower above all others. It was a success, which meant that his tall building did not remain the only one for long. Manhattan was built up, irregularly, chaotically, impossible from the design point of view, but imposing nonetheless. The first tall brick buildings, if they have not yet made room for still taller buildings, have long since become dwarfs among the giants. After the event, the rise of skyscrapers has been explained with great plausibility: high ground prices, shortage of land, rationalized management, concentrated production and much else. But in arguing in this way, the effect is mistaken for the cause.

It was once more primarily the need to dominate which led to the first gigantic building. The desired effect was certainly achieved, even if not so much for the individual as for the island of Manhattan as a whole, which moreover became the symbol of the entire town and of the United States itself.

As well as the desired results, there were a number of un-intended consequences: over-concentration at points attracted traffic and the consequent traffic congestion, inflated land prices, uneconomically long journeys to work, and over-organ-ization were all in evidence in New York until the introduction of zonal control put a brake on the building of new skyscrapers. Is the European highrise building modelled on the skyscraper? In America, at least in the beginning, skyscrapers arose from the need for an impressive demonstration of economic power. Architecture played a decidedly subordinate part. When the Chicago Tribune Building, a concrete-framed structure clad with slabs of gothic motifs, was inaugurated, Erich Mendelsohn was to write sarcastically: 'Even the pointed iron arches on the turrets cannot transform the powers of the press into the spir-itual sovereignship of the cathedral.' When architects, partic-ularly Sullivan and Wright, subsequently fought for the better design of skyscrapers, they were not the instigators but the critics of an event; especially Wright, with his definite tendency to low and medium height building. Besides, in the case of the skyscrapers, solely business premises were involved.

In that category, Europe, too, produced several examples of highrise building before the Second World War. There was a tall office block built in Dusseldorf in 1924 and there was the Schiekade building in Rotterdam in 1929. In Switzerland, there were the Bel-Air at Lausanne, the town hall at Wipkingen and the Walchetower in Zurich. These were not inspired by Amer-ican models, but came into being because of the need for local contrast and emphasis, and remained entirely without wider influence.

The general change-over to tall building took place only after the Second World War. The change was demonstrably fur-thered by the architectural profession. Post-war architects were governed, however, by motives different from those underlying the original creation of skyscrapers. They were in-terested neither in giving distinction to individuals or groups, nor in demonstrating any power, but simply in creating a ver-tical spatial element which would effectively articulate and punctuate the horizontal mass of banal housing that was rapidly spreading around large cities.

Admittedly, in one respect the originators of European highrise building, especially the residential type, had social motives in mind. Starting with the theory that architectural environment influences man's way of life, they hoped, by means of differ-entiated, accentuated building, to promote the re-emergence or strengthening of human values and individuality instead of the growing tendency towards collective behaviour. They were successful.

Thus the idea and the motives behind European highrise build-ing may be said to have originated in history, too. But this evolutionary aspect is not under discussion, nor is the search for stylistic patterns in the past. We are concerned with the emergence of a completely indigenous feature, which is giving rise to so many questions precisely because nothing quite like it has ever existed before. European highrise building is new.

Social change

No idea, however valid in itself, can flourish unless the ground on which it falls is socially prepared. This holds good for the idea of highrise building too, no matter how closely it may also correspond with man's primeval endeavours. It was surely not by chance that the idea of highrise building emerged at this moment in time, nor that it was sympathetically received and adopted with astonishing speed. The most striking proof of the change-over from the preceding rural/artisan/aristocratic so-ciety to today's industrialized democracy, lies in the enormous increase in the size and number of cities. The traditional pattern of hamlets, villages and country towns that used to character-ize the countryside is becoming more and more overlaid with the sprawl of cities of all kinds. In the industrialized countries of the West, more than half the population lives in towns and the proportion is steadily growing. Heavy industry has long since ceased to be the sole begetter of cities, the various light

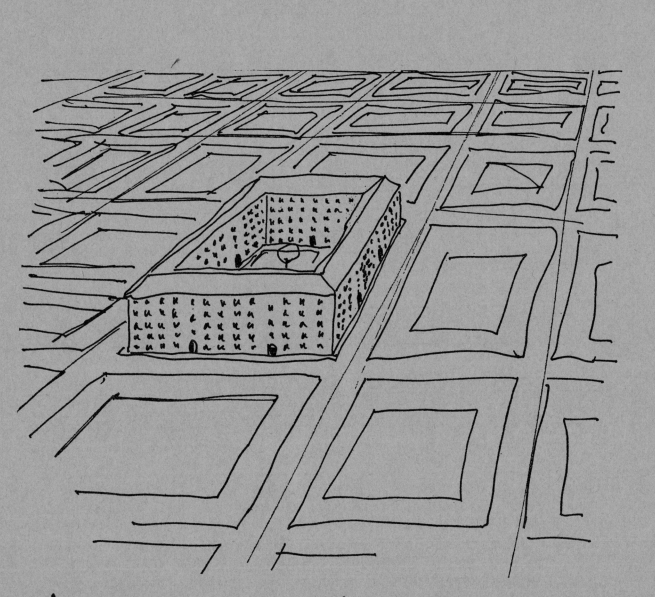

19.th century solution to town-planning problems

Local streets in the 19th century

and service industries play an even larger part. At the same time, there is a population increase such as the world has never seen before. Periods of expansion favour deeds of pioneering. In the face of insecurity and danger, our epoch carries the unmistakable signs of success. Even so, one of its central problems, the modern city, remains totally unsolved, both architecturally and functionally.

Liberated from the stranglehold of late-medieval fortifications, European cities gained much-needed space, but lost both security and order at the same time. Cities were not only freed from the pressures of constriction, but laid bare to the open country beyond. When, as the result of new, fast-developing industries, the accelerated growth of the cities first began, no one could have foreseen the extent of this growth. In order to keep pace with the flood of requests for living and office accommodation, town-planners of the nineteenth and early twentieth century still clung to the simple square grid of housing grouped round courtyards and surrounded by streets, a form which could be extended indefinitely, provided there was no topographical obstacle. Layout of this kind provides comparatively high land utilization and ensures simple access on all sides. In addition, it makes no great demands on urban design. In the suburbs and outlying districts, chequerboard groups and serpentine rows of one-family dwellings appeared, providing better housing, but of equal monotony. These too could be extended at will and were relatively fast to produce. Urban design elements were thus reduced to squares and districts equally standard in storeys and height.

The width of the streets in such districts was generally determined by the essential light-angle requirements. The roads frequently proved inadequate, even in the days of the horse, and there were hardly any green spaces. Indiscriminate additions of similar buildings created hopelessly dreary urban districts without contrast or animation. Tenement blocks, justly referred to as barracks, were flooded with an endless stream of people, migrants from the countryside, and often from the very lowest social levels. Here, removed from their familiar environment, they were uprooted and bewildered. The social problems that followed all too soon are well-known.

Perturbed by these slum-like mass dwellings and the social ill-effects, social workers, urban designers, architects and politicians tried to remedy the evil by attempting to change the architectural environment which had allowed such conditions to develop. That it was a British parliamentary shorthandwriter, Ebenezer Howard, who in a brief but impassioned pamphlet successfully pleaded for the creation of pleasantly organized green-studded garden cities in contrast to the congested metropolis, is perhaps less surprising than may appear. He was, after all, a constant witness of parliamentary debates dealing with slums and their social effects. Architects, especially, propounded the theory of the influence of environment on the nature of man. They pointed to cases and produced visible evidence that seemed irrefutable. Through this thesis and the desire to create better cities, fit for men, came a gradual change in urban design, leading by degrees to the less rigid form of the garden-city.

In the course of time, this theory has lost much of its original force. It became apparent that perfectly healthy communities could develop in architecturally inadequate quarters as long as enough inhabitants had sufficient civic experience to have found their feet. It was striking that certain social evils regularly reappeared in the new towns, even in areas of one-family housing, although these were far superior to the old tenements. It was for a new science, sociology, to explain the complex process of adjustment that faced the newcomer from the country. Later, experience was to show that new arrivals adapted themselves to urban life more easily when the greatest proportion of the existing population was urbanly integrated.

Consequently, the greatest conflicts appeared where the new, as yet unintegrated arrivals formed the majority. As a rule, the newcomer is more than willing to adjust to the urban environment. Indeed, he will look for it in its most concentrated form, but where he is not able to find and follow an example of acceptable behaviour, he will constantly be tempted to revert to his old village ways, or, even worse, make a misadjustment. It would be, therefore, a definite mistake to try and solve the city problem according to the behaviour pattern of not yet integrated newcomers.

Efforts to transplant the village to the metropolis only achieve

17

exactly the opposite effect of well-meant intentions and reveal a number of mistakes in the town-planners' postulations, specifically those intended to alleviate the difficulties of social adjustment. One example is the neighbourhood concept, developed as a meaningful unit in the town fabric; another is the idea of borough piazzas analogous to village centres.

When such features of urban planning are rejected, it is not the inhabitants who are at fault, but the original concepts. What the town-dweller wants is the town. Even if lately he seems to escape to the country, he is far from looking for village life, but seeking another, more acceptable form of urban existence. He creates suburban regions because the city of today can no longer give him what he wants: quiet, healthy, comfortable living conditions. The problem of town-planning thus remains unsolved. It cannot be solved by introducing the forms of a bygone way of life. Against this background, the appearance and quick acceptance of highrise building becomes more understandable. Its character is definitely urban. It promises advantages that conventional housing can no longer offer: more green open spaces and less noise in consequence, better air, better views. Even when highrise buildings are planned in conjunction with park-like landscapes, they never lose their urban character, as they themselves remain urban in scale and proportion. Moreover, they express so exactly all that is chararcteristic of urban society today — a concentration of equal accommodation for equals — that the town-dweller regards them as made to measure for his needs. Where a highrise building appears to have strayed into a rural area, it is placed deliberately as an urban symbol. Indeed, highrise building could well become a valid symbol of the proud, invulnerable town. By this, it would accomplish a not unimportant social purpose.

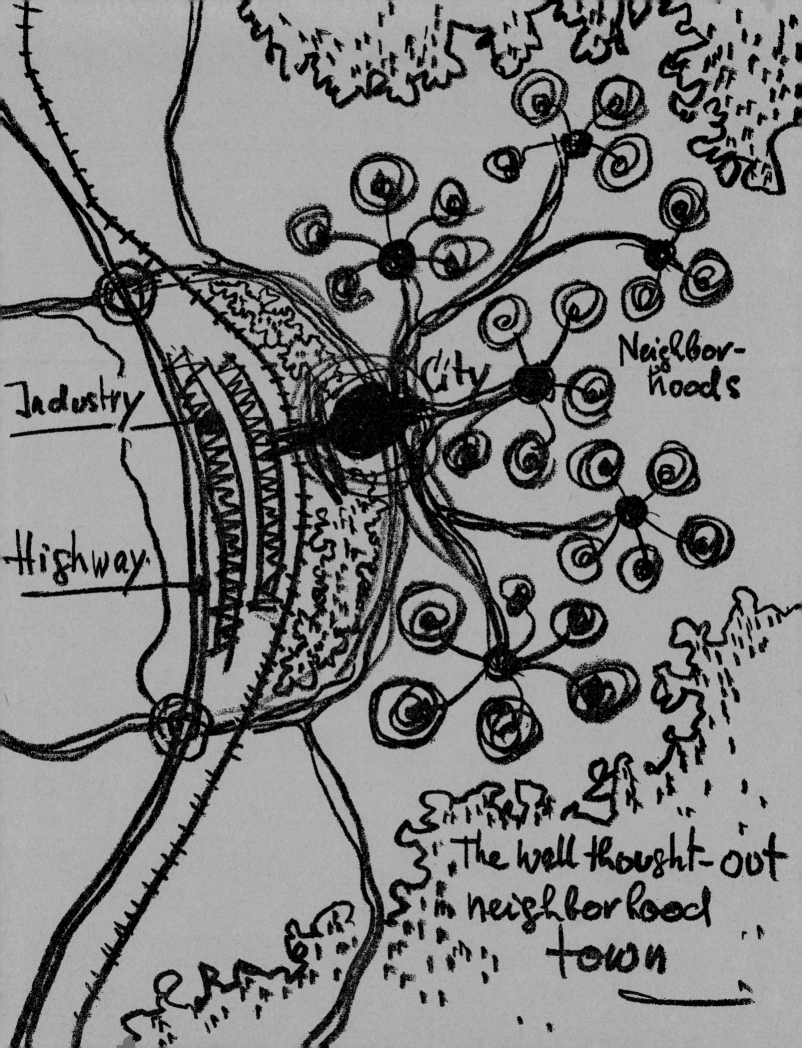

Industry

Highway

City

Neighbor-hoods

The well thought-out
neighborhood
town

The high-rise is the symbol of an urban society

Town-planning in flux

When we spontaneously respond to medieval cities, it is not because we recognize them as the models for our own cities, but because they arouse our latent feelings for the romantic. We respond to their apparent repose and security. Not least, we are attracted by the variety of the shapes and forms of buildings within the framework of an overall discipline. In comparison, today's mass housing schemes evoke feelings of distinct unease. They emanate a sense of constant stress and strain, the signs of a hard and often cruel struggle for existence, and repel by their architectural monotony, which seems outside any visible co-ordinating discipline. Furthermore, today's cities are inadequately equipped for the demands of modern life. The contrast is striking; the city of the past suggests development evolved from a social order, the city of today testifies to the hasty, unthinking, unrelated piling up of buildings.

Many well-meaning excuses could be made to explain what is, after all, an inexcusable state of affairs after almost a century of town-planning: unpredictable shifts of population, commercial interests, defective land acts, muddled regulations out of step with the times, lack of insight on the part of the government, inadequate town-planning authorities, lack of training for the rising generation, and much else besides. Each excuse contains an element of truth. Together, they represent formidable difficulties. But the question remains: why do the inhabitants of such cities put up with such shortcomings?

Yet, cities are not as black as they are often painted. There are the unsatisfactory mass-housing developments. There is monotony, traffic congestion and lack of adequate sanitation. However these faults have not been blindly and unthinkingly perpetuated. After the rectangular tenement block with its enclosed inner yard, came the larger grass-covered courtyard, then rows of more widely-spaced houses, then the single block development with larger green areas, and finally, the more spacious layout of the garden-city. Simultaneously, the small house, singly or in perfectly acceptable terraced rows, was enjoying a positive renaissance. Cities have certainly become more humanized, always excepting the slums

which in some cases still house the majority of the inhabitants.

City-planning has a twofold task: slum clearance and expansion appropriate to the times. Beyond that, there is the desire for a co-ordinated, unified town. Neither task has been properly accomplished. The character of the buildings themselves may be better, but there is no improvement from the town-planner's point of view. The tenements have risen again, improved in ground-plan and with new façades, but still suffering from the old ills: unsolved traffic problems, insufficient sunlight, trapped street noise, and lack of open space for relaxation. Many of these shortcomings have been dealt with in the new suburbs, but these too leave much to be desired. Blocks of flats flank noisy arterial roads. The impression of the sprawling town remains. In contrast to the monotony of the central districts, the suburban developments often look confused and arbitrary, like a gigantic experimental architectural model. There seems to be no recognizable overall design. The increased loosening of the town fabric often amounts to the disintegration of the town itself, the surrender of its function and denial of its character. For instance, American statistics show that the incidence of crimes is highest in such parkscaped, town districts.

Town-planners and designers understandably try repeatedly to gain inspiration and instruction from the cities of the past. The motif of the historical town keeps reappearing in new urban developments: the piazza (borrowed from the towns of the south), criss-crossed by traffic, is pushed between blocks of flats. Strictly geometric road-grids alternate with sweeping, curving streets. In the place of large zones built up to a uniform height, there appear small-scale height differentiations with no apparent relationship. The symmetry of old towns, the skill in the layout of the squares and parades of royal cities, and the ambitious avenues of historical capitals, none of these contributions of the past serve a purpose in the modern city.

It would be unjust to say that urban-planning and design had not progressed at all, but had only marked time, during the past hundred years. Certainly, it has failed in many respects and frequently lagged behind the times. But this in itself reflects

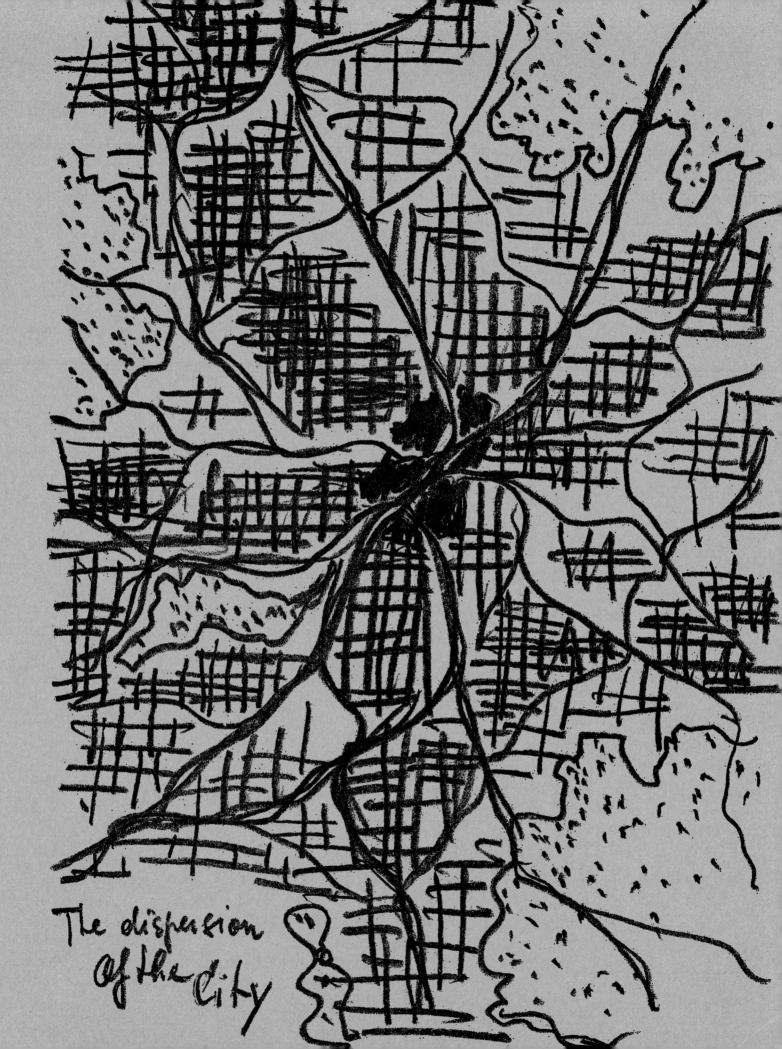

The dispersion
Of the city

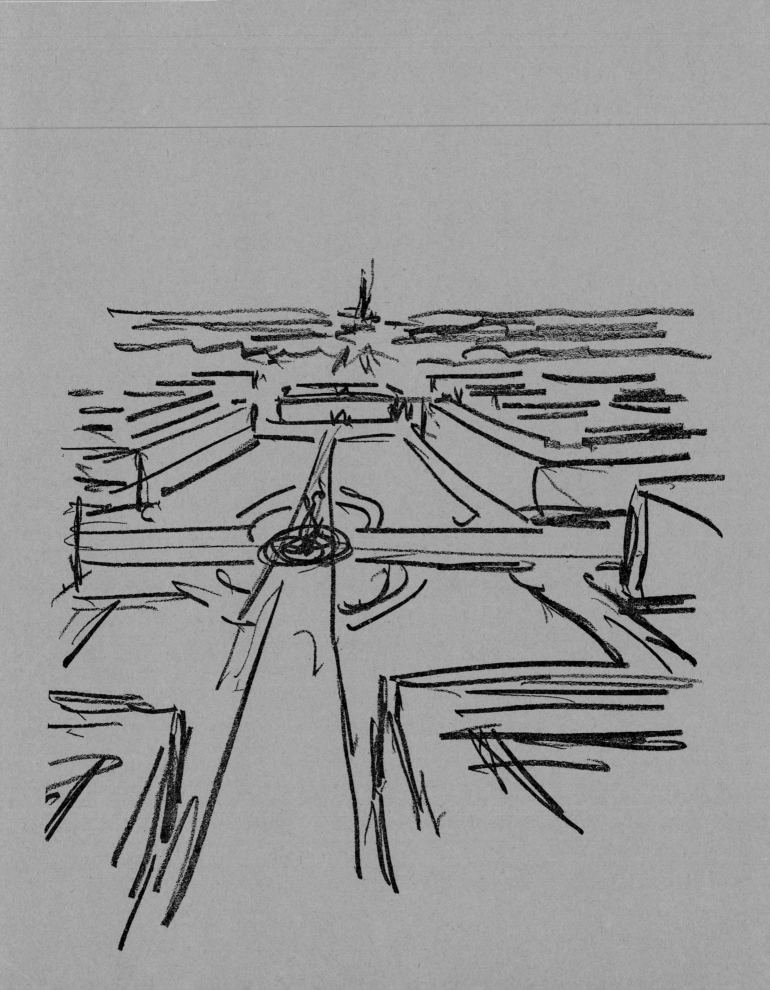

social conditions and society's attitude towards town-planning. Overshadowed by the need for essentials, consideration for greater co-ordination, elementary rules of hygiene and aesthetics, and concern for the future did not get much of a hearing. In the effort to do only the minimum necessary, the appropriate was often left undone. For instance, there was no adequate provision for roads, even at a time when cars were forming long queues at intersections. A society which is too exclusively orientated towards the pressing needs of the moment, and which, in any case, tends to project its private business methods on to its public affairs, would regard attempts to create a forward-looking unified over-all plan as rather suspect. It values actions, not ideas and this is clearly apparent.

The foregoing is not so much a criticism as a statement of fact. Not the town-planners, but the prevailing socio-economic order has the final say in the layout and building of housing. The effect of recognizing this, commonplace though it may appear, meant a real breakthrough in the theory and practice of town-planning. Until then, town-planning had been in conflict with a society that apparently refused to understand its purpose and thereby made the realization of it impossible (even when town-planners themselves entered the political arena). They gradually began to see the necessitiy of coming to terms with society if they were to build its cities. As a result, town-planning, as it is generally understood, was organized in three separate categories: urban research, urban planning and urban design.

If modern city development is not to be judged a failure, but recognized as a socially conforming process with unmistakable, though not unavoidable, defects which result from the lack of definite rules, then there is reason for hope in a future for town-planning. Above all, there needs to be an unbiased examination of the problems. First of all, there is the city user. Present-day society is difficult to analyze because it is so changeable and varied in its needs and characteristics. Modern society is pluralist and no satisfactory form of enclosed city can emerge from this kind of social structure, in contrast to the Middle Ages, when the city was the product of a mainly singularist society. This circumstance alone prevents the existence of a unified city-image or the realization of a monocratic town-picture such as town-planners with leanings towards the classic like to visualize.

In the light of this diversity, the modern city appears as a homogenous arrangement, but one with variations and differentiations. There are several types of town centres, shopping centres, various forms of residential areas and differentiated areas for commerce and industry. Even an apparently single concept, such as the town centre, proves to have many facets. The multiplicity of demands could never be satisfied in an over-rigid urban plan, quite apart from the autonomous economy that, by its own dynamics, is likely to break through any constriction. Perhaps the town-planner of the turn of the century may now be easier to understand. He based his cities on the coarsest possible grid in order to do justice to every possible future requirement. Later efforts to correct the shortcomings of the system, by superimposing a finer zonal grid, failed because of the dynamics of the times and the constantly developing new requirements.

We must consider not only the variety of urban phenomena, but also the city's approaches, its structure and its size. Several almost convincing theories of urban planning seem, at closer inspection, plainly to presuppose the building of an entirely new town. There is, for instance, the theory of organic development, which stipulates a city's growth according to the rules of plant morphology. However, towns are not organisms subject to natural laws, but (more or less) planned works of man. Major cities, moreover, are always conglomerations of different building periods, and, for that reason alone, the notion of enlargement by an annual ring is absurd. It is also strange how obstinately the *art nouveau* approach has lingered in town-planning. So-called organic growth frequently serves as a euphemism for the failure of a badly, or not at all organized, town plan. The existing buildings in any town normally make for difficulties in planning, and the absence of any definite boundaries makes even more. How can a road grid be designed, public transport planned, central installations sited, when nobody knows how many inhabitants and what area are finally to be served. Staggered town development, with pre-arranged intervals for the provision of new installations aiming at achieving the continued entity of the city, seems even further in the future. However, the fact that there are no boundaries to the cities of today has expanded town-planning into regional planning. Because the city is no longer an entity in time and space, it can only be understood, or limited, in its wider sphere.

These then are the principal town-planning problems. There are also some additional, practical, day-to-day difficulties. Most important is the question of volume. The constant and increasing growth of today's major cities results in an ever-growing demand for both living and working accommodation. Widely standardized living requirements make for fairly stand-ardized building. The architect's careful attention to detail, which was bestowed even on single dwellings in time of mod-erate building activity, can no longer be applied to buildings on such a vast scale. Repetition of the same kind of housing is unavoidable. Moreover, it is a delusion to believe that each multiple dwelling becomes an architectural achievement when the same ground-plan is constantly repeated, even if there are slight variations in the façades. The number of buildings required, and their similarity of purpose, demands industrial production, even pre-fabrication. This increases the danger of architectural monotony far more than the unfairly denounced zonal height regulations ever did. Urban measures other than opportunities for mere height variation are needed if monotony of housing is to be avoided, but it must be remembered that a certain uniformity in building is the result of uniform require-ments. That also is an integral part of the major city. The grow-ing desire for differentiation on the one hand, and the need for a large number of similar or identical housing units on the other, pose urban designers with both contradictory and difficult problems.

Solving such problems, especially in their design aspect, is made even harder by the notion of and structure of private property. Private ownership of land is too precious a posses-sion, too tenaciously fought for by a politically emancipated population, to be given up lightly. It is still considered to be the surest token of freedom. This feeling has a deep historical justi-fication in countries where the freeing of bonded subjects fol-lowed the purchase of a piece of land. Even though in practice

24

only the minority actually own land, the majority share the right to do so, a right too highly valued to be quietly relinquished. Perhaps everyone likes to imagine himself a potential land-owner. In any case, it is understandable that the sanctity of private property is guarded with special vigilance. Even justified modifications, suggested for the common good, meet with considerable resistance. Although the growing rate of private group ownership and the rise in ground prices must sooner or later lead to a modified concept of private ownership, it seems hardly likely that private property in itself will disappear. For town-planning, however, private ownership means yet another independent element that grows in power with the numbers of owners participating.

There is one last problem that should be mentioned to round off the picture of present-day town-planning: traffic congestion in the cities. Nothing is more conducive to people's sympathy than a threat to their own comfort. Thus, there is an insistent demand for a solution to the traffic problem. Plans are drawn up requiring massive encroachments of the town fabric, and are even accepted, but it remains difficult to make people see the simple truth, that there is a close relationship between the town fabric and traffic flow. Authorities who, at great expense, rationalize the traffic in their town centres, but simultaneously step up building densities there, illustrate how little this inter-relationship is understood. Urban traffic planning is a part of town-planning. If the problem is to be solved, traffic and city-planning must go hand in hand, and a flexible attitude to city expansion must be maintained. Traffic, more than anything else, has revealed the inadequacies of our urban design, and calls for a totally new conception of the town. Squares and parades are redundant in the modern townscape, but urban motorways, multiple-storey crossings and traffic filters, parking areas and multi-storey car parks, and proper provision for public transport are vital. Roads were always an important element in urban design. Today, an efficient road-grid is an absolutely basic necessity, but it can only be designed when the layout of the town, or at least its most important elements, have been planned. This, in itself, should ensure that urban traffic is never considered as a separate problem to be independently tackled.

If all the aspects of town-planning, which can only be roughly indicated here, are to form a harmonious entity, then the appropriate means to achieve this must be found. Although classic town-planning has admitted merits, its elements can no longer provide for the diverse needs of the modern town. The intellectual conditions are now at last right for comprehensive town-planning, experience has been fairly gained and it now needs only the courageous application of our knowledge.

What does highrise building mean in terms of urban planning? Town-planners have positively demanded it as a new design element. But an important decision has to be made before its fitness in urban design can be judged. Should highrise buildings be employed as dominating features, as a substitute for the church spires that no longer seem to make their point? Or should they be the means of enlivening and visually organizing otherwise uniform areas? Where the highrise building is intended to create a focal point, a landmark, it must be sparingly used and carefully sited. It may mark the central point of an area, an important approach to a city, or some really notable place, but in this capacity it will not tolerate neighbours of similar construction set in meaningless sites, since it would then lose its position of dominance. A possible exception is the town centre, where a more massive emphasis would not be out of place. There, highrise buildings could be represented by several examples without losing significance. But enticing though the idea of adding significance may be, the problem, in terms of the overall town structure, is great. If we started off with a closed city, where boundaries are defined and functions locally fixed, then it would be legitimate to use highrise buildings as points of emphasis in the manner of the fortified towers of the past. But when we consider the cities of today, subject as they are to constant change, attempts at final emphasis of a single point in any area becomes a questionable enterprise. It must also be remembered that highrise office or residential buildings do not have the integral functional distinction of, say, a palace or cathedral. Here, Erich Mendelsohn's words regarding the Chicago Tribune Building apply again. Height alone cannot lend significance, that only emerges with ideological content. People will become accustomed to regarding 27

highrise office and residential buildings as no more than exceptionally tall office and residential buildings, unless they are remarkable achievements of architecture or happen to house an especially distinguished firm.

This only leaves highrise buildings to function as leavening, loosening elements in the townscape, except where, collectively used, they form highrise districts. Correctly handled within a zonal development, especially in residential districts, they can indeed exert this kind of visual effect horizontally and vertically. Horizontally, because of the open green spaces that are achieved through the small area the building takes up; vertically, through their towering height. Highrise buildings are not, of course, ground-savers, at least not when they are built according to the town-planners' and not the speculators' ideas. But they leave room for planting and for more variety in development without the use of additional land and this is in itself a great advantage. It is possible to set a highrise group into a park-like landscape, indeed, only highrise buildings could bring such parks into existence and this too speaks in their favour. For town-planning purposes, highrise building is a definite gain, even though it has not fulfilled all that its advocates promised. Its value as an accent is smaller than it originally appeared to be. On the other hand, its spatial contribution in leavening and shaping residential areas is considerable, even though horizontal organization remains as important as ever. Whether highrise building is suitable for the rationalization of antiquated central areas is still relatively unknown. Here, existing over-development usually argues against it. But in this case, the disadvantage lies not with highrise building, but with established over-development which would be difficult to reduce to sensible proportions. Nevertheless, continued efforts to clear up these antiquated districts could be profitable. In actual district redevelopment, there is no reason why redundant street areas should not be built up. That would leave fewer, more efficient roads in the place of a greater number of inefficient ones. One- or two-storey shops and office buildings could cover the greatest possible part of the area, their flat roofs could be turfed and the rest of the space used for highrise housing which would, by these means, at least stand in bearable surroundings.

Highrise building offers distinct advantages in commercial districts too, although here it is a question of gaining parking space instead of parkland. In such districts, some massing of highrise buildings can be very much to the point. As long as such development would not overload the traffic system, it could achieve a distinctive contrast and emphasize the structural make-up of the town to advantage.

Highrise building is one of the elements of urban design, and a most welcome one. If it does not become fashionably or speculatively overused or misused, it may well become a continuing feature with a distinctive influence on the look of our cities.

Higher building and highrise building

When highrise building is mentioned, it is tacitly assumed that everyone using the term means the same thing, but discussions with professionals or laymen quickly reveal that this is not so. Professional journals also express different concepts by the term, even as regards height alone. Moreover, with the passage of time, the concept of highrise building has changed. When the idea of highrise building first occupied the minds of planners after the Second World War, it was mainly considered in relation to the existing conventional development of the surrounding zones. The Swiss United Land Planning Commission made this quite clear when it described highrise building in the following way: 'The term "highrise building" defines buildings which considerably exceed the height laid down in zonal building regulations, or which, where no such regulations exist, considerably exceed the height of existing buildings.'

This apparently useful terminology could not work in practice. In one- or two-storey developments, the conventional four- or five-storey block of flats would thus be counted as a highrise building which hardly did justice to the latter's multi-storeyed character. The adoption of this definition has the unmistakable undertones of a desire to impose limits on highrise building, of not allowing 'the trees to grow up into the skies.' If the usual height of local building is indeed to be used as the yardstick for highrise building, there will be little difficulty in setting the upper limit for 'considerably exceeding' that height. However, the height of highrise building cannot be determined by what is usual locally, but only by the deliberate intention of building higher. Even when highrise building is not primarily intended as a means of urban emphasis, it should and must at least be able to appear as something out of the ordinary and special. Therefore no terminology which attempts to define the characteristics of highrise building in terms of the number of storeys of existing buildings will ever be convincing.

' ... to define those buildings as highrise buildings which exceed the permitted number of storeys in any building zone by a certain number (i. e. five or more storeys)' (from *A study of the question of highrise building, North-Eastern Swiss Planning Group*).

Building height in relation to nature

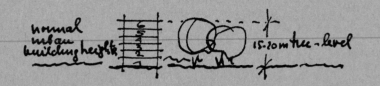

normal
mean
building heights — 15-20m tree-level

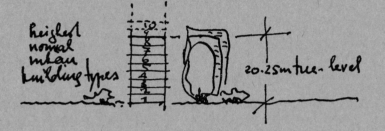

highest
normal
mean
building types — 20-25m tree-level

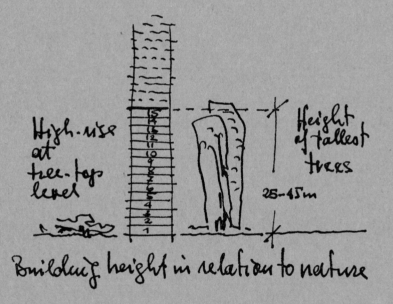

High-rise
at
tree-top
level — Height of tallest trees 25-45m

Building height in relation to nature

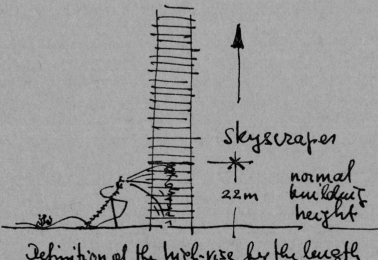

skyscraper — 22m — normal building height

Definition of the high-rise by the length
of the fire department ladder.

Thus, among single-storey buildings, a six-storey house would appear in the role of a highrise building, and nothing could be less relevant. Highrise buildings are not relatively but absolutely high. Both the above definitions characterize not the highrise, but the higher building.

Absolute standards come closer to the highrise idea than relative ones. German regulations about highrise building for building authorities use the following definition: 'The definition of highrise buildings according to these regulations are buildings with rooms for the permanent accommodation of people, and whose floors on the uppermost storey are situated more than 72 feet above ground level on any one side of the building.'

This measure, arrived at from the length of ladders used by the fire-brigade, no doubt makes good sense, but for urban planning purposes it is the lowest limit, because already there are cities whose building regulations permit occasional zonal development up to nine storeys, and five- or six-storeyed buildings are an integral part of the usual urban core development.

While it is not easy to prove conclusively, experience shows that there is a recognizable pattern in the height determination of buildings. In practice, it works in threes:

1–3 storeys   village and suburban building;
4–6 storeys   conventional urban building, multi-family and commercial blocks;
6–9 storeys   metropolitan building.

The question is not whether highrise building is to be limited to six storeys, but whether it is to be limited to ten. Only a few years ago, there would have been undisputed agreement on eight storeys, at least in German-speaking districts. In the meantime, however, several buildings of about that storey-level have appeared. This height has become increasingly recognized as a useful design factor within the total development, which is still an effective means of introducing variety into an urban group of multi-family housing. But there, such buildings recognizably fulfil the function of the higher block. It must also be remembered that the eye has become used to the higher block without seeing anything extraordinary in it.

Awareness that this may lead to a possible widening of the term 'highrise building' should logically place it in the category into which it already seems to belong:

1–6 storeys   regulation building;
7–9 storeys   non-standard building of higher blocks, particularly within the framework of differentiated total development;
10 and more storeys   highrise building.

This is, of course, not a constructively proved, nor economically derived, insurance or technical term, but an attempt to define highrise building as it fits into the urban scheme, a height definition that only experience will prove right or wrong. As a working thesis, however, it is useful provided it does no more than clarify what is meant by the term highrise building.

The distinction between the higher block and highrise building proves useful in town-planning practice. Even when the higher block is intended to make its effect as an individual unit, the rules regarding its siting are far less strict than they are for highrise building proper.

There is one last question regarding terminology according to height. Should there not be a terminological upper as well as lower limit? Should the term apply to something like the Empire State Building with its 1,250 feet? Or should another name be found for such giants among buildings? Traditionally, Manhattan's tall buildings are known as skyscrapers. Professionally, they are all called highrise buildings. Experience shows that buildings up to 328 feet high are regarded as highrise buildings even by the proverbial man in the street, so there seems no reason for searching for a further term to differentiate between heights. It may well be left to people's inventiveness to find a suitable name for high-rising giants, in so far as they will eventually rise at all in the cities of Europe.

Purpose and function of highrise buildings

Not every tall building is a highrise building. Industrial and technical structures such as factories, silos, etc., are excluded, as are churches. The essential exterior characteristic of highrise buildings is a façade organized in storeys. Roughly the following functional categories can be defined:

Residential highrise building: this includes student and nursing hostels as well as multi-storey dwellings

Office highrise building: office space only

Commercial highrise building: generally a combination of shops, storage and office space with perhaps a few dwelling units

Hotel highrise building: here hotel accommodation may be combined with dwelling units and office space

Hospital highrise building: wards and treatment departments.

Discussion of highrise buildings at first dealt with their general visual effect, but it was soon concentrated on the residential highrise building in particular. The functional suitability in the other categories had never been seriously in doubt, but the idea that highrise building could be suitable for domestic purposes was more or less completely dismissed.

Domestic highrise building

The residential highrise building is still the subject of so much argument that it must be separately examined. Its opponents include not only timid spirits and backward-looking champions of the traditions of yesterday, but also perfectly open-minded modern people who register concern at the thought of highrise buildings for the accommodation of large families. They do not as a rule object to this form of housing in the case of students, old people, etc. They admit that highrise living offers undeniable advantages to single people or couples. Their main objection, therefore, concerns the use of highrise dwellings for family accommodation. In circles that are against highrise living for families, 'differentiated building' is once again the slogan. This time not for reasons of aesthetics, but because of social considerations.

The champions of differentiated housing expect to attract a socially mixed group of residents by offering more varied accommodation. Principally, they count on people's moving among the various types of flats and houses within the same housing estate as their family circumstances change. If this premise is accepted, then highrise building and even higher blocks must be confined to offering single-room or small-flat accommodation and only form part of a total development. There is something attractive about the idea of the housing group as a social unit. But it comes dangerously close to the non-functioning architectural neighbourhood concept, and, so far as one can judge today, the idea of the residential group does not work either. Examples quoted to prove the contrary unfailingly reveal stronger binding factors than mere neighbourhood spirit or local pride. Where houses change hands within the same circle, it usually turns out to be a case of a co-operative estate, or an exclusive interest group. No valid conclusions can be drawn from cities suffering from a latent housing shortage. There, local pride often means no more than lack of opportunity to move elsewhere. In the case of people who have lived for a long time in a city, a certain loyalty to the locality can sometimes be discerned, but neighbourhood spirit is not usually the basis for this. In the case of exchanging a smaller for a larger flat, the system of accommodation-to-measure does not work at all. When, on the other hand, it is a question of looking for a larger flat, then other considerations come before local pride. The housing market has many facets and that of neighbourhood relationship is the least significant. But all this does not settle whether highrise buildings offer suitable accommodation for families with children.

During the time that Europe became accustomed to residential highrise building, Frank Lloyd Wright and other eminent architects in America pronounced more and more strongly in favour of single-storey or at least single-family dwelling as the correct form of housing. European architects are not agreed on this question. Le Corbusier and his disciples recommend highrise buildings as the contemporary form of housing. Many other notable architects accept highrise building as suitable for single people and small families while denying its suitability for multi-family housing.

Those between the camps must inevitably ask themselves how there can possibly be such differences of opinion in a profession that spends its life grappling with questions of town-planning and home-building. The answer that is sometimes heard — that architects put artistic vision and the desire for structural achievement before the interests of human beings — totally

ignores the sense of responsibility and the seriousness with which these theories are propounded and fought for. Both points of view are definitely based on social considerations. Their points of departure, however, are utterly different.

Le Corbusier's thinking is based on the appearance of the Urban Colossos, his model doubtlessly being Paris, the crowded city, with its brilliant urban marvels on the one hand, and its immense slums on the other. More than one million Parisians live in antiquated houses, lacking hygiene or comfort. Yet, the idea of rehousing the roughly 7½ million inhabitants of Paris in single-storey dwellings is so patently absurd that no such notion could have arisen there. Incidentally, properly laid out, this would require an area of 770 square miles. Even the clearance of slums, provided they are not to rise again with all their old shortcomings, presents enormous problems, because without exception it concerns overcrowded districts. Seen from this point of view, Le Corbusier's giant building Unité d'Habitation with its one thousand or more residents, no longer appears so extraordinary. This approach would be a means of organizing the shambles of a huge city without increasing its spread, of improving living conditions and traffic flow, and creating open spaces for recreation at the same time. Building height and mass make a different impact in a city the size of Paris than they would in a medium-sized town. It is a question of proportion.

Frank Lloyd Wright lives in a country where low dwellings predominate. Of course, the U.S.A. too has its share of residential highrise buildings. European architects like Mies van der Rohe and Gropius have used them as points of emphasis in a town plan. Wright does not visualize the compact metropolis, but landscape-orientated living. His theory of ground-level housing has emotional overtones. He stresses the value of daily contact with nature, a value that cannot be demonstrated by facts and figures. Wright's concept is that of wide open space, lived in by a population less daunted by the need of covering vast distances than their European counterparts, who still have visions of living and working in the same place. For Wright and Le Corbusier, holding, as they do, diametrically opposed views on housing, no common denominator can be

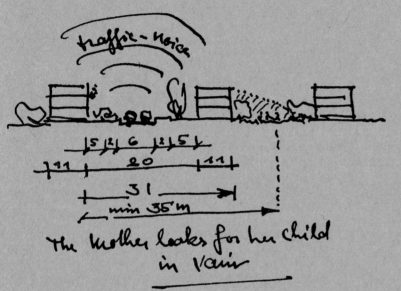

the mother looks for her child
in vain

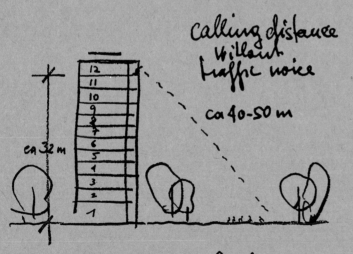

Calling distance
without
traffic noise

ca 40-50 m

the mother sees her child
the mother calls her child
without difficulty.

found. They cannot be compared — their points of departure are too different.

Meanwhile, between the two extremes, the 'machine for living in' and 'the house in the landscape', there is another faction of architects and town-planners, conscious of the problems of dense and crowded cities and the value of living in contact with nature. They are trying to find a solution by differentiating between user categories. They say that single- and double-storey housing and, as a concession, three-storey multi-family units should be reserved for the use of families, in the sense of married couples with children. Recognizing the importance of daily contact with natural surroundings, they mean to secure this amenity especially for the children who can then enjoy and experience nature at first hand during their formative years, as well as benefit physically from daily periods spent in the open air. With some justification, they fear that children living in upper storeys of highrise buildings may, because of the difficulty of adequate maternal supervision, become practically house-bound. Living in the upper storeys of highrise buildings has its very human problems. The psychological effect of living above the tree tops may lead to a certain presumptiousness over nature itself. The landscape may present itself as mere scenery, the seasons as theatrical spectacles, and only the changes in the weather provide direct contact with natural events. Adults might be expected to live in such a world, as it offers such considerable advantages, such as muted street noises, better air, wider views. But children would miss a whole range of experience that may damage the growth of their personalities. It could be argued that highrise buildings in fact allow for green open spaces where children can play. There are lifts to ease the mothers' journey down. It would be all to the good if, in order to look after their children, mothers were obliged to spend a few hours each day in the open air. While this may be a practical possibility where there is only one child in the family, it becomes a purely theoretical argument where there are more. Then there are further proposals, such as the employment of a communal child-minder, the building of safe playrooms, the creation of a safely laid-out, turfed playground on the roof which would effectively half the distance. All such proposals, however well meant, are substitute solutions, conceding that highrise building as we know it is basically unsuitable for larger families.

However, what about conditions in the central areas of cities? They are often no better and frequently much worse, even when houses are only three or four storeys high. The environment all too often consists of nothing but streets, although in specially fortunate cases there may be a closed-in, asphalt-covered courtyard at the back. Supervision of the children is as difficult or as impossible as in highrise buildings, but the dangers are infinitely greater. The temptation of bringing up children indoors, at least until they reach school-age, is equally great, and moreover in such districts, outings to play-parks usually require a real effort. Compared with conditions such as these, highrise building would, after all, offer considerable advantages.

It could be justly argued that downward comparisons are basically invalid. The thing to remember is that highrise buildings, except for their lower storeys, have disadvantages for larger families. But these disadvantages will be more than offset if family tower-blocks are the only available means by which to improve living and housing conditions in the over-crowded, antiquated central areas. On the other hand, highrise building offers many benefits to single people, couples, and small family units. Urban man, in contradiction to the neighbourhood theory, values and seeks privacy in housing. He deliberately avoids his neighbours, differing fundamentally in this from the villager. This behaviour has been acquired through bitter experience. Working in town forces upon him such a volume of human contact that he tries, understandably, to restore the balance by keeping his home life as private as possible, whereas people in villages, who do not have much human contact during working hours, round off the day by social activity. Also, in the city, social relationships do not depend on local proximity. These, among other reasons, explain the urban preference for anonymity in housing. Contrary to general opinion, privacy is more easily achieved in highrise buildings than in conventional multi-family blocks, and more easily there than in single-family houses. The vertical arrangement of the apart-ments isolates them more than a horizontal layout, especially when, as in the case of highrise buildings, chance meetings on the stairs are negligible.

The intrinsic advantages of highrise buildings have already been enumerated. In addition, there are those of better amenities. Highrise buildings are usually more carefully planned than conventional housing blocks, fitted more luxuriously and comfortably, and the architectural environment is in many ways pleasanter or at any rate further away. All these advantages explain why the residents, the people who finally matter, are satisfied with their highrise homes.

Answers to Swiss and German questionnaires clearly show this positive result. Criticisms are generally concerned with specific points of layout or construction, such as insufficent insulation against changing weather conditions or noises in other flats, faults in planning, lack of storage space for suitcases, skis, shoes, etc., badly-designed balconies and inadequate lift installations. These criticisms, quoted here in order of frequency, are not fundamental. They are often encountered in conventional blocks, only there they are less significant than in the case of highrise buildings, as the sum total increases their importance. And, above all, they can be dealt with. Other shortcomings are mentioned besides, but these without exception are voiced as often and with as much justification, in ordinary rented housing. The proportion of highrise residents who reject this form of living for one reason or the other is small. So is that of people, about one-fifth of the total, who, without rejecting it outright, would prefer some other form of accommodation. However, it would be a great mistake to conclude from this that, with few exceptions, the entire nation, so to speak, longs to live in highrise buildings. The questionnaires are, by necessity, addressed to highrise residents. The still infrequent vacancies naturally attract people looking for this form of accommodation, although there are cases where people rent highrise apartments because they cannot find anything else. Questionnaires to discover potential highrise residents returned proportions of only 8%–10% of the population of medium-sized towns and 10%–12% of the major cities. With more and better offers, the proportion is expected to rise a little. 35

Separation in better guaranteed vertically than horizontally

Research based on the characteristics of highrise buildings to discover potential highrise residents produces similar figures. In conclusion, it has been established that the residential high-rise building offers acceptable and suitable accommodation for a certain part of the population, single people, couples and the smaller families. For the housing of larger families, it should only be used in exceptional circumstances: in selected sites, in central areas, if there is no other way to achieve considerable improvements in present housing conditions, and then only if ground plan and roof layout provide adequate open play space for large numbers of children.

Forms of highrise building

Two main shapes of highrise building have emerged: the point block and the slab. The point block is accessible by central circulation, the slab by additional access balconies. Both basic plans come in many variations. Besides the square, the original plan of the point block, we have the rectangle, the star, the T- and the Y-shaped ground-plan, in twin arrangement and even in circular, triangular and honeycomb layout. The slab, too, is used with variations, with staggered or curving façades, as well as contrasting heights.

The tower effect of the point block forces comparison with the surrounding building heights, whereas the slab attracts attention not so much by its height as by its mass. Height comparison is less immediate than in the case of the point block; here, comparison with the neighbouring building mass comes first. Slabs dominate their environment, eliminating an appreciable section from the range of vision. Point blocks on the other hand frame and accent the view. The linear shape of point blocks casts shadows which are less disturbing and annoying than those cast by the slab. They permit their neighbours a wider view, unlike the slab which can easily block it. On the other hand, point blocks cannot be used to produce real exterior spaces. Spatial effects can only be created by the surrounding lower development. That is precisely what makes point-building all the more suitable for integration into a development of different-iated heights. It creates a sufficiently large surrounding neutral

area, confining itself to being the vertical spatial element and leaving the task of horizontal shaping to the lower buildings.

The choice of one or the other basic form is not only, and for the most part, not even mainly governed by aesthetic considerations. Usually the purpose for which the building is to be used, and the economics connected with it, determine the choice of form. For offices, hospitals or hotels, the slab would, in most cases, be more suitable. When it is a question of residential highrise building, the choice remains open. From the point of view of the user, the point block would certainly be preferable. It incorporates the most important advantages for highrise living, mainly the optimal layout for privacy. Highrise buildings are not only architecturally new, they represent, when they are well-planned, a new way of life. Apart from some exceptions, it cannot be claimed that they are only a sideways-up version of the old tenement barracks of the turn of the century. The slab's advantages do not point so strongly to its residential use. The temptation to add vertically to a twelve-unit floor-plan of a multi-family block until it becomes a highrise slab is far from negligible. It is hard to erase completely the impression of a barracks even when the slab is well-designed. Living conditions are not so very different from those in conventional blocks. Only high-storey living will emerge as an advantage or disadvantage. Of course, maisonettes and other interesting kinds of accommodation can be used to advantage in the slab. But all of these can generally be included in regulation height blocks, except that highrise building might incorporate a greater number of them and therefore be more economical.

Apart from town-planning motives, economic considerations soon move into the foreground in the case of the slab. In spite of the fact that it offers similar or better housing value when compared with regulation height blocks, these economic factors cannot be dismissed out of hand.

Both of the plans in use today have their particular functions, advantages and disadvantages. One simply cannot say that one form is better than the other. The choice may fall sometimes on the one, sometimes on the other, depending on the requirements of the client, the situation as well as legal and economical considerations.

Profits of highrise building

So far, we have examined highrise building mainly for its aesthetic value as an urban architectural element that should be welcomed even were it to yield no measurable material advantage beyond increasing the order and visual appearance of our cities. But as originally pointed out, there must always be a material side to architecture and town design. They serve a set purpose and therefore must profit somebody. The identity of this person must be established, however, before profit can be discussed. Who makes a profit from highrise building? The community? its neighbours? the site-owner, the builder, the landlord or the tenant? And it cannot solely be a question of profiting, of building or house-production as such, but of highrise building in particular.

The tenant, to begin with, regards highrise building in the light of abstract as well as material profit. Is highrise living better as well as cheaper? To some categories of tenant, residential highrise building indeed offers better conditions than traditional housing, but financial profit can scarcely be one, as the flats which incorporate the special highrise advantages tend to be more expensive than those on the lower floors or in comparable multi-family blocks.

Material profit is perhaps possible for tenants of highrise commercial and office-blocks where their efficiency is increased through the greater concentration and organization, but no direct gain through saving of rent is to be expected there either. Nor do builders and owners derive any special profit, as costs are still 10%–15% more than with ordinary buildings. The extra cost can be partly balanced by more rational and therefore cheaper traffic circulation, but where large parking areas have to be created, the savings may be partially or entirely swallowed up in the extra expense. The balance of the extra expense must be found in correspondingly higher rents, paid, usually, willingly enough in view of the extra advantages. In many cases, costing profits by the levy of a small surcharge, for which permission is often granted in connection with zonal development to a unified plan.

The site owners are most likely to profit from highrise building

main advantage of high-rise buildings: free ground area

where lan dprices have risen strictly according to possible profit yield and the extra surcharge can be counted on from the start. The fact that permission for these surcharges is granted for better urban redevelopment in the shape of mixed building, proves that the special highrise and taller building methods do not offer sufficient economic incentive in themselves. Still, the building industry is competitive by nature and it is likely that in due course it will manage to reduce one or the other cost factor in its favour, and, if such a saving is made without harm to the value of the accommodation or the urban plan, there is nothing against it. At most, the surcharge, intended to be an incentive and cost-equalizer, will then become problematic from the legal point of view.

People living next door to highrise buildings may have the advantage of wider views and higher sunshine incidence than they enjoy would with standard building. On the material side, there may be a profit when neighbouring sites rise in value. In today's conditions, however, we should not look for the main advantages of highrise building in individual profit, nor even necessarily on the material side. If we accept that the density-rate of highrise building must equal that of other zonal development, except for a limited increase in total redevelopment, then the principal benefit of highrise building by its vertical utilization of small areas is the gain of open space that does not have to be separately acquired. By highrise building it is possible to avoid the main disadvantage of the compact city: lack of space for relaxation. The spaces gained must be carefully watched, they must not be misused for, say, the parking of cars; in any case, all open spaces should be subject to a special vigilance in case, one fine day, they fall victim to exploitation by profiteers. The lack of recreation space in our cities is most serious. It is partly made up for by the ante-urban regions to the cost of other communities, or by private individuals who have land in attractive natural settings in their possession. No one who is familiar with this problem and conscious of the cost of the traffic trying to escape from our cities, would ever lend a hand in speculating for the sake of private avarice or public expedience, in the open spaces so inexpensively gained by highrise building.

The mixed development achieved through higher and highrise building also permits, in most cases, more rational circulation and better traffic flow. Finally, taking the long view, sanitation will be cheaper in the less compact zones and highrise building is a means to create less compact areas with high, though not excessive, density.

Are there any drawbacks to the use of highrise buildings? When all architectural, sociological, legal and town-planning requirements are fulfilled, highrise buildings have as few disadvantages as any other solution to the same housing problems. So there remains the question of its advantages. So far, the people to benefit are mainly the tenants and the public. It would be good if things could continue this way.

Selection of site

Highrise housing continues to be the exception to the rule, and the reasons are in its positioning and its impact. The responsibilities arising from this begin with the selection and the critical assessment of the site. For idealistic and ideological reasons alone, there cannot be the same freedom in siting highrise building as in standard schemes. Selection of position must follow even stricter rules when, for reasons of town-planning, further siting restrictions are imposed, usually through zonal regulations. The visual impact of highrise building, however, has an equally limiting effect. First of all its towering height results in the apparent widening of the site itself. Its greater size appears to be aggressive exhibitionism in a setting where traditional housing would merge into the landscape. The highrise block cannot disappear behind trees or in small hollows of ground, and when it towers above such natural screens, it attracts all the more attention.

Highrise buildings must be aesthetically satisfying from a distance as well. This is the first siting condition. Yet already here, two opposing theories exist. The contrasting versus the merging setting. Should the highrise block be seen, or should it, as far as possible, blend into its surroundings and make only the smallest possible impact? Bluntly put, the question is whether the highrise building should stand in front of, on top of, or behind the hill. Unfortunately, this is not so easily, and certainly not irrefutably answered.

Highrise building is the embodiment of contrast. It must be seen or else it would be, on town-planning grounds, a contradiction in terms. Therefore the highrise block set behind the hill is a simple image wrongly placed. Any attempt to hide a highrise building in its surroundings is misguided. If it is not to be seen, why build it at all? In such cases, traditional building forms, with their many variations, are always at one's disposal. To be sure, this is not to deny highrise buildings the use of sheltered positions, should this prove desirable for other reasons. The argument here concerns only the visual effect of highrise buildings, especially from a distance. The vital point is that the site is not made more desirable by the fact that the building would be out of sight. The people and authorities in charge indicate loss of the courage of their own convictions, if the positioning of a highrise building has to be explained away.

Much more difficult, because it depends so much on each individual case, is the actual assessment of the site according to whether it is better suited for adaptability or contrast. Although highrise building should make a strong visual impact, the effect must not be exaggerated. It would be a mistake to judge by historical precedents, although these are often quoted as parallels. The examples cited usually include watchtowers and fortresses, always built on high ground, or castles and churches, which were often built high up as well. In such comparisons, the function, purpose, significance, and appearance of the various buildings must be appropriately related to their actual dimensions. None of the historic buildings were set on rising ground purely for architectural effect.

The positioning of watchtowers and fortresses was functional, and the placing of churches and castles motivated by the desire to emphasize spiritual content and to demonstrate power. In such buildings content, form and position combine in an indivisible impression, so the spectator sees them with more than the usual feelings of polite boredom, which is described by Lessing as the reaction to beauty as such. A good building is beautiful, imposing and interesting at the same time. Even when the simplest man looks at such buildings, he remembers snatches of history and experiences vague feelings of something great and significant, though he may not have the least idea of what this has to do with the building itself.

With few exceptions, highrise blocks, on the other hand, have to exist by their looks alone. A pedestal is often the only thing between the V.I.P. and the braggard, and the highrise building remains a block of flats or offices even when it stands on top of the hill.

The decision whether the highrise house is to be adapted to its environment or contrasted with it cannot be made theoretically, by its appearance alone. Where there is freedom of choice, the preferable position will have to be decided in each individual case.

In the meantime, experience with the effects of highrise building has shown that there is something very like a basic rule, even though it is rather general. Highrise buildings enter the field of critical vision not only by their particular height, but also by their proportions and visual weight.

No perspective drawing of a project, however masterly, in which highrise buildings seem to float above ground level, can disguise this fact; indeed the very need to make the buildings appear, graphically, to be almost weightless reveals that their true effect is otherwise. There are, of course, considerable variations. The sensation of heaviness is determined by ground-plan design and the proportioning dimensions. Much less important, especially from distance, is the design of the façade. The more finely designed the highrise building appears, the more contrast it can stand.

The shape and size of the natural base on which the highrise building is to stand are not without importance, and the more massive it looks, the more visual weight it can be expected to carry. As far as the sensation of weight is concerned, the most critical height is probably that of other vertical elements, similar in height to the building itself. As highrise carriers, hills can easily lose their own significance, especially when they themselves are fenced round with standard housing. As a rule, the more contoured and massive they are in themselves, the more visual weight they can carry.

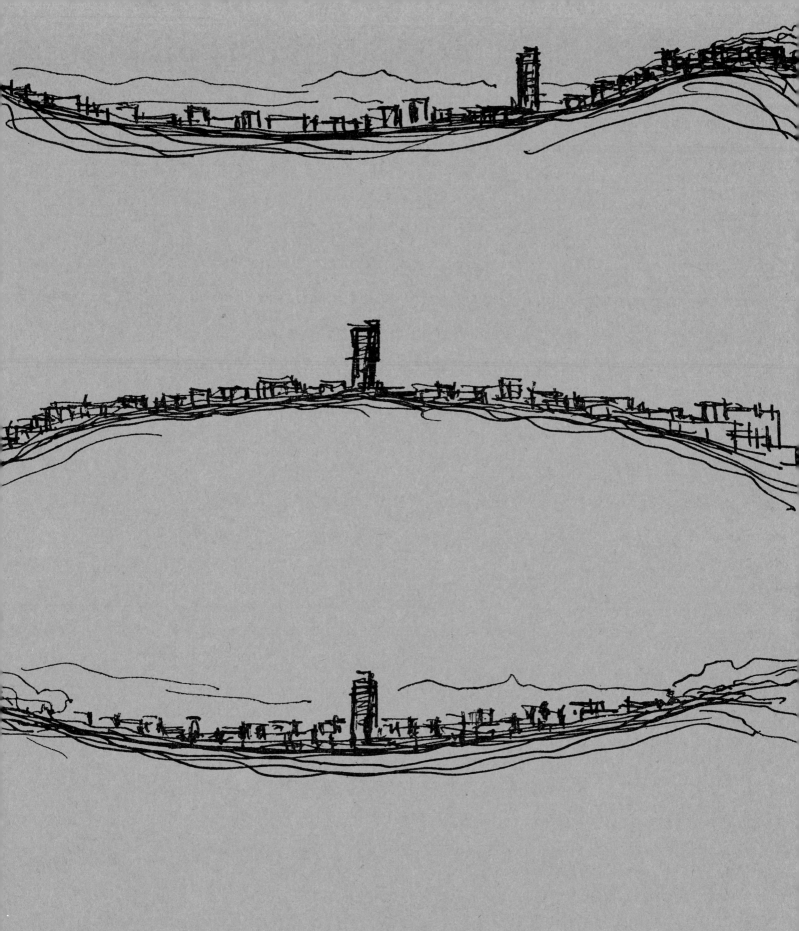

de gustibus non est disputandum!

*unlucky pride
of the citizens*

The effect of highrise buildings from the distance is not only determined by their own position, but by the background and scenery. In a plain, apart from the surrounding buildings, the question does not, of course, arise. This, incidentally, is the most appropriate situation for highrise buildings. Here the effect of its height becomes absolute, determined only by its own dimensions. The problems of visual effect only begin where surrounding heights appear to be in competition.

The effect, then, also depends on the surrounding scenery and its proportions in relation to the highrise building. If there is a clear difference in height between building and back-drop, the image is unambiguous and clear. Where, on the other hand, the height is only slightly exceeded or not quite reached, the picture is one of muddled relationships and disturbing effects. These impressions are stronger or weaker according to the proximity of building to background. They are strongest of all where the highrise building stands, so to speak, in the middle of the scenery and thereby becomes a part of it.

Of course, there are always vantage points from which a highrise building will not look well. But these should not be the criteria for the assessment of the site. Finding the critical vantage point is at least as important as choosing the site itself. Both points are the basic pre-requisites for the system of visual assessment. This should be self-evident, but often is far from being so. Frequently enough, in order to further or hinder highrise projects, vantage points of extreme advantage or disadvantage are chosen to judge its effect. This is as unfair as asking a dwarf to judge the hair style of a giant.

When choosing the vantage point, objective and subjective viewing procedures should be adopted. Objective viewing takes place from the proposed highrise building position. Subjective viewing must take into account the points from where the highrise block will be most frequently seen. In practice, that means from popular walks, views, approach-roads, railway-approaches, residential areas in close proximity to schools, or points of tourist interest. There may be some special cases of scientific or military interest, but generally these individual cases need not be considered. However, the assessment must not neglect to include any planned, though not yet built-up residential areas, although potential approach roads, walks or views must be rejected as invalid.

The effect of highrise buildings from a distance must be given the greatest possible attention, because experience has shown that this is far more significant that the close-up effect. There is nothing mysterious in this. From a close-up view there are no points of comparison to lead the eye from the height of the building to its environment. From close to, the building may seem high but never disturbingly so. If any sensation of restriction or oppression should arise, the cause does not lie in the height of the building, but in the lack of surrounding space, and this is discussed in another chapter.

The building position must of course be judged on more grounds than only those of visual effect. A great many other considerations, which may make a site just as unsuitable as the building's effect from a distance, play a far from unimportant part. This criterion, however, is the most important in the preliminary selection, where in practice the choice between adapting to or contrasting with the environment must be made. Then follow other considerations affecting site-selection such as: fitting the highrise building into the urban plan, its effect on the landscape or townscape, its relationship to existing or planned building environment, its position with regard to traffic, size, function and accessibility, and finally marginal conditions such as air-traffic security, subsoil water levels, etc.

Not very long ago, the consistency of the ground itself would have been an item on the list of criteria, but technological progress in the securing of foundations has been such that this point need not override town-planning considerations.

In the assessment of the site, its position must take precedence over all other criteria, since it establishes the scale that must be applied. As has been explained, no judgement of highrise housing can be absolute, and from the point of view of the building it becomes a question of its relationship with its environment. What may appear as no more than a dot in an immense townscape may disfigure a village with its visual brutality. There is also the question of whether there is any point in highrise building in villages. As, unfortunately, nowadays our concepts of future development are far from clear, there can

be no unequivocal answer, and it becomes necessary to examine highrise building within the range of various forms of development. In the main, these can be reduced to three characteristic cases: the city, the village and the open landscape.

Highrise buildings in the city

When we talk here about the city, it is principally meant in the sense of the major city with 100,000 or more inhabitants. It was basically for cities like these that highrise building was intended. Its advantages come into full focus here, and it is here that it can be most successful. The major city is generally the ideal place for highrise building.

How is highrise building to be incorporated into the existing structure of the city and what is its part in urban expansion? In other words: is there an urban overall plan, can it be created, is it at all possible? The structure of the compact city is usually based on the following pattern:

- Core: Ancient city with historical features
- First ring: Business and cultural 'town-centre'
- Second ring: Dense 5- to 6-storey residential area, with small traders, service industries and local shopping centres; square block developments
- Third ring: 3- to 4-storey dwellings, mainly terraced development
- Fourth ring: Urban area, small dwellings
- Fifth ring: Allotments, goods-yards, playing-fields
- Sixth ring: Open, free and reserve areas
- Seventh ring: Suburbs, from rural to independent rural character.

Industrial areas are often inserted between the second and third ring, and these sometimes spread as far out as the fifth ring. Often, for no apparent reason, a certain social differentiation occurs according to the points of the compass, even when there seems to be no topographical reason. Roughly speaking, the tendency is as follows:

Towards west and north: working class areas
Towards east and south: so-called better-class districts

city | core / old | city 1 | 2 | 3 | 4 | 5 | 6 | suburb 7 | landscape

schematic section through the compact city

Using these urban schemes as points of departure, it is self-evident that highrise building has no business to be in the core, the historical part, of the city. In addition to the need for preservation of this area (in which the fitting scale of the buildings plays a part), and to the protection of ancient monuments, the road network is usually narrow winding streets, quite unsuited to traffic. Such a layout could not support extra loading-points, even if highrise building were to be considered from the urban design point of view. However, the historical part of the city is not the place for architectural experiments. This at least is one point on which there seems to be general agreement. There may be exceptions where the buildings in the old parts are of questionable value, but as a rule doubtful cases should be decided in favour of historical areas. Even where the preservation of these districts has been neglected and their architectural content is not beyond criticism, they still play an important part in the structure of the town, sheltering craftsmen and cranks, artists and antique dealers, pawnbrokers and prostitutes; in these areas will be found bookshops and galleries, old-established firms and street-traders. In short this is a district which is animated, contradictory, yet full of originality and life; it is an essential element in any city. Only a puritan would wish to replace the nooks and crannies with quasi-hygienic, strictly geometric shapes and cubic experiments. There should be no highrise building in the city's historic core.

It is more debatable how far the first ring, the 'town-centre', is suitable for the siting of highrise building. Office blocks are the least controversial form of highrise building and should be appropriately placed in commercial districts, which are distinguished by a relatively high density of non-industrial work-places in a small area. As a rule it comprises no more than 3%–5% of the total urban housing area, though it accommodates more than half of all urban work-places. Generally the utilization rate in commercial districts is already high, and it can be increased further by highrise building. The regulation of such building (distances between blocks, open spaces etc.) is far less stringent than in residential areas. Living accommodation in these areas need scarcely be considered: it amounts to little more than floors occupied by caretakers, etc. It may be possible

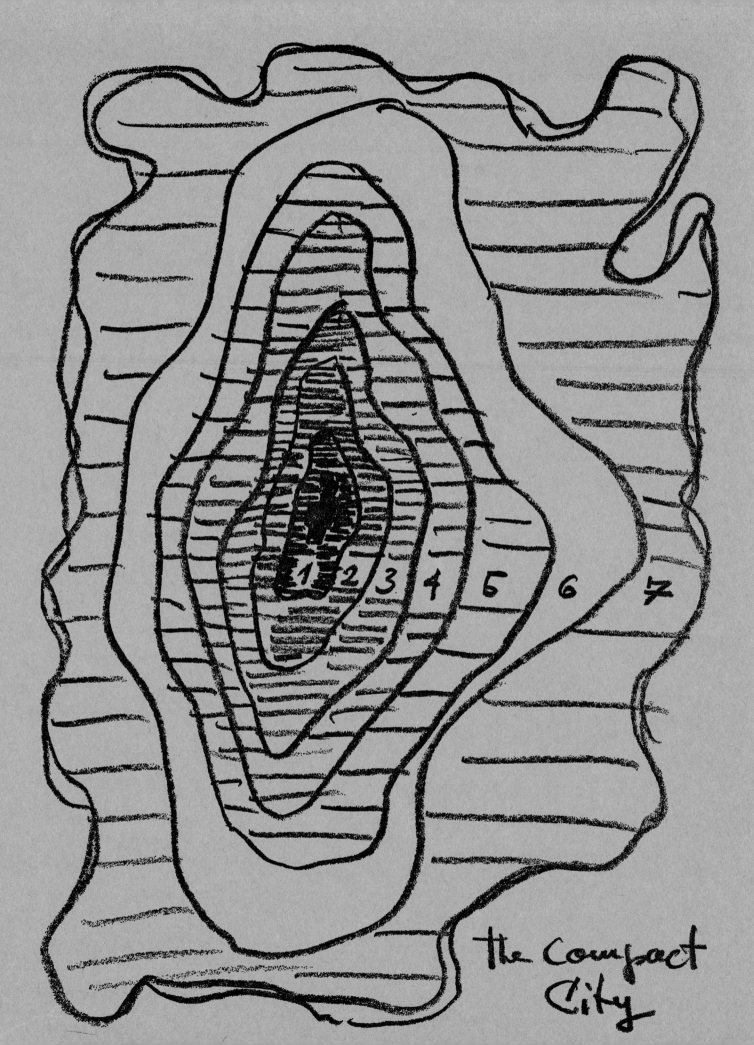

1 2 3 4 5 6 7

the Compact City

Frequency of visitors in the City

in very many cases to increase the utilization rate without producing overcrowding. The increase in office area will be welcome in many cities. This area will increase in any event, but will do so externally, at the expense of the second ring with its residential density. It would seem desirable to stabilize the town centre and contain this encroachment for some time to come.

There are, however, two serious obstacles to this course. Visually the concentration of highrise development may be unpleasant, and it will be disastrous if it surrounds and overshadows the old quarters with their churches and narrow streets. The practical obstacle to this development is the traffic congestion it produces. The main traffic sources, the residential districts, cover a far wider area than the commercial district. Business premises (in the area belonging to the tertiary circle: commerce, banking, insurance, management, etc.) have an average visitor incidence of from 5–7, compared with an incidence of 2 for premises in the rest of the town. The commercial district thus has a visitor density three times greater than the average, in an area twenty times smaller. Shopping and traffic to and from work swell the business traffic. The only remedy for this congestion is to reduce building in proportion to the absorption capacity of the street-grid. Attempts to keep the traffic moving by means of urban motorways, improved crossings and filter facilities are like the labours of Sisyphus. The problem of parking is almost greater than that of traffic-flow. Even if public transport were more widely used as a means of going to work there is still insufficient space for visitors' parking. However, the best means of keeping the business centres of large towns alive is a really efficient public transport system.

In its absence, many organizations will move away to districts accessible without so much expenditure of time and nervous energy. It follows that in business areas, the traffic absorption rate must determine the amount of building and not the other way around. This, however, limits the use of highrise building in the area where it most naturally belongs. In considering siting, it is necessary to add to the testing points discussed above the possibility of providing multiple parking facilities and improving the road-grid in the commercial city centre. If, thanks to highrise buildings, open spaces can be gained, so much the better, but in commercial districts this cannot be the main consideration.

A theory of town-planning which, so to speak, turns the urban fabric inside out, has been put forward in connection with highrise building in the commercial centres. At present, the density of buildings and utilisation in a town, forms something like a cone: the density is highest in the middle and decreases towards the outside. This theory proposes that the ratio should be reversed, with the lowest density at the centre, the highest on the periphery. The distribution of density would then form a sort of funnel. These proposals mainly concern building height and suggest the periphery as the proper place for highrise buildings. There are, however, so many objections to this restructuring of the city that one may as well forget about it. Yet the theory has its uses, if it does no more than reveal the problems of the business district as a central organism. This central position is far less sacrosanct than it would seem. It is the result of the pedestrian's town of the past. The majority of people were able to get to work and to the shopping and service centres by the shortest, most convenient route from dwellings that formed a dense ring around the commercial area. Basically, the same holds good for the motorist's town, but the concentration should be less dense to make the ratio between traffic-area and traffic-aim more favourable. Technically, this is quite appropriate, as cars can cover greater distances in the same time. The 'car-adjusted' city should have a central but expanded business section. Cities, however, are not 'car-adjusted' and can hardly be rebuilt to become so, or at least not in a reasonably short time. The purely 'motor-car city' is not to be thought of in connection with the evolved European town. In towns with more than half a million inhabitants, only an efficient public transport system, which at least at the core is disentangled from private traffic, will ever effectively solve the traffic problem.

Such transport must radiate from the town centre to points on the periphery. It is appropriate to think of the town centre as an axis or even a cross on the basis of the public transport routes.

Development in this direction can be observed in some major cities. If they have not yet come to much, the reason frequently lies in the shortcomings of public transport, with over-large distances between stops, lack of inducement to zoning and an unsuitable road-grid. Contrary to the liberal view that the principle of self-regulating development can be transferred from economics to urban design, this cannot be done. Towns need to be planned. If an expanded commercial sector seems desirable in the interest of the motorized city, then a deliberate policy of highrise building, coupled with correspondingly higher utilization possibilities, can provide the inducements to bring it into being. This would not mean the disappearance of the central sector, only the lightening of its load. The point would be to deflect businesses, by offers of better sites, to more suitable localities, instead of blindly allowing the unsatisfactory conditions to reproduce themselves, to the point of total disaster, in the bordering residential areas. Whether new town centre development is to be ribbon-like or in single points, as auxiliary centres to a new point of focus yet to be developed, is a secondary question which, in the event, will have to be answered by planning authorities. But if the aim is to examine the positioning of highrise buildings in relation to an all over urban plan, then the possibility of the expanding town centre becomes one of great importance, as this is where the problem of highrise building in the business sector lies.

In the second town ring with its dense dwelling areas, highrise building comes up against the same problems. In logical terms, its presence here would be well justified in the city structure, even if represented in smaller numbers than in the business sector. Moreover, as already indicated, it could improve to a marked degree the standard of living in these, for the most part antiquated, areas. But this proposal is once again confronted by the excessive utilization of existing buildings. Residential buildings, if they are to comply with social and hygienic requirements, must show a utilization figure of, at most, 1.0 (= usable storey area divided by the total area of the site). Anything above this figure means a reduction in living standards, regardless of the type of dwellings. A higher utilization figure can only be defended when the advantages of the site counter- 47 balance the diminished standard. This would apply in the second ring. However, even when siting advantages are taken into account, the figure may not be arbitrarily raised, particularly as larger families will have to be considered. The figure 1.5 could still be regarded as reasonable, but in such districts, the existing utilization figure is invariably higher as development occurred without utilization limitation, with minimum building distances. The solid sweep of buildings is invariably set alongside the building line. Their courtyards admit only the minimum incidence of light. Utilization figures of 3.0–4.0 are no rarity, and at corner sites the figure can reach 5.0 and more.

Even attempts to reduce the figure to 3.0 would only become feasible if parking areas for motor vehicles were provided underground as a matter of principle; and if, furthermore, the areas which are not yet built up, such as redundant road areas, were utilized. Also, a considerable part of the development should be executed in one- and two-storey base blocks to be used for commercial purposes, so that a justifiable amount of space for living accommodation would remain above the base.

There may be other solutions, but there is no way of redesigning the dense old districts without highrise building, although here again the question of increased traffic is raised. However, there seems to be a solution to this. For one thing, one is dealing with a source, not a traffic attracting area. Of course, a certain number of business premises would have to be taken into account, but they would cause less visiting traffic here than in the commercial sectors. In any case, residential areas produce less traffic. Thus the redevelopment of such zones would only be sensible on the basis of an appropriately improved road-grid, with fewer intersections, and designated functions for the various streets.

It is well worth giving every attention to the question of re-designing of town centres and the redevelopment of the crowded districts in the residential ring which are ripe for improvement. Anything of architectural value must of course be protected, but it would be quite wrong not to take the necessary steps because of misguided sentimental feelings for picaresque and romantic ugliness.

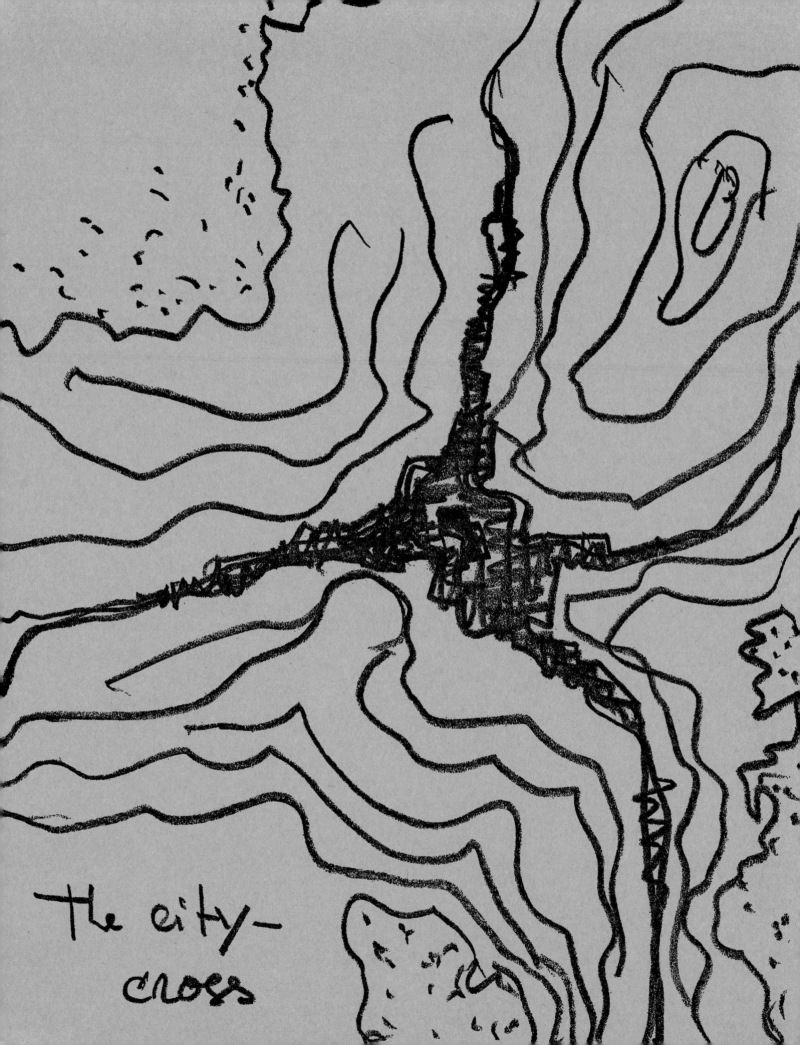

the city—
cross

City - axis

coefficient of use
2,5-3,5

The conception of a new district is comparatively easy, but it is very difficult indeed to make the interior of a compact city stay alive and worth living in. All the same, as many dwellings as possible must be preserved in the second ring, although some of the border areas will have to go to the business sector, which in most cases can no longer expand vertically but only horizontally unless another solution is found. The second ring should accommodate all those people whose tasks take them to the business sector at irregular times. Besides, it would be undesirable for sociological reasons alone to depopulate the central area. There is something ghost-like about an empty commercial centre in the evening. It would be worse if this area were enlarged, and it must not be overlooked that such dead zones tend to invite crime.

The central areas, with the exception of the historical core and its immediate surroundings, would be the natural home for highrise building, and it is unfortunately just there that the obstacles are most serious. There highrise building can at least fulfil its task of loosening the compact fabric. No doubt a more courageous time will come, when the excessive utilization figures will be drastically lowered. From the socio-economic point of view, this would be much less costly than the massive investments necessary to keep the traffic flowing in the inner zones alone. Only when there is a balance between architectural utilization and the traffic capacity of the streets will we have cities that are not a danger to themselves, and in this respect highrise building may be an encouraging portent.

With its 3- to 4-storey houses in terraces, rows of free-standing blocks, the third ring offers urban living conditions which are, depending on their character and position, perfectly tolerable, except where rows of terraced houses face directly on to the road and the noise considerably reduces living standards. There highrise housing, coupled with differentiated development, could introduce a real improvement. However, where living conditions are satisfactory, where 2-, 3- or 4-storey multi-family dwellings are surrounded by trees and gardens as in a garden city, it would be very wrong to substitute these by highrise blocks and mixed developments. The third ring, as a result of the desire for light, air and sunshine and the influence of the English and continental garden city movement, represents the residential zone proper for larger families and must be preserved for this purpose. The same holds good for the fourth ring, the zone of small urban dwellings. These zones, however, are more threatened for economic reasons than their multi-family neighbours. Small house areas are unjustly blamed for being ultimately uneconomical, in that they show too low a utilization rate, and so offer too few people the opportunity of living in favourable proximity to the central working locations. This reasoning, in as far as it is not based purely on speculatory interests, is wrong. It arises from a notion of equality, often labelled democratic, that where many suffer under bad conditions, it is wrong for the few to enjoy advantages. In practice, it is wrong mainly because it more or less ignores the modern traffic needs connected with modern town-planning. The traffic problem in the major cities cannot be solved by continued concentration, only by decentralization according to traffic capacity. Within such decentralization, the single-family dwelling is quite justified and not at all out of place, even if it cannot be the only form of accommodation in the European cities with their fine-meshed grids.

The fifth ring, with its allotments, sports grounds and goods yards, used to be the belt of reserve ground. Now, through increased building development, it has moved farther and farther away from the city into the country, although it is beginning to be stabilized wherever the city boundaries approach the suburbs. At the same time it is becoming more attractive. The sports grounds and goods yards overshoot the suburban belt and begin to settle on the newly established edge beyond the suburbs. The temptation to build up intensively this reserve belt also, is great. But from the dense inner ring outwards and sometimes even as far as the third ring, major cities suffer from a terrifying lack of space for sport, recreation and relaxation, and although such amenities in the fifth ring are at a considerable distance from the densely populated areas, it is better to have them there than not to have them at all. It would therefore be a serious mistake to build up the fifth ring, in as far as it is still able to overshoot the neighbouring suburbs. It should and must remain green.

Outside the fifth belt, urban development, usually determined by public transport routes, is linear and based on the bordering suburbs. In the sixth belt, in as far as it has an independent existence and is not simply to be a demarcation strip free of any building, between the fifth and the seventh, there are again good opportunities for highrise building. This is the urban expansion zone proper, the area for total development. Here, there are rarely any obstacles in the way of higher or highrise building. Single-dwelling zones are economically undesirable. Site utilization of the remaining ground reserves, generally makes it imperative to develop this area rather more densely than the fourth belt, and this is best done by a mixed development of high and low buildings. Nor is highrise building in these areas undesirable on visual grounds, as it can, in some cases, mark the city boundaries with great effect. In the interest of the greatest possible independence for the suburbs, a boundary that is distinguishable by horizontal green belts and vertical highrise blocks is definitely preferable to a feeble diffusion on the border area. This presupposes, however, that no such similarly distinguishable buildings are used in the suburban zones, as this would negate any attempt at distinction between the housing elements.

For the seventh suburban belt, a structural distribution of highrise building similar to that in the core could be envisaged. Whether such distribution is useful in practice must depend on the spread of the suburban area. As a rule, this area is considerably smaller than that of the core and a structurally recognizable disposition of highrise buildings only makes sense when the area is big enough for a large-scale effect. Also, as mentioned before, it would be a mistake in urban planning to counterpoint possible boundary demarcation of the city core by a similar suburban development. In suburbs, except for cases of potential twin or sister cities, highrise building should be confined to the centre. Suburbs do not need to produce the residential density of the city core. A looser, more rural way of housing is more appropriate and, in the framework of mixed development, highrise housing could make a great contribution.

52   The creation of distinctive centres in suburbs helps them to

depopulated inner city

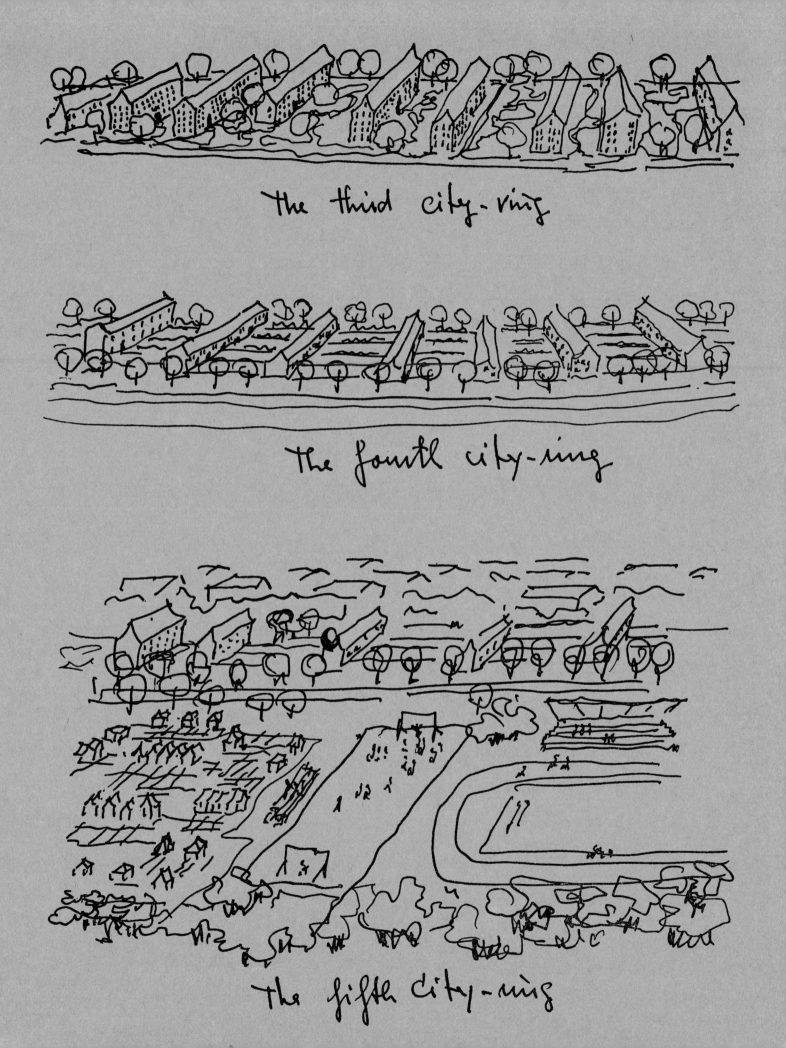

The third city-ring

The fourth city-ring

The fifth city-ring

The sixth city ring

emerge as independent urban elements instead of mere accommodation units, and is well worth aiming for in the urban plan, especially when it is not possible to separate the town from its suburbs by a sufficiently wide green belt. Furthermore, if a suburb is to be more than a mere dormitory, it needs its own shopping and cultural centre, designed to complement and thereby to ease the burden of the central core.

Experiences with the central urban sector show that it would be inadvisable to try to develop the suburban centres on the grid of the old village centres. The opportunity to create enough traffic space and, more important still, parking areas must not be wasted. Often the question arises whether it would not be better to place the centre in an entirely new position, instead of where it had been in a previous development. If this question was exclusively technical, the answer would be an unreserved affirmative, because the conversion from village to modern suburban centre is always a difficult, time-consuming process. Nevertheless, the more difficult process of gradual change is usually preferable, unless the old village centre represents an architectural achievement worth preserving, in which case the new centre must give way. However, the suburb must be one of considerable size if the new centre is to flourish while the old one remains in architectural existence. As a rule, the position of what the inhabitants regard as the centre of their region cannot be wilfully moved from one place to the other. A town centre is not merely made by architectural design, nor by the presence of one or the other amenity, but by being an unquestioned central point of the city and identified as such by everyone. Such key points can only form when siting, architecture and amenities represent an inner unity. If that is lacking, the centre disintegrates and the various elements scatter over the entire building area. The result is a meaningless collection of buildings, such as can, unfortunately, often be seen in the residential regions of our major cities.

Highrise building could be particularly effective in counterbalancing the characterless, undesigned regions of urban expansion. It would certainly be effective in stressing the centres of suburbs, but it cannot actually bring them into being. Experience has shown that the arbitrary scattering of highrise

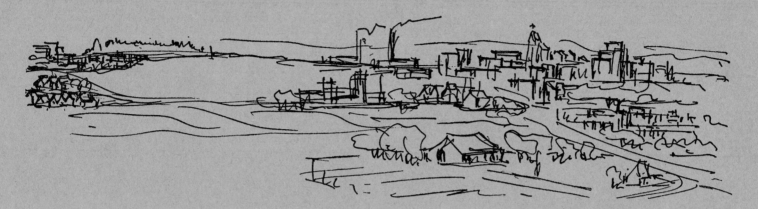

buildings over urban and suburban regions fails to achieve the desired result of giving shape to the building mass. It merely adds yet another element to the amorphous urban structure. While it makes many local improvements feasible, it, surprisingly, does not help articulate the various building elements. This proves, beyond all doubt, that the use of highrise building as a local emphasis is not in itself meaningful. It only becomes significant when the separate buildings express a distinctive idea beyond their physical presence.

If highrise building was incorporated into the urban structure for aesthetic reasons alone, it would be no more than an empty gesture. There are two ways of determining whether or not to use highrise building: by the structural character of the city, or by specific suitability of the highrise block. In the latter case, however, highrise building loses its ordering or stressing characteristics, and if this approach were to prevail, highrise buildings would be regarded as no more than huge residential or office blocks. The exterior of a highrise building does not indicate a business sector, a central residential district, a town boundary or a suburban centre. No one, having been once or twice misled by the signs, will pay any further attention to them. The more frequently highrise building appears on the urban scene, the more familiar it will become.

Observing the development of highrise building in the cities of Europe, the tendency to use it arbitrarily within the over all structural order clearly emerges, although visible efforts have been made to take into account as far as possible its specific characteristics and requirements. This tendency, however, demonstrates a defeat, a retreat to the lines of expediency, which correspond to the pluralistic character of contemporary society, which cannot agree on a common concept of total regional planning.

This state of affairs is inevitable. It will therefore only be possible in the rarest cases to incorporate highrise buildings into a total urban order. There should at least be an attempt to state in local regulations where highrise houses should not be built, even though the attempt to prescribe where they would be acceptable, or even, welcomed would pose many problems. There are four zones in the urban structure where highrise

buildings should be barred: in the historic core and its immediate neighbourhood, in well-kept and well laid-out districts of 2- to 4-storey multi-family housing, in areas of small dwellings, and in the green belt with its sports and recreation facilities. In the central sectors, always excepting the historic parts, the toleration of highrise building depends, next to its visual effect, on the traffic conditions. In all other urban areas, it must always be a question of specific suitability.

If the use of highrise building in major cities depends in the main on its specific suitability, this applies all the more in the case of small and medium-sized towns. A small town with up to about ten thousand inhabitants is, properly speaking, too small to accommodate the massive effect of a highrise block within the framework of a planned development. The small town should be content with taller blocks. The critical size of a city capable of providing sufficient space for highrise building lies in around twenty-five thousand inhabitants with a residential area of about two and a half to three miles square. Below this general minimum, highrise buildings tend to look rather brutal and out of proportion, but even in a city of fifty thousand, this building form should at most be used to emphasize the centre or to mark the approaches. If it was more widely used, it would soon lose its distinguishing effect.

The choice of sites for highrise buildings is rarely based on the requirements of the overall plan, but rather on the specific suitability of the highrise block. This makes the consideration of the site even more important. In the absence of an urban plan that would regulate the siting of highrise buildings, the greatest care must be taken in assessing the effect of highrise buildings on the whole townscape, with regard to the possibility that first one or two and finally a considerable number of highrise blocks may appear.

It has already been established that there is no place for highrise building in the historical core and its vicinity. Generally, a horizontal distance of at least six to sixteen hundred feet, depending on the height and mass of the building, is necessary to avoid visual competition between highrise building and the sector which is to be protected. Features such as steeples, gables or any other tall buildings are usually the points to watch.

development of the village center into a suburb

The higher building in the small towns

city-village

Particularly vulnerable are historic settlements by the seashore or on river banks, or those set against large grassy slopes, where their full silhouette can be seen. Here, nothing too tall or massive should be built even at a considerable distance. The minimum distance must be at least sixteen hundred feet. The topographical position can, of course, ease or aggravate the problem.

Equally sensitive to visual competition are buildings that already have a distinctive character of their own, even when they do not form part of the historic sector. Their effect can easily be spoilt when a building rises even to the same height. This is similar to the disturbing effect when over-tall buildings are set around the edge of a square, which should evoke a feeling of space. The lower the surrounding heights, the more spacious the effect. When the building height equals the building distance, the effect is lost, and the square seems to become a mere courtyard. Even if the height exceeds the limit on one side only, it produces a tight, constricting feeling, unless the other three sides are particularly low. On the other hand, a square edged with low buildings can increase the apparent height of any individual building.

After the effects of highrise building, both close-up and distant, have been carefully examined, another aspect needs to be considered. According to the theory of the intensifying effect of opposites, a highrise building is capable of transforming an older, but well-preserved district into a visual slum. Highrise building still carries the aura of the new and modern, and is likely to do so for some time to come. As a result of its height and mass, it tends to overpower its surroundings not only by its size, but all the other aspects of its appearance.

Therefore it is not enough to estimate the effect of highrise building on the urban silhouette and the wider urban scene alone. The same attention must be given to its impact on its immediate neighbours, particularly when it is to be introduced into an existing or previously planned development. Wherever it is provided with suitable surroundings within the framework of a mixed development, its success is solely dependent on the skill of the architect, and in such cases only the suitability of the building complex as a whole needs special examination. 57

In the case of the individual highrise block, however, there is already an existing framework which was created with no intention of including a higher edifice. Whilst there can be some modulation between the old and the new in a mixed building development, this is not so with the individual highrise block. This does not mean that there ought to be a compromise with the existing environment; any insignificant difference of, say, only one or two storeys is definitely to be rejected. Any such device, though very useful in the contrasting and shaping of long rows of conventional housing, would deny highrise building its characteristic impact. Highrise buildings ought to be taller than their neighbours not merge with them. In the field of standard building, no such merging would be possible. It is precisely here that highrise building appears as something special and specific. An initial adjustment in the building mass rather than in actual height can lead to a certain reduction in volume which makes for good proportions.

When a city opens its gates to highrise buildings, inhabitants and authorities must clearly realize that the town picture will now begin to change. What was flat and even, interrupted at most by a few spires, will be replaced by something less calm and more dramatic. Small towns, in particular, will lose a certain ambiance of intimacy and modesty. Highrise blocks have something loud and aggressive about them. That is their strength and their weakness. On the other hand, highrise blocks create an urban atmosphere, even when they are used in a loosely built-up area, and that is their contribution. Where highrise building gives character to a newly developed area, it has found its best application. Where it has been used sporadically in a district quite differently conceived, it will never seem at home, no matter what else can be said in its favour. In such districts, some sort of group treatment should be aimed for, which would more clearly and satisfactorily express the duality of the urban conception. Districts with a certain unity of their own may be robbed of their only strong accent when highrise buildings are introduced.

Urban designers naturally prefer to plan the effect of such groups in advance. It goes against the grain to leave it to chance. When there is no overall scheme, this is far from easy

old town and skyscraper in silhouette

to achieve. It cannot be forced, only stimulated and encouraged. Efforts should be made, even so, to regulate the distribution of highrise blocks in the evolving urban structure, even if present conditions do not favour more precise and, as a result, stricter controls.

Highrise in the village

After all that has been said about highrise building in the city, it is clear that it must be out of place in a village and rural structure. In the context of building, the concept of the village consists of one- to two-storey houses. The make-up of a village is characterized by the predominance, or at least the noticeable presence, of a peasant population. Villages are typed, and named, according to their layout: roadside village, squared village, clustered village, etc. The village is, in effect, the opposite form of settlement to the town. Its distinguishing marks contrast completely with those of the city: low buildings rather than high ones; loose, not dense development; isolated houses surrounded by green spaces; communal life based on local proximity instead of privacy; a daily routine dependent on the sun and the seasons; and close contact with nature. The characteristics of the village are not only in complete opposition to those of the town, but also to those of highrise building, which stands for all that is urban in thinking and feeling. No further argument is needed to show that highrise building is to be rejected in villages.

However, in practice, the concept of the village is no longer so clear-cut. The influence of the spreading town and the industrialized economy have produced forms of settlement which, in the absence of a more suitable term, are also called villages. Generally, they emerged from true villages. Frequently, they borrowed architectural manners from the villages. But in their social structure, and therefore in the behaviour of their inhabitants, they more nearly approximate to the town. These settlements may reach considerable size. There are all those villages which generally, in time, reach the statistical urban minimum, but which prefer to pretend that they are not towns at all. Their ground plan usually develops after the village pattern, even

when the resulting disadvantages are quite evident. These townlets, to distinguish them by this term, will sooner or later have to decide whether to open their doors to highrise building. Both population and authorities are usually divided in their views. One side sees highrise building as an unrural element, to be rejected for that very reason; the other side is ready to welcome it, just because it could show that village status has been outgrown. Both sides, however, obstinately cling to the rural layout. They build narrow roads with no pavements, tolerate building distances with insufficient light-incidence, omit the provision of private and public parking areas, and boast of the freedom they have preserved, only to create a confusion of buildings and uses which will be hard to disentangle later. These townlets are far from ready for the highrise block. Such an approach gives one good cause to fear that highrise blocks will be misused, to become little more than up-ended barracks. There are already enough examples, in places such as these, of highrise buildings which are inappropriately sited or built. The plans of the flats are usually based on those in conventional blocks, often on below-average types at that, lacking all the specific additional amenities of highrise building as well as open spaces.

But even when all the rules are observed, highrise buildings in townlets remain a problem. A highrise block is simply too massive in relation to the existing architectural scale, and too urban for what are, after all, surroundings of a rural character. In townlets with only a modest expectation of growth, highrise buildings would be absolutely out of place. The effect of such blocks, usually left standing in isolation, is reminiscent of such dilapidated monuments of misguided civic pride as the single blocks of flats frequently seen near the railway stations of smaller villages.

In the smaller townlet of under five thousand inhabitants, as in the village proper, no higher and certainly no highrise building should be introduced. In the larger townlet, the higher block alone would be able to offer enough scope for differentiation, urban contrast and lively treatment.

Highrise building in suburban communities in the process of being transformed into suburbs proper are particularly hard to assess. Such districts often present themselves in rather rural garb, though they are usually interspersed or surrounded by urban-looking buildings. Only in rare cases is the development suited to the character of the position. This is especially true in the case of sloping and seaside sites, where single-family houses, farmhouses or multi-family blocks of modest mass, surrounded by greenery, usually spring up by themselves. In such cases it is not difficult to change, reorganize or even preserve the original village. Although the building forms may alter, the scale and impression of rural grouping remains. In such suburban settings, highrise and higher blocks seem like interlopers and are indeed generally met with unanimous opposition by population and authorities. Even people who do not usually take much part in public affairs will sometimes be moved to oppose highrise buildings because they wish to continue in their accustomed way of life and therefore object to changes in their surroundings.

Often, landscape, traffic, geographical situation and existing buildings leave a free choice between rural- or urban-orientated building methods. Often, there is no set policy to suggest development in one or the other direction. The impetus to development does not, after all, rest with the community itself. It comes from outside, from the expanding city, and affects the community whether or not it desires this state of affairs and even if it wishes to prevent it. The number of inhabitants grows without much concern on the part of the newcomers, who are usually only too pleased to have found partially suitable accommodation, to worry about the further development of their new environment. The policy decisions thus rest with the old inhabitants who, in such cases, often suffer a peculiar inner conflict. They are usually the owners of property. By origin and nature, they would prefer to preserve a village, or at least a rural atmosphere. But, being land-owners, they are naturally interested in the rise of land prices which they sometimes mistakenly expect from urban building. Thus quite often, there is the spectacle of the dyed-in-the wool countryman, the peasant and the rural craftsman playing the role of protagonists for urban building methods and highrise building, in particular. They try to still their consciences with practical-sounding phrases about progress that must not be opposed. Discussions of highrise building, in particular, tend to mobilize another section of the population that suddenly remembers that it is actually living in the country. From this sector come the counter-prophets who, either out of true affection for the country or from the fear of suddenly finding themselves in a pseudo-city of little promise, denounce the city and highrise building. Apart from noting attitudes tinged by financial interest or emotion, it is difficult to give professional advice on the right approach. It would certainly be a mistake to force rural building methods, soon to become anachronistic, on to a suburb rapidly growing into a town. It would be equally wrong to encourage spasmodic and slow-growing suburban communities to experiment with urban forms which, because of their isolated appearances, would for a long time to come turn them into rural hermaphrodites. Of course, a suburban community which will later be incorporated into an urban region must, as far as architectural activity is concerned, be judged differently from independent rural communities, whether villages or townlets. The dicisive factor must be the rate of devlelopment. If the change to urban status is expected within, at the most, fifty years, it would be justifiable to judge the architectural treatment in terms of the probable total development. The rather disturbing appearance of such a locality caused by the proximity of rural and urban features will then have to be accepted during its metamorphosis. There is no other way of achieving a transformation in urban design, it must be done with careful attention to detail, as well as to all the stages of the overall plan. In these circumstances, it would be wrong to prettify or waste good design solutions through misplaced anxiety. It would be foolish to create a city which would already be out of date before the first foundations had been fully excavated. If the higher or the highrise block could contribute to a satisfactory solution, then there is no reason why it should not be built, even if to begin with cows still graze in its vicinity.

A slow degree of acceleration offers a different problem. If the urbanization of a suburb seems improbable within a housing generation, an intermediate building plan, of the kind roughly appropriate for a townlet, should be introduced. A higher block

The acceleration of
Development

Suburb   Village   Town

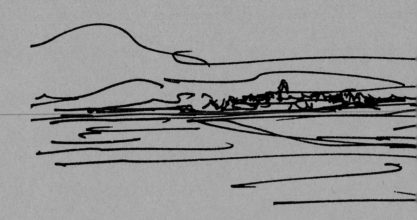

of modest dimensions might be considered, but not a highrise building. Planning and design should then concentrate more on the departure point of the development than on the finalization, which should be the prerogative of a later generation. No generation appreciates having issues prejudged which in its opinion ought to follow different lines.

From this point of view, even a fifty year span seems too long. Urban planning, however, must reckon with different periods of time than, say, traffic planning. Town building, however accelerated, is still rather slow and once built, it is not so quickly altered. From the economic point of view, the ammortization period is held to be roughly fifty years, after which period fresh urban changes might reasonably be considered.

It may seem timid not to settle the development of a community once and for all, and to act accordingly. Some may still remember the slogan which declared that town-planning could affect centuries to come. Experience has proved otherwise. One thing however is true: while architectural appearances may change, the ground plan, and in particular the road layout, remains the same. Therefore, when a transitory phase is deliberately planned in a suburb-to-be, it has to be based on a road layout adequate to carry the later, denser development. This applies especially to the traffic capacity of the road, the design of junctions and the distance between building lines.

Highrise and landscape

If highrise blocks are to be barred from villages, they must equally be banned from the open countryside, and it seems superfluous to say more. Buildings in the rural landscape are as a rule only sympathetic when they serve for its conservation or enjoyment. As long as they are built of natural materials like wood or stone, modest in dimension and successful in execution, they can look pleasing to the eye. Other buildings, though quite small, can be most disagreeable in their effect. A small electricity sub-station or a stray suburban villa may painfully disrupt the natural harmony of an otherwise unspoilt landscape. How much more disturbing would be the effect of a highrise block.

Technology has, in any case, made visible inroads on the landscape. Railways, funiculars of all kinds, electrical wires and telephone lines, power stations, aerodromes and other technical installations 'decorate' the landscape like so many cobwebs and fly blowings on a work of art. Necessary accessories of civilization though they may be, they are nevertheless disturbing. Then there are the scattered buildings, holiday houses, and even stray factories, that rob the landscape of its original impact.

Yet, it is still relevant to consider whether or not highrise buildings should be set in the open landscape. The suggestion of replacing the traditional village with a single highrise block to house all its inhabitants is well-known, the argument being that not only would valuable productive land be saved, but also living standards would be raised and furthermore, the necessary services better and more cheaply supplied. Intellectually, these arguments are valid. If a rural settlement was only a question of accountancy, the collective highrise block would no doubt be a solution which deserved further consideration. However, farming is much more than an arithmetical problem. It is also a craft strongly influenced by emotional attitudes, not least because of its close link with the seasons, which also determine its daily and annual routine. Age-old production methods have over the generations produced an entirely separate culture and behaviour. These are, of course, subject to change with the changing times, but they remain basically the same. Farmstead and soil form an entity and whenever this is disturbed, every effort is made to re-establish it. Present-day Swiss conditions seem to favour the one-man farm with its farmer occupant. The large villages that used to represent the great unity of farm and land are being penetrated by other branches of the economy and architecturally interspersed with alien buildings. There is also the frequent parcelling up of land as a result of inheritance laws. Modern farm-collectivism promotes renting of rural establishments and thereby favours individual or group settlements. This leads to the farmer's exodus from the village. It aims partly at economically short journeys to work, but also partly secures for the farmer his traditional, entirely appropriate way of life. The collective highrise building, however, would stand in the way of this process, which seems likely to bring about real improvements in Swiss agricultural conditions.

It is possible that agriculture, regardless of property considerations, may move increasingly towards collective management. There are certainly signs of this trend even in the countries of the West. Part of this will be communal stabling, machine and repair co-operatives and even communal administration. A communal residence would seem less questionable than it at first appears. It is interesting to note that the collectivism of farmers, even in countries where it is otherwise well advanced, such as in Israel, has stopped just short of communal housing. The Russian experiment of gathering farmers into agro-cities evidently did not progress much beyond the inception of the original idea. Strangely enough, efforts towards collective farming have two opposite causes: lack of labour, or the overabundance of it. Figures show that production is highest where the individual farmer is his own master, and attempts at collective farming in the West are expedients to aid him in preserving his self-employing status. But the most meaningful expression of this effort is the unity of farm and soil, even if part of the scheme is run collectively for economic reasons. Although it may be theoretically possible for the farmer to remain a free agent even in a communal highrise block, the strongest bastion against total collectivism, that of living on his own soil, would have fallen. It cannot be ignored that the residential highrise block, like any multi-family dwelling, expresses a significant change in the social structure: the relative decrease in self-employment and a corresponding increase in the numbers of employees. This feature, which is inherent in industry proper as well as in the service industries, is what has led to our housing conglomerations. There is nothing to be done. The director's villa, once common and now already out of date, signifies in answer to this no more than a comforting illusion, a reaction in a battle that has been lost before it has begun. In agriculture, the trend goes in the opposite direction. Agricultural establishments consist more and more of family units, even couples. This leads to isolation instead of agglomeration. Here lies the deeper reason for the depopulation and consequent

63

change of the farming villages, which very nearly seems like self-destruction. This trend is expressed by the farmhouse, not by the highrise building, which, as an idea, still remains bewildering and without cultural, social or economic justification. And when free-standing highrise buildings in the open landscape cannot be justified even by reasons which are difficult to argue against, how much less chance of justification remains in other cases.

There are other cases: convalescent homes in favourable climates, hotels in tourist districts, residential blocks for local industries, or freehold holiday flats. At the turn of the century, a great many, far from modest hotels were set in the most beautiful natural surroundings. True, they were disguised as castles and fortresses, and if ever they had to be justified, it was said in explanation that castles and forts had always been set in the open countryside. Although their dimensions obviously did not approach those of highrise buildings, many reached those of the higher block, so there is no lack of illustrative evidence. It may well be an attractive thought to contrast the free organic shapes of, say, the mountains, with the strictly geometric building mass, and there are examples which are interesting in this way. But in the majority of cases, such buildings look like interlopers, all too frequently monstrosities spoiling the very landscape they were built to commercialize. The tourist trade is part of the modern world, and if it is concentrated in the regions most worth seeing, that is only logical. But it is equally logical that the tourist installations should be adapted and subjugated to their surroundings. Highrise and higher buildings are not adaptable in this sense and are therefore to be rejected in the open landscape.

The same applies in the open country to highrise and higher buildings with other functions. Modern architecture offers many other building forms which could be made to fit into the landscape without detrimental effect to their appearance or purpose, should the building's function require such siting. To ask for abstention from highrise building on such sites is therefore not an unreasonable demand, only a request for the now essential consideration of the little in nature that is left in the highly industrialized regions of central Europe.

Highrise building – single or grouped

According to the original concept, individual highrise blocks coupled with lower buildings express all that is most meaningful in highrise building. The highrise block, landmark and dominator in one, can then ideally do justice to its function of accentuation and loosening the uniform mass of the compact city. But its use in this sense would presuppose a strict adherence to an over-all plan. As we have seen, no such plan exists nor is possible within the present structure of our pluralistic society, particularly in connection with a form of building capable of serving more than one purpose. Highrise building, in isolated application within today's town structure, only confirms that modern towns have grown from architectural entities into many-sided organisms, in contrast to the towns of the Middle Ages which were characterized by architectural variety within a general urban harmony. As a matter of fact, no city has yet made an attempt to work highrise building into its fabric within a wider urban programme. After some early beginnings in this direction, the tendency is now to assess highrise blocks according to their requirements in a specific position and their suitability in the areas for which they are planned. This must inevitably lead to the dispersed, apparently arbitrary distribution of highrise building in our cities. It may well be the reason why the initial aesthetic motivation to highrise building has given way to a sociological one.

The idea of visually uniform districts broken up by highrise buildings has given way to the concept of the highrise building being introduced into a socially undifferentiated district to allow the population to be socially more widely integrated. Thus highrise building has moved increasingly into new zones where it can help in the creation of a social intermingling from the start. This, however, will only work when dwellings of different sizes and price ranges can be offered. Locally limited housing programmes of this sort preclude, *a priori*, the mere addition of similar housing. On the contrary, there must be greatly differentiated housing, which in turn must provide a good variety of accommodation. It follows that the development must consist of building or housing forms which have now found acceptance under the term of differentiated development.

Residential schemes like these are composed of low buildings, such as rows or clusters of single-family dwellings, higher multi-family blocks and a few highrise buildings. Larger families with four or more children should live in the low buildings, normal-sized families in well-designed multi-family blocks of no more than three or four storeys, and small families, couples and single people especially, in the highrise blocks. The differentiated appointments of the flats and the different attractions of the various sites should achieve a social mixture of considerable breadth, besides attracting households of various sizes and different age groups. The doctrine of differentiated building has been so whole-heartedly accepted that it has almost become the exclusive field for highrise building. The housing group has much to be said for it, but as an idea, it has already been riddled with holes before it has properly established itself. At best, it usually provides a number of different-sized flats according to the building type. In this way, there should be at least a mixture of households of varying sizes. But even this modest programme has only in part been realized. The highrise buildings in such schemes also contain larger flats. The multi-family blocks often resemble rather massive high slabs. One-family houses are not infrequently rejected, so that what is left is a differentiated estate with a population fairly similar in household size, age and social status. Such estates are no more than groups of buildings and are not socially satisfactory. Often enough, they are pseudo-aesthetic creations with no inner meaning. Occasionally they degenerate into a sort of colossal landscape sculpture without an artistic message. Certainly, large open spaces can be achieved in this way. Circulation is more rational. The flats get more sun because of the larger distances between buildings. But living standards do not rise in proportion to the pretended monumentality. The barrack-like character of such groups both in use and appearance differs only very slightly from the traditional tight square development with courtyards. Compared to the landscaped four-storey zones which were built before and particularly after the Second World War, they seem a retrograde step.

mixed
building types

It is no doubt praiseworthy to try and counteract the all too great effect of monotony in urban districts. The exclusive company of people of similar social status in a neighbourhood is conducive to a blinkered outlook, whatever the status of the inhabitants. If the composition of an estate population is moreover limited by age, profession and origin, the inhabitants will adopt a picture of the world that will gradually exclude any consciousness and understanding of the variety of life. However, if the aims are not too ambitious and the mixture is not expected, after the rural pattern, to contain anyone from a cabinet-minister to a labourer, then they may well be capable of achievement. If the new estates are more mixed than the old ones, then this state of affairs is more easily maintained in differentiated building groups. Mixed building favours a mixture corresponding to the population, unless uniformity of accommodation should cancel it out again. Differentiated building should not be confined to the mere differentiation of the formal elements, but must be expressed first of all in a difference of size and type in the accommodation provided. That this is best achieved by the specific suitability of the various building forms for a particular type of accommodation should be self-evident. Highrise blocks therefore seem most appropriate for small apartments and one-room flats.

Beyond this, the special requirements and the strong visual impact of highrise blocks argue for their use within a framework of mixed building. Requirements regarding shadows cast on neighbouring buildings and the protection of their outlook, sufficient surrounding greenery in relation to height, sufficient parking facilities and the blending-in with the environment can only rarely be fulfilled in a combination with any existing development. There, highrise buildings tend to look like intruders. This danger also exists in the case of a group of new buildings. Highrise buildings must always be the determining factor; and the rest of the development has to be adapted to them. In an existing development, however, the environment dictates the setting for the highrise block, which by its nature is so little adaptable. Basically, it is not suitable for use outside the framework of an overall design, and even within a group it can be unconvincing. It is at its most effective when used in a scheme that has a considerable area at its disposal. Experience shows that a group with only a single highrise block would require an area not smaller than two and a half acres and those with several, at least seven and a half acres. These are the minimum requirements, and if such minimum groups are placed too close together, the result can easily look like an arbitrary development. If green belts or streets with planting do not visually divide the various complexes into separate groups, the impression produced is one of a city in disintegration. Thus it is not surprising that there is a clear call for the more compact city, a reaction to the arbitrary fragmentation of the city area. This danger could be avoided if these residential schemes were planned to cover areas at least the size of small districts. Occasionally this is indeed the case, but then it is mostly a matter of luck, and such conditions are not usual. It would be quite possible to set up a plan designed to create harmony not only within building groups but also between them. The realization of such a plan, however, would depend on so many and such varied contingencies, and on the understanding of all the participants and their readiness to become a part of a larger whole, that it would have to lie under a particularly propitious star to succeed. There is little point in trying to find out the exact conditions needed for the creation of model cities. The task of urban planning must be to cope with the multiplicity of requirements, forms and ideas within a larger design, at least to the point where the ideal model city can become a city model.

The pure highrise complex must be regarded as the exception among building groups, although it would be justified in cases where parklike areas with fine trees need sensitive, yet economic development. Such groups could also be used to link two zones or regions where, for some reason, total separation was no longer possible but visual building density had to be reduced. For estate developments proper, the use of highrise complexes is questionable. Apart from the monotony of such repeated monumentality, it would mean a misuse of highrise building, and achieve, precisely what it was designed to prevent, a district of nearly uniform height. This is not by any means to say that the solitary, isolated highrise block should be rejected. In the business sectors, when there are no special obstacles (such as proximity to historic areas or the usual traffic chaos), as well as in zones of dense development, it could render useful service. But the motivation must come from urban design and the block must be able to be integrated into an already existing environment. A highrise block of flats or offices must not be set in a busy traffic area, where its own traffic would only increase the congestion. As far as possible, its own parking area should be confined to its own site and, wherever possible, in the basement. Children living in highrise buildings should have enough green open spaces to play in safety and in peace. Roof gardens may, at a pinch, fulfil this purpose, although there is no justification for regarding them as our answer to the hanging gardens of Babylon.

The appearance of our cities will be far more changed by isolated highrise buildings than by differentiated building groups. The feeling of nicely-proportioned scale, too hastily denounced as monotony, will be replaced by an irregular, restless picture. It may be that this is far more appropriate to the spirit of modern man than the over-reticence of previous urban design. In addition, the scale of highrise building suits our modern, over-wide streets better than the close-fronted sweeps of five-storey buildings. Thus, our city plans are overlaid with yet another layer, that of tall houses and wide streets, although the previous layers will not totally disappear in consequence. In many cases, regrettably, it will mean the loss of a certain intimate cosiness. Yet, it is a sign of a society that has remained lively, and is striving for an appropriate way of expressing itself in architecture and urban design. This explains why it is impossible to fight against such signs of vitality with a doctrine or ideology of urban planning. Mountain streams cannot be explained away, but they can be controlled so as to do no harm. With all the yearning for a strict overall urban plan, it is creditable indeed when something new and different finds a place for itself without destroying what is old and good. Thus highrise building is best situated where cities are expanded and legitimately renewed. And it is the mixed building group rather than the isolated highrise block which is most suited by character to serve as a new regenerating element in the process of urban design.

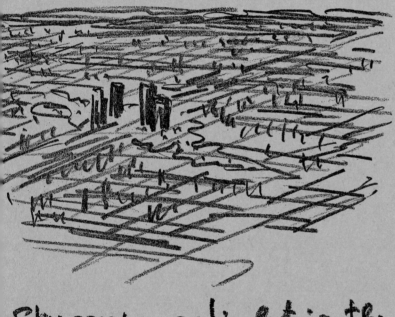

Skyscraper articulating the
cross-point of a metropolis

Rule or exception?

What contractors long for, the legal profession advocates (against its own interests), and architects half wish and half fear, is town-planning capable of execution according to a few handy rules. But where mixed building schemes are recommended as the better form of urban design, and where highrise building is required as a design element, town-planning approaches the other extreme; not a total absence of rules, but rules governed by individual circumstances. Highrise blocks cannot be forced into total development schemes when they are to exist in the framework of a mixed building group, nor when they are to be integrated into an existing development. Highrise building is the exception in urban planning and likely to remain so. It would only be logical if it were so regarded in building law. The principle of equality before the law does, after all, not say that the same rules apply to every case. It only requires that similar facts are treated similarly, and binds the authorities to similar decisions in similar cases. It is in the nature of zonal building regulations that, provided the regulations are adhered to, every project constitutes legally a similar case. Urban plans are no longer realized by the sum of individual buildings but by the development of whole districts.

The highrise block, on the other hand, is always a special case. According to its specific position and conditions, it presents a problem of individual assessment in each individual case. If considerations regarding sufficient green spaces and sunlight incidence take second place in the case of a city office block these are the very things that matter most in the case of the residential highrise tower. In these circumstances, any attempt at producing general building regulations must result in a collection of exceptions. Of course, there may be laws and regulations enumerating subsidiary conditions to be met if permission to build is to be granted. The principal requirement, however, of justification and suitability in the urban plan can only be basically outlined and must be decided case by case. Since highrise buildings may be prohibited on legal grounds, as well as by conventional zonal regulations, it would be an offence against the principle of legal protection to expose the same area to two different sets of building regulations, both claiming to be legally binding, quite apart from the obvious impracticability of such procedure.

Therefore it is not by chance that highrise building is in most cases subject to special building regulations. These provide the necessary flexibility for practical adjustment and at the same time, the chaotic urban scene which would be the result of proclaiming highrise building the general rule is thus avoided. What the law-makers cannot achieve, is even less likely to be achieved by inflexible rules. It would therefore be a very questionable enterprise to provide local authorities with something like a recipe to simplify their decisions about highrise building for those cases where they have the right to make such decisions on their own. Where they lack professional competence, it should be self-evident that professional advice should be sought. One would hardly expect a councillor to fill in medical certificates on the strength of his having a seat on the board of health. Therefore, when the criteria of highrise projects are summarized below, they are not offered as a rigid set of rules, but in an effort to sum up the complexity of highrise building in simple terms.

1 What is highrise building?

Where the law or regulations define the term, the legal definition is valid. Where no definition exists, the following rule of thumb may be applied:

Buildings with multiple storeys and corresponding height over and above the regulation of usual height – higher blocks
Buildings with ten or more storeys and corresponding height – highrise buildings
Average storey-height from floor to ceiling may be assumed to be 9 feet 3 inches.

2 Geographical position

Open countryside: neither higher nor highrise buildings
Village: neither higher nor highrise buildings
Townlet under five thousand inhabitants: neither higher nor highrise buildings
Town areas over five thousand inhabitants: higher blocks
Suburban areas with slow growth: as town area
Suburban areas with faster development and suburbs: higher blocks and judicious use of highrise buildings

Small country towns worth preservation and historic towns, including a surrounding distance of at least 1,650 feet: neither higher nor highrise blocks
City built-up area – according to scale of architectural development, local traffic situation, showing care for residential areas of high standard: higher blocks and highrise buildings.

3 Effect on the landscape

Special attention to slopes and brows of hills and the avoidance of a walled-in appearance, the protection of views from popular public vantage points and the protection of exposed points in the landscape. If used, higher and highrise buildings should neither be hidden nor over-exposed.

4 Effect on the townscape

Competition in height between taller buildings should be avoided in cases of mixed building groups. Give attention to characteristic silhouettes, e.g. coastline. Avoid highrise massing except in the centre or on the main axes, and misleading signpost effects. Care should be taken to prevent visual depreciation of well-preserved older districts. Questionable effects of dominance should be rejected.

5 Effect on adjacent sites

Observance of possible regulation development. Shadows cast on existing or potentially inhabited regulation façades: at most two hours at the time of the equinox. Minimum distance opposite the shadow-free zone: at least half the height of the building. In the business sector, distance requirements can be reduced opposite uninhabited façades.

6 Effect on the vicinity

Suitable proportions in relation to surroundings. Clear, but not exaggerated contrast. When in doubt, follow the proportion of the golden section. Squares: attention to the rules of visual effect, the lower the surrounding buildings, the greater the effect of space and vice-versa. Streets: axes with conflicting traffic movement should be avoided.

7 Architectural exploitation of the site

Higher and highrise buildings are unsuitable for increasing density. Architectural utilization should correspond with zonal plans and be appropriate to position and suitability. Surcharge in the case of building groups should be no higher than what is required to balance the cost of additional amenities. The so-called inducement premium to be rejected on the grounds of equality before the law.

8 Immediate surroundings and children's playgrounds
These should be green and to be walked on. If there are flats for families with children, provision of a safe infants' playground of at least one-fifth the usable storey-area. In the case of mixed building groups, playgrounds for larger children, partly hard-covered, should be provided.

9 Traffic
Well organized approach drive. At least one parking space per flat, if possible this should be collective and subterranean. Also uncovered parking space for visitors and tradesmen: one space for every five flats. Inhabited façades should not face streets or squares with busy traffic, as traffic noises reach even the upper storeys.

10 Proportions and façades
Proportions of height and mass are more important than the details of façade design. Façades should not look dead, but not be too fussy in design.

11 Plan
Sufficiently large rooms should be provided with south orientation or sun from two sides in the living-rooms. Balconies should not project excessively, but should be sufficiently large and are best in the form of loggias. Each flat should have one storage room. In residential highrise buildings with children, a safe playroom every second and third storey, perhaps combined with interior circulation, should be provided. Parapets must be sufficiently high.

12 Interior circulation
At least one lift for every ten storeys. One lift should run all the way through, capable of transporting goods. Allow for a rubbish-shoot.

13 Insulation
First-class insulation against noise, cold and heat must be provided.

14 Fire authorities
Rules and regulations of the insurance companies must be taken into consideration.

15 Use
Mainly in mixed building groups in combination with low-rise buildings and multi-family housing. Isolated highrise blocks for special purposes in urban areas.

16 Principles
Highrise buildings should only be permitted: when they are set in a mixed building development; when their isolated appearance is justified by the demands of the urban plan; when they do not disturb the town- or landscape or their immediate surroundings, can show good utilization, and meet specific local requirements including those of the police.

Taking leave of the reader

The above summary of the special points of assessment may give the impression that highrise building should be subjected to niggling regimentation. But it must be remembered that highrise building makes demands on the scene and in its turn must be prepared to meet high demands. Without wishing it ill, it must not become an ill in itself. A slightly reserved attitude is far from signifying rejection. Neither good architecture nor urban design depend on highrise building, and where an area is under the illusion that it can only achieve urban status by highrise building, life will certainly not be very attractive there. Rather fewer, but better highrise blocks should be the aim.
This book contains mistakes, omissions and errors, for human beings are fallible. But it is meant to stimulate rather than to instruct. Highrise blocks and wide streets alter the urban scale. They are a sign of the times and cannot be avoided. The question is whether we mean to endure them or control them. The answer will lie in the appearance of our cities in ten or twenty years' time. And this is not only the concern of the professionals, but of everyone whose fate it is to live in a town.

The single skyscraper will change our cities.

Otto Glaus   Documentation   29 examples

Examples

Price Tower
Bartlesville, USA (1953–1955)
Frank Lloyd Wright

The design for the Price Tower is based on an idea Wright had in 1929. He planned a concrete and glass tower in St. Marks, N.Y., the exterior planes to be formed by a glass and metal skin. Only twenty-five years later this idea has been realised true to the original project. The floors are suspended from a windmill-like horizontal skeleton. Three of the wings contain offices, the fourth, flats.
The individual character of the plan is lost to some extent in the three-dimensional structure.

Der Entwurf für den Price Tower basiert auf einer Idee Wrights vom Jahre 1929, als er einen Beton-Glas-Turm in St. Marks (New York) geplant hatte. Die Außenfläche wurde durch eine Glas-Metall-Haut gebildet.
Erst 25 Jahre später wurde diese Entwurfsidee für den Price Tower projektgetreu realisiert. Vom windmühlenartigen Tragskelett schwingen die Etagen frei aus. Drei Flügel wurden auf der ganzen Höhe mit Büros, der vierte mit Appartements ausgebaut.
Der eigenwillige Grundrißcharakter verliert im kubischen Aufbau etwas von seiner Aussage.

Le projet de Price Tower est basé sur une idée de Wright remontant à 1929, année où il élabora les plans d'une tour béton-verre à Saint Marks (New York). Les façades étaient constituées d'une enveloppe verre-métal.
L'idée-projet de Price Tower ne put être réalisée conformément aux plans que 25 ans plus tard. Les étages s'élancent librement du squelette porteur en forme de moulin à vent. Trois ailes sont occupées sur toute leur hauteur par des bureaux, la quatrième par des appartements.
La structure cubique fait perdre au caractère volontaire de l'esquisse un peu de sa valeur expressive.

Erdgeschoß / Ground floor / Rez-de-chaussée

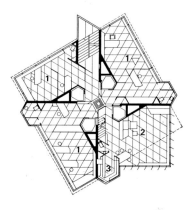

Zwischengeschoß Wohnung / Mezzanine flat / Appartement entresol

Normalgeschoß / Typical floor / Etage type

0 10 M
0 30 F

Erdgeschoß / Ground floor / Rez-de-chaussée:
1 Parkplätze für Büros / Office parking area / Parkings pour bureaux
2 Gedeckte Parkplätze / Covered parking area / Parkings couverts
3 Eingang Büros / Office entrance / Entrée bureaux
4 Parkplätze für Wohnungen / Parking space for flats / Parkings pour appartements
5 Eingang Wohnungen / Entrance to flats / Entrée appartements
6 Fahrweg / Drive / Voie de desserte
7 Ausfahrt / Exit / Sortie
8 Laden / Shop / Magasin

9 Wohnung Hauswart / Porter's flat / Conciergerie
10 Öffentliche Dienste / Service area / Services publics
11 Vortragssaal / Lecture theatre / Salle de conférences
12 Bühne / Stage / Scène
13 Halle / Foyer / Hall
14 Kasse / Cashdesk / Caisse
15 Kundendienst / Customer's Service / Service clientèle
16 Toiletten / Lavatories / Toilettes
17 Büro / Office / Bureau
18 Besprechungszimmer / Consulting room / Salle de réunion
19 Telephon / Telephone / Téléphone

20 Kiosk / Kiosk / Kiosque

Normalgeschoß / Typical floor / Etage type:
1 Büro / Office / Bureau
2 Wohnung, Wohnraum / Flat, living room / Appartement, sa'le de séjour
3 Küche / Kitchen / Cuisine

Zwischengeschoß Wohnung / Mezzanine flat / Appartement entresol:
1 Schlafzimmer / Bedroom / Chambre à coucher
2 Bad / Bathroom / Salle de bains

Schnitt / Section / Coupe:
1 Büro / Office / Bureau

2 Wohnung / Flat / Appartement
3 Zwischengeschoß Wohnung / Mezzanine flat / Appartement entresol
4 Buffet / Buffet / Buffet
5 Konferenzraum / Conference room / Salle de conférences
6 Chefbüro / Office / Bureau directorial
7 Dachgarten / Roof garden / Jardin sur le toit

Photo: Ansicht von Westen / View from the west / Vue de l'ouest (Reproduced by permission of the publisher, Horizon Press, N.Y., from 'The Story of the Tower' by Frank Lloyd Wright. Copyright 1956.)

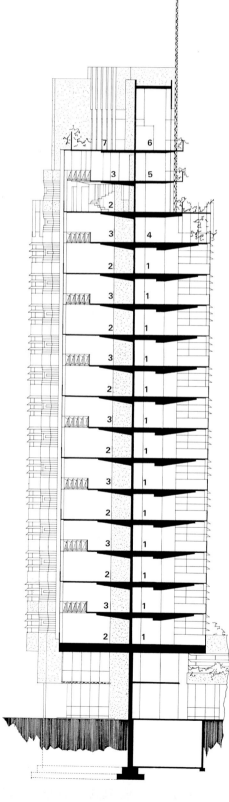

Lever House
New York (1951/1952/1955)
Skidmore, Owings and Merrill, New York

hebt sich der 24 Stockwerke hohe Hochhausteil im Stahlskelettbau klar vom eingeschossigen Flachbau ab. Es ist vor allem die fein proportionierte Verkleidung der Glasaußenwand, die dem Gebäude den ätherischen Charakter gibt, der das Lever-House zu einem weltweiten Begriff gemacht hat.

Height: 305 ft. Lever House rises above one of the busiest streets in New York. The twenty-four floor highrise part rests on slender supports and the steel skeleton building is clearly separated from the single-storey one. The finely proportioned glass-clad exterior is mainly responsible for the ethereal character of the building, which has brought Lever House worldwide recognition.

Hauteur: 93 m. Lever-House s'élève le long d'une des rues les plus fréquentées de New York. Les 24 étages de son ossature d'acier, reposant sur des piliers élancés, se détachent nettement de la partie basse (un étage) de la construction. C'est au revêtement finement proportionné de sa façade de verre que le bâtiment doit le caractère éthéré qui a fait sa renommée mondiale.

Bauhöhe: 93 m. An einer der verkehrsreichsten Straßen New Yorks steht das Lever-House. Auf schlanken Stützen ruhend,

Erdgeschoß / Ground floor / Rez-de-chaussée

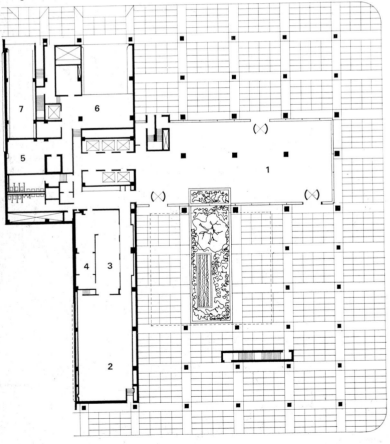

Typisches Bürogeschoß / Typical office floor / Etage de bureaux type

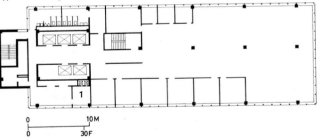

Erdgeschoß / Ground floor / Rez-dechaussée:
1 Halle / Lobby / Hall
2 Versammlungsraum / Assembly hall / Salle de réunion
3 Küche / Kitchen / Cuisine
4 Ausstellung / Display area / Exposition
5 Abfallraum / Garbage / Déchets
6 Laderampe / Loading / Rampe de chargement
7 Abfahrtsrampe zur Garage / Ramp

down to garage / Rampe d'accès au garage

Typisches Bürogeschoß / Typical office floor / Etage de bureaux type:
1 Postverteilanlage / Mail conveyer /

Distributeur de courrier

Photo: Lever-House von der Park-Avenue gesehen / Lever House seen from Park Avenue / Vue de Park-Avenue

Seagram Administration Building
New York (1954–1958)
Mies van der Rohe and P. Johnson, Chicago

Bauhöhe: 160 m. Das Seagram-Verwaltungsgebäude ist einer der architektonischen Merkpunkte von Manhattan. Es steht diagonal gegenüber dem Lever-House, drei Stufen erhöht, 30 m von der Park-Avenue zurückgesetzt. Durch diese besondere Anordnung des Lageplans wird das Hochhaus von den umliegenden Gebäuden losgelöst und eine außergewöhnliche Repräsentation erreicht.
Die Stahlskelettkonstruktion des 39 geschossigen Hochhauses wird von einer aus Bronze und bräunlichem Sonnenschutzglas bestehenden Fassadenhaut umschlossen.
Mies van der Rohe erreicht durch einfachste, aber wohlproportionierte Verhältnisse größte architektonische Wirkung.

Height: 525 ft. The Seagram Administration building is one of the architectural landmarks of Manhattan. Its position is diagonally across from Lever House raised on three steps and set back by 98 feet from Park Avenue. By this imaginative siting the highrise building is dissociated from the surrounding buildings and so achieves an extraordinary effect.
The steel-skeleton structure of the thirty-nine floor high building is enveloped in a skin of bronze and brownish anti-glaze glass. Mies van der Rohe achieves a maximum architectural effect by very simple but well-related proportions.

Hauteur: 160 m. Le bâtiment administratif «Seagram» est un des points de repère architectoniques de Manhattan. Surélevé de trois degrés, en retrait de 30 m de Park-Avenue, il est situé en diagonale de «Lever-House». Cette ordonnance particulière du plan de situation le fait apparaître détaché des bâtiments environnants et lui confère un aspect exceptionnel.
La construction en squelette d'acier des 39 étages est enfermée dans une enveloppe de façades faite de bronze et de verre anti-solaire brunâtre.
Des rapports simples mais bien proportionnés permettent à Mies van der Rohe d'atteindre un très grand effet architectonique.

Erdgeschoß / Ground floor / Rez-de-chaussée

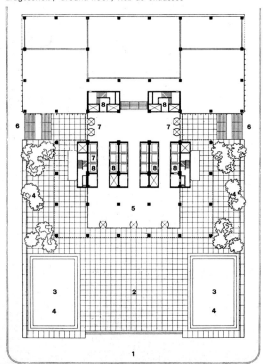

11.–27. Obergeschoß / Upper storeys / Etage

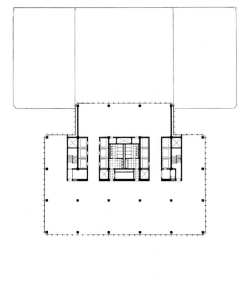

Erdgeschoß / Ground floor / Rez-de-chaussée 1:1000:
1 Park Avenue
2 Platz / Square / Esplanade
3 Wasserbassins / Basins / Bassins
4 Springbrunnen / Fountain / Fontaine
5 Haupteingangshalle / Main entrance / Hall entrée principale
6 Treppen Nebeneingänge / Staircase, side entrances / Escaliers, entrées latérales
7 Nebeneingänge / Side entrances / Entrées latérales
8 Verkehrs- und Installationsschächte / Circulation and installation wells / Espaces souterrains pour circulation et services internes

Photo: Seagram-Gebäude von der Park-Avenue aus gesehen / Seagram Building seen from Park Avenue / Vue de Park-Avenue

CBS Building
New York (1965)
Eero Saarinen and Associates
Hamden, Connecticut

Saarinen gestaltet dank dieser Lage und vor allem mit der eigenwilligen Stützenausbildung ein Hochhaus mit einmaliger Aussage.

Height: 410 ft. The new headquarters of The Columbia Broadcasting System in New York stands completely free as a street block. Triangular supports 5 ft. wide appear to 'grow' out of the ground, stretch upwards and end abruptly at the thirty-eighth floor. The columns are clad in dark granite, the metal windows and doors are of equal width. On this site and by these means Saarinen has created a unique architectural statement.

Bauhöhe: 125 m. Das neue Hauptgebäude des Columbia Broadcasting System in New York steht als Straßenviereck vollständig frei. Dreieckige Stützen von fünf Fuß Breite scheinen aus dem Boden zu «wachsen». Sie streben ohne Verjüngung in die Höhe und enden unvermittelt im 38. Stockwerk. Die Pfeiler sind mit dunklem Granit verkleidet. Metallfenster und Türen haben Einheitsmaße.

Hauteur: 125 m. Quadrilatère au milieu d'un carrefour routier, le nouveau siège de la société «Columbia Broadcasting System» s'élève seul, monolithique. Revêtus de granit sombre, les piliers triangulaires de cinq pieds de large semblent surgir du sol et tendre vers le haut pour prendre brusquement fin au 38e étage. Les fenêtres de métal et les portes ont des dimensions standard. Grâce à la situation et surtout au caractère des piliers, Saarinen réalise une maison-tour d'une expression unique.

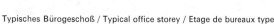

Typisches Bürogeschoß / Typical office storey / Etage de bureaux type

Erdgeschoß / Ground floor / Rez-de-chaussée

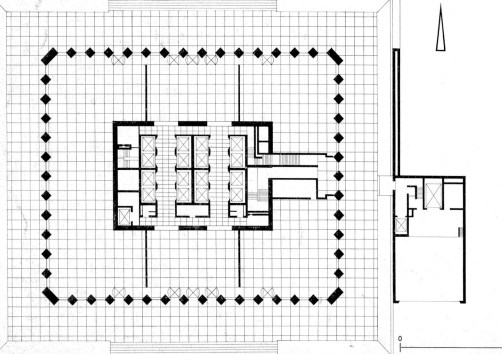

0   10 M

0   30

Photo: CBS-Hochhaus von der anderen
Seite der Sixth Avenue aus gesehen / CBS
Building seen from the opposite side of
Sixth Avenue / Vue de Sixth Avenue

Park Lafayette
Detroit, USA (1955–1963)
Mies van der Rohe
and Ludwig Hilbersheimer, Chicago

The development at Lafayette Park is half a sq. mile in area and contains terrace houses of one and two storeys as well as high-rise buildings. The living quarter is reached by secondary roads which lead off from a main traffic ring road. Parking spaces are adjacent to these and foot paths lead to the houses. The high-rise building so far completed using a skeleton building system rests on two floors of columns which contain communal rooms. The residential floors contain one to three room flats. Here, in spite of the strict three-dimensional treatment a lively urban atmosphere has been achieved.

Die Hochhaus-Siedlung «Lafayette Park» ist 290 ha groß und enthält ein- und zweigeschossige Reihenhäuser und Hochhäuser. Von einem Hauptverkehrsring wird das Wohnquartier durch Stichstraßen erschlossen, an denen Parkplätze liegen, von wo aus Fußgängerwege zu den Häusern führen.
Die bis heute fertiggestellten Hochhäuser in Skelettbauweise stehen auf zwei Säulengeschossen, in denen Kollektivräumlichkeiten angeordnet sind. Die Wohngeschosse sind unterteilt in Ein- bis Dreizimmerwohnungen. Hier ist trotz strengster kubischer Ordnung lebendige urbane Atmosphäre erreicht.

S'étendant sur 290 ha, «Lafayette Park» groupe des maisons en ordre contigu de un et deux étages et des maisons-tours. Le quartier est relié à une ceinture routière par des routes pourvues de parkings, d'où des chemins conduisent vers les maisons. L'ossature des maisons-tours actuellement réalisées repose sur deux étages-piliers, dans lesquels ont été aménagés des espaces collectifs. Les étages d'habitation se subdivisent en appartements de une à trois pièces. Une vivante atmosphère urbaine règne ici malgré la stricte ordonnance cubique.

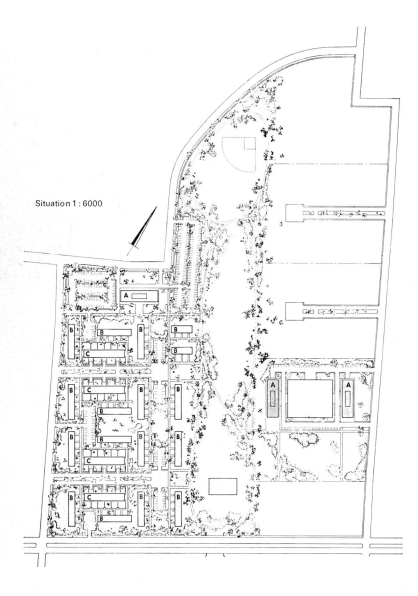

Situation 1 : 6000

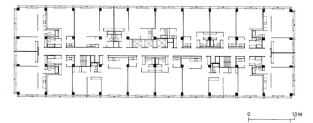

Wohngeschoß / Residential floor / Etage de jour

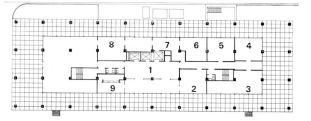

Erdgeschoß / Ground floor / Rez-de-chaussée

Situation 1:6000:
A Hochhäuser / Highrise buildings / Maisons-tours
B 2geschossige Häuser / 2-storey buildings / Maisons à deux niveaux
C 1geschossige Häuser / Single-storey buildings / Maisons à un niveau

Erdgeschoß / Ground floor / Rez-de-chaussée:
1 Eingangshalle / Entrance hall / Hall d'entrée

2 Büro / Office / Bureau
3 Laden / Shop / Magasin
4 Kinderwagen / Baby carriages / Poussettes
5 Lagerraum / Storage / Entrepôt
6 Wiederverkauf / Retail / Revente

7 Zubringerdienst / Messenger service / Livreurs
8 Vorräte, Lagerraum / Stores and warehouse / Provisions, entrepôts
9 Postbüro / Post office / Bureau de poste

84

Photo: Ansicht Hochhaus mit 1- und 2 geschossigen Reihenhäusern / View of highrise building with single- and double-
storey terrace houses / Vue de la maison-
tour et des maisons à un et deux niveaux
en ordre contigu

Married Student Dormitories, Harvard University
Cambridge, Mass., USA (1964)
José Luis Sert,
Huson Jackson and Ronald Gourley, Cambridge

staltung der Kuben und Fassaden gibt dieser Studentensiedlung eine ausgesprochen persönliche Note.

The main square which forms the centre of the student campus is surrounded on three sides by low buildings and accented by three highrise hostel blocks; the third one being only visually connected. The buildings are constructed from pre-fabricated concrete units. Circulation corridors every third floor are reached by subsidiary stairs. There are six living units on each floor. The singularly plastic form of mass and façade give a special personality to this student campus.

Centre de la cité universitaire, la place principale est entourée de constructions basses et de trois maisons-tours qui en soulignent le caractère, une de celles-ci n'ayant qu'une influence optique. Toutes les constructions sont en éléments de béton préfabriqués. On accède aux étages par des couloirs de communication, aménagés tous les trois étages, et des escaliers latéraux. Chacun de ceux-ci dessert six unités d'habitation. La cité tire sa forte personnalité de la plastique particulière des cubes et des façades.

Der Hauptplatz, der den Mittelpunkt der Studentenwohnsiedlung bildet, wird an drei Seiten durch niedrige Bauten eingefaßt und akzentuiert durch drei Wohnhochhäuser, wobei das dritte lediglich optisch hineinwirkt. Alle Gebäude bestehen aus vorgefertigten Betonelementen. Durch Erschließungskorridore werden je drei Etagen über Nebentreppen erreicht. An diesen liegen je sechs Wohneinheiten. Die eigenartige plastische Ge-

10., 11., 13., 14., 16., 17., 19., 20. Obergeschoß im Hochhaus / Upper storey in highrise building / Etage de la maison-tour

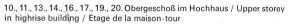

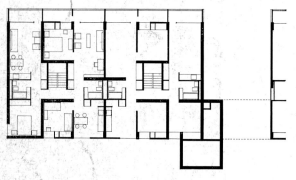

9., 12., 15., 18. Obergeschoß im Hochhaus / Upper storey in highrise building / Etage de la maison-tour

Erdgeschoß / Ground floor / Rez-de-chaussée

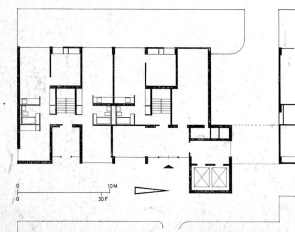

Situation

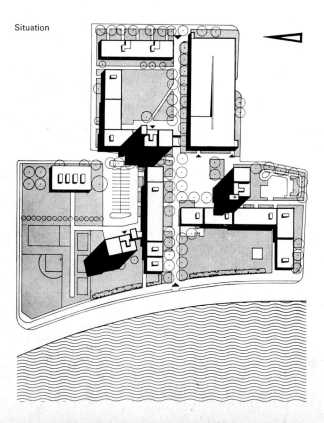

Photo: Ansicht von Westen / View from the west / Vue de l'ouest

Marina City
Chicago (1962–1964)
Bertrand Goldberg Associates, Chicago

Bauhöhe: 179 m. «Marina City» besteht aus einem rechtwink-ligen Platz, auf welchem fünf Gebäude errichtet wurden. Theater, Ausstellungsgebäude, Bürohaus mit allen Gemein-schaftsanlagen, Lager und Empfangshalle sowie zwei 65-geschossige Wohnhochhäuser. Die unteren 18 Etagen bieten Parkierungsmöglichkeit für 900 Autos. Der Kern enthält Auf-züge, Installationen und Treppen. Von hier öffnen sich die Ap-partements strahlenförmig nach außen und werden durch einen Balkon erweitert.

Height: 587 ft. Marina City consists of a rectangular piazza on which five buildings have been erected, a theatre, an exhi-bition building, an office block (with all the offices, a store and reception hall) and two highrise residential blocks of sixty-five floors each. The lower eighteen floors offer parking facilities for nine hundred cars. The core contains lifts, service installations and stairs. From there the apartments radiate outwards and are extended by balconies.

Hauteur: 179 m. «Marina City» est une parcelle rectangulaire sur laquelle cinq bâtiments ont été érigés. Théâtre, bâtiment des expositions, bâtiment administratif pourvu de tous les équipements collectifs, d'entrepôts et d'un hall de réception, et deux maisons-tours d'habitation de 65 étages. Les 18 étages inférieurs, aménagés en parkings, peuvent abriter 900 voi-tures. Ascenseurs, services internes et escaliers sont au centre. De là les appartements s'ouvrent en rond vers l'extérieur où un balcon les prolonge.

Situation und Erdgeschoß / Site and ground floor / Situation et rez-de-chaussée

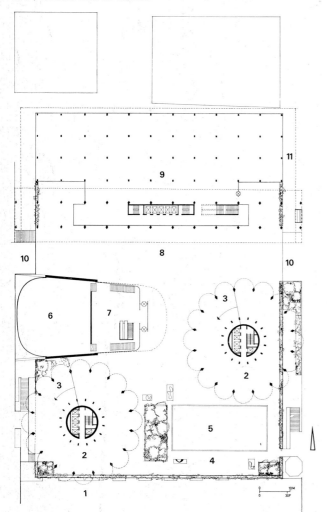

Normalgeschoß Wohnungen / Typical floor / Appartements étage type

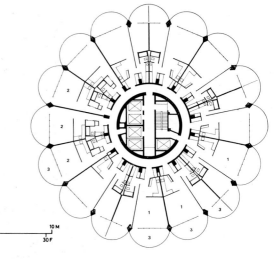

Situation und Erdgeschoß / Site and ground floor / Situation et rez-de-chaussée:
1 Chicago River
2 Wohntürme / Residential towers / Tours d'habitation
3 Auffahrt zu Parkgeschossen / Ap-proach to parking floors / Accès aux parkings
4 Skulpturengarten / Sculpture garden / Jardin des sculptures
5 Eisbahn im Untergeschoß / Ice skating rink below / Patinoire souterraine
6 Theater / Theatre / Théâtre
7 Halle mit Rolltreppen / Lobby with escalators / Hall et escalier roulant
8 Platz / Piazza / Esplanade
9 Bürogebäude / Office building / Bâti-ment de bureaux
10 Abfahrtsrampe / Ramp from garage / Rampe de descente
11 Autobank / Car storage / Banque pour automobilistes

Normalgeschoß Wohnungen / Typical floor / Appartements étage type:
1 Zweizimmer-Wohnungen / 2-room flats / Appartements de 2 pièces
2 Einzimmer-Wohnungen / 1-room flats / Appartements de 1 pièce
3 Balkon / Balcony / Balcon

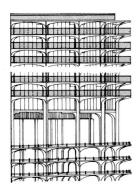

Ansicht Parkierungsrampen und Zwischengeschoß / View of parking ramps and mezzanine floor / Vue des rampes d'accès aux
parkings et de l'entresol

Photo: Ansicht von Südosten / View from
the south-east / Vue du sud-est

Newton Medical Research Laboratories
University of Pennsylvania, USA (1958–1960)
Louis Kahn, Philadelphia

Die Türme bestehen aus vorgespannten Säulenscheiben, die mit Backstein verkleidet sind.

On the outskirts of Philadelphia, Kahn has designed a medical laboratory. The scientific work demanded the division of the working space into small units which could also, if necessary, be connected. Each 'Studio-Working Laboratory' has its own emergency stairs and chimney and these are contained in three towers. The fourth is reserved for vertical intercommunication. The towers consist of prestressed columns which are clad in brickwork.

Am Stadtrand von Philadelphia hat Louis Kahn ein medizinisches Laboratorium entworfen. Die wissenschaftliche Arbeit verlangte eine Unterteilung der Arbeitsplätze in kleine Arbeitsgruppen, zudem sollte die Möglichkeit der Verbindung vorhanden sein. Die sogenannten «Studio-Arbeitslaboratorien», die je ihre eigene Nottreppe und Kamine haben, sind in drei Türmen untergebracht. Der vierte wurde für die vertikale Verbindung reserviert.

Kahn a projeté un laboratoire médical à la périphérie de Philadelphie. Le travail scientifique imposait une subdivision des postes en petits groupes de travail devant communiquer entre eux. Les «studios-laboratoires de travail» pourvus de leurs propres escaliers de secours et cheminée occupent trois tours, la quatrième étant réservée aux liaisons verticales.
Les tours sont des piliers en éléments précontraints revêtus de briques.

Nordfassade, Endausbau / North front, final stage / Façade nord, stade final

Erdgeschoß / Ground floor / Rez-de-chaussée

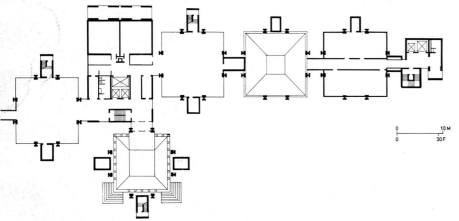

Typisches Laboratoriumsgeschoß / Typical laboratory floor / Etage de laboratoires type

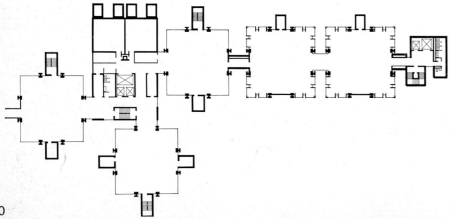

Photo: Ansicht des Gebäudes zusammen mit den Studentenunterkünften / View of the building together with campus dormitories / Vue du bâtiment et des logements des étudiants

Photo: Ansicht von Norden, Laboratorien- und Verwaltungstürme / View from the north, laboratories and administration towers / Vue du nord, tours des laboratoires et tours administratives ▷

Congress Hall
Brasilia
Oscar Niemeyer, Paris

Height: 295 ft. Brasilia consists of two axes. The north-south axis is the residential area, across which is a smaller, wider axis which contains the administration buildings, ministries, parliament, senate, city hall and other public buildings. The congress building is on the east of this axis and consists of two vertical slabs of many floors standing close together, which give this axis its emphasis. Niemeyer has achieved with the highrise elements and the rounded shapes of the Congress halls a truly urban character.

Bauhöhe: 90 m. Brasilia besteht aus zwei Achsen. Die Nord-Süd-Achse ist die Wohnzone – eine breitere, kürzere Achse kreuzt diese Zone und enthält die administrativen Bauten, Ministerien, Parlament, Senat, Rathaus und andere öffentliche Gebäude. Im Osten erhält diese Achse durch das Kongreßgebäude, das aus zwei vertikalen, eng beieinander stehenden Scheiben von vielen Etagen besteht, seinen Akzent. Niemeyer erarbeitet mit den Hochhauselementen und den Rundformen der Kongreßsäle monumentale städtebauliche Wirkung.

Hauteur: 90 m. Brasilia repose sur deux axes, l'axe nord-sud de la zone résidentielle et un axe plus large et plus petit coupant perpendiculairement ladite zone et comprenant les constructions administratives, ministères, Parlement, Sénat, Hôtel de ville et autres bâtiments publics. Cet axe est dominé par le bâtiment des Congrès, construction constituée de deux corps verticaux étroitement rapprochés. Niemeyer obtient grâce aux éléments des maisons-tours et aux formes circulaires des salles de congrès un effet urbain monumental.

Erdgeschoß / Ground floor / Rez-de-chaussée 1:2000

1. Obergeschoß, Niveau der Säle / First floor, hall level / 1er étage, niveau des salles

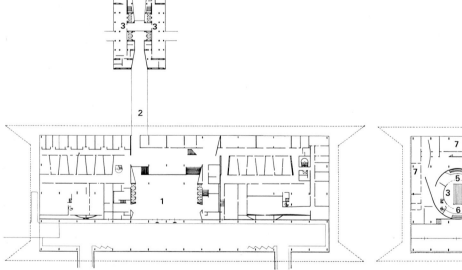

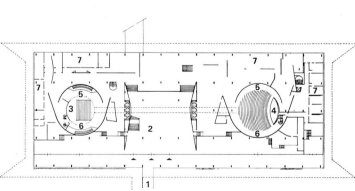

Erdgeschoß / Ground floor / Rez-de-chaussée:
1 Halle für Abgeordnete und Senatoren / Assembly Hall for deputies and senators / Hall réservé aux députés et aux sénateurs
2 Rampe zu Kongreßgebäude / Ramp to congress building / Rampe d'accès au bâtiment des congrès
3 Halle / Lobby / Hall

1. Obergeschoß, Niveau der Säle / First floor, hall level / 1er étage supérieur, niveau des salles:
1 Rampe / Ramp / Rampe
2 Publikumshalle / Public Hall / Hall réservé au public
3 Senatssaal / Senate Hall / Salle du Sénat
4 Abgeordnetensaal / Deputies' Hall / Chambre des Députés
5 Gäste / Guests / Visiteurs
6 Journalisten / Journalists / Journalistes
7 Büros / Offices / Bureaux

Ansicht von der Längsachse her / View from the longitudinal axis / Vue de l'axe longitudinal

2. Obergeschoß, Niveau der Kuppel bzw. der Schale / Upper floor, cupola level / 2e étage, niveau de la coupole

Schnitt / Section / Coupe 1:2000

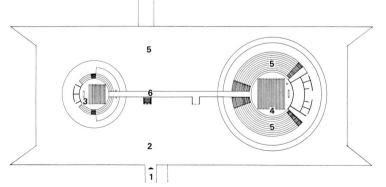

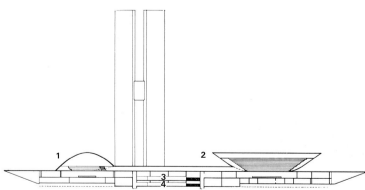

2. Obergeschoß, Niveau der Kuppel bzw. der Schale / Upper floor, cupola level / 2e étage supérieur, niveau de la coupole:
1 Rampe / Ramp / Rampe
2 Terrasse / Terrace / Terrasse
3 Senatssaal / Senate Hall / Salle du Sénat
4 Abgeordnetensaal / Deputies' Hall / Chambre des Députés
5 Gäste / Guests / Visiteurs
6 Verbindungsgang / Linking passage / Couloir de communication
7 Büros / Offices / Bureaux

Schnitt / Section / Coupe:
1 Senatssaal / Senate Hall / Salle du Sénat
2 Abgeordnetensaal / Deputies' Hall / Chambre des Députés
3 Publikumshalle / Public Hall / Hall réservé au public
4 Halle für Abgeordnete und Senatoren / Hall for deputies and senators / Hall réservé aux Députés et aux Sénateurs

Ministry of National Education and Public Health
Rio de Janeiro (1937–1943)
Costa, Leao, Moreira, Niemeyer, Reidy, Le Corbusier

bestzementlamellen. Es wird dadurch eine konsequente Ordnung mit lebendigem Spiel von Licht und Schatten erreicht.

Height: 271 ft. The administration building rests on two-storey high stilts. It has a concrete skeleton with three rows of stilts. A low block contains lecture halls and exhibition hall as well as service rooms. A special characteristic of this highrise building is the splendid system of sun protection which consists of vertical concrete ribs and adjustable horizontal, asbestos-cement louvres. This creates an orderly façade pattern with a lively play of light and shade.

Bauhöhe: 82,5 m. Auf zweigeschossigen Stützen erhebt sich das Verwaltungsgebäude. Es ist ein Betonskelett mit 3 Stützenreihen. Ein niedriger Querriegel enthält Vortragssaal und Ausstellungshalle sowie Wirtschaftsräume.
Das besonders Charakteristische des Hochhauses liegt in der Abschirmung der Sonne durch ein ausgezeichnetes System von vertikalen Betonrippen und verstellbaren horizontalen As-

Hauteur: 82,5 m. Squelette de béton, le bâtiment administratif s'élève sur trois séries d'appuis de deux étages. Un bas verrou transversal circonscrit une salle de conférences, une halle d'exposition et d'autres locaux utilitaires.
La maison-tour est caractérisée par son système de protection anti-solaire constitué d'éléments de béton verticaux et de lamelles d'amiante horizontales réglables. Ainsi obtient-on une ordonnance précise alliée à un jeu vivant d'ombres et de lumières.

Erdgeschoß / Ground floor / Rez-de-chaussée

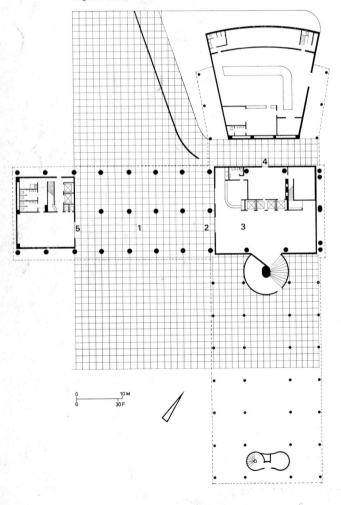

Normalgeschoß / Typical floor / Etage type

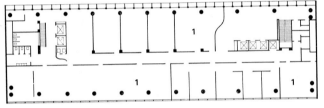

2. Obergeschoß / Upper floor / 2e étage

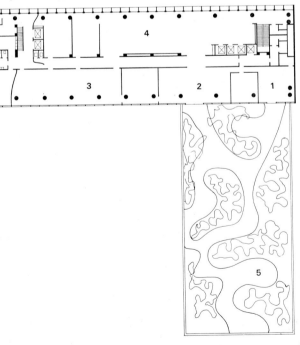

Erdgeschoß / Ground floor / Rez-de-chaussée:
1 Portico / Porch / Portique
2 Publikumseingang / Public entrance / Entrée publique
3 Halle / Lobby / Hall
4 Eingang für den Minister / Minister's entrance / Entrée des ministres

5 Angestellteneingang / Staff entrance / Entrée des fonctionnaires

2. Obergeschoß / Second floor / 2e étage:
1 Räume des Ministers / Ministerial suite / Bureaux du ministre
2 Sitzungssaal / Conference hall / Salle de conférences

3 Büros / Offices / Bureaux
4 Wartehalle / Waiting room / Salle d'attente
5 Dachgarten / Roof garden / Jardin sur le toit

Normalgeschoß / Typical floor plan / Etage type:
1 Büros / Offices / Bureaux

Photo: Ansicht der Nordseite mit den verstellbaren Sonnenschutzelementen / View of the north side with adjustable sun blinds/ Vue du nord; éléments pare-soleil réglables

94

Toronto New City Hall
Canada (1961–1966)
Viljo Revell, Helsinki – John B. Parkin Associates
Toronto

vexen Betonmauer und einer inneren konkaven Glasfront. Die Geschoßdecken kragen von der Betonwand über die Pfeiler-reihe bis zur Glaswand aus.

Height: 328 ft. The city hall of Toronto is a group of three buildings. The circular city hall itself is enclosed by the two half-moon shaped office towers which symbolize the administration structure of the city. Each of the two towers consists of an outer convex concrete wall and an inner concave glass front. The ceilings of each floor are cantilevered from the concrete wall beyond the row of supports up to the glass wall.

Hauteur: 100 m. L'Hôtel de ville de Toronto est constitué par un groupe de trois bâtiments. Deux tours de bureaux en demi-lune, symbolisant la structure administrative de la ville, entourent la Salle du conseil de forme circulaire.
La façade convexe de chaque tour est en béton, la façade concave en verre. Soutenues par des séries de piliers, les dalles relient la façade de béton à celle de verre.

Bauhöhe: 100 m. Das Rathaus von Toronto besteht aus einer dreiteiligen Gebäudegruppe. Die beiden halbmondförmigen Bürotürme, welche die Verwaltungsstruktur der Stadt symbolisieren, umschließen den kreisförmigen Rathaussaal.
Jeder der beiden Bürotürme besteht aus einer äußeren kon-

Schnitt / Section / Coupe

Ratssaal und Normalgeschoß Bürotürme / Committee room and typical office floor / Salle du Conseil et étage type des tours de bureaux

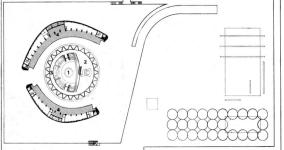

Erdgeschoß / Ground floor / Rez-de-chaussée

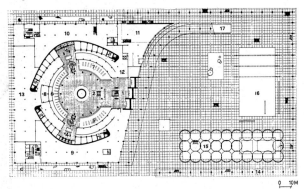

1. Obergeschoß / First floor / 1ᵉʳ étage

Ratssaal und Normalgeschoß Bürotürme / Committee room and standard plan office towers / Salle du Conseil et étage type des tours de bureaux:
1 Ratssaal / Committee room / Salle du Conseil
2 Wandelhalle / Members lounge / Hall
3 Umgang / Gallery walkway / Promenoir
4 Typisches Bürogeschoß Turm / Tower typical office floor / Etage de bureaux type

Erdgeschoß / Ground floor / Rez-de-chaussée:
1 Haupteingang / Main entrance / Entrée principale
2 Gedächtnishalle / Memorial Hall / Hall du Souvenir

3 Aufzüge und Treppen zum Ratssaal / Lifts and stair to committee-room / Ascenseurs et escaliers vers la Salle du Conseil
4 Turmaufzüge / Lifts to highrise section / Ascenseurs de la tour
5 Patentregister / Patents register / Bureau des brevets
6 Gemeindebuchhaltung / City treasury / Service comptable de la ville
7 Personal, Kreditinstitut / Personnel, Credit institute / Personnel, institut de crédit
8 Lager / Storeroom / Entrepôts
9 Grundbuchamt / Registration office / Cadastre
10 Regionales Grundbuchamt / Regional registration office / Cadastre régional
11 Städtische Bibliothek / City library /

Bibliothèque municipale
12 Telephon / Telephone / Téléphone
13 Buchhaltung / Accounts / Comptabilité
14 Überdachte Wandelhalle / Covered lounge / Hall couvert
15 Parkanlagen / Park / Parcs
16 Teich / Pond / Plan d'eau
17 Rampe / Ramp / Rampe

1. Obergeschoß / First floor / 1ᵉʳ étage:
1 Empfang / Reception / Réception
2 Bürgermeister / Mayor / Maire
3 Stadtrat/ Chairman / Conseil municipal
4 Büros / Offices / Bureaux
5 Stadträte-Räume / Committee rooms / Bureaux des conseillers
6 Bibliothek / Library / Bibliothèque
7 Regionalstandesamt / County registry office / Etat civil régional

8 Gemeindestandesamt / City registry office / Etat civil municipal
9 Lunchraum / Dining room / Salle à manger

Schnitt durch Ratssaalgebäude und Bürotürme / Section through committee building and office towers / Coupe transversale du bâtiment de la Salle du Conseil et des tours de bureaux:
1 Erdgeschoß / Ground floor / Rez-de-chaussée
2 Kellergaragen / Underground garages / Garages souterrains
3 Installationsgeschosse / Installation floors / Etages des services

Photo: Ansicht von Süden / View from the south / Vue du sud

Lend Lease House
Sydney, Australia (1961)
Harry Seidler, Sydney

Height: 150 ft. This nineteen floor high office building stands above Sydney harbour on a peninsula. The highrise building was erected between two parallel streets with a difference in height of two and a half floors. The building contains four car parking floors, a two-storey high exhibition room, fourteen office floors and a penthouse with offices. All service installations are housed in a broad cube at the top. The length of the façades is equipped with individual movable louvre blinds.

Bauhöhe: 45,7 m. Das 19geschossige Geschäftshaus steht auf einer Halbinsel über dem Hafen von Sydney. Das Hochhaus wurde zwischen zwei Parallelstraßen gebaut, die etwa 2½ Geschosse Höhendifferenz aufweisen.
Der Bau enthält vier Parkgeschosse, einen zwei Stockwerke hohen Ausstellungsraum, 14 Bürogeschosse sowie ein Attikageschoß mit Büros. Darüber sind in einem breitgelagerten Kubus alle technischen Installationen untergebracht. Die Längsfassaden sind auf ganzer Höhe mit individuell beweglichen Sonnenschutzlamellen ausgerüstet.

Hauteur: 45,7 m. Maison-tour de 19 étages, «Lend Lease House» est implantée sur une presqu'île à l'entrée du port de Sydney, entre deux rues parallèles situées à des niveaux différents (2½ étages).
La construction comprend quatre étages de parkings, un hall d'exposition de deux étages, 14 étages de bureaux et un étage de bureaux en attique. Au-dessus, un large cube où sont aménagés tous les services techniques. Les façades longitudinales sont équipées sur toute la hauteur de lamelles pare-soleil réglables individuellement.

Erdgeschoß / Ground floor / Rez-de-chaussée

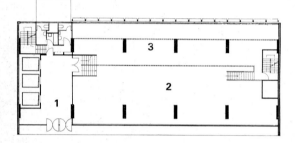

Normalgeschoß / Typical floor / Etage type

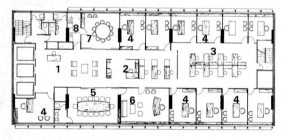

Typisches Kellergeschoß / Typical cellar / Etage souterrain type

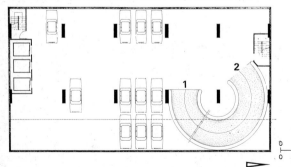

0 — 10 M
0 — 30 F

Schnitt / Section / Coupe 1 : 600

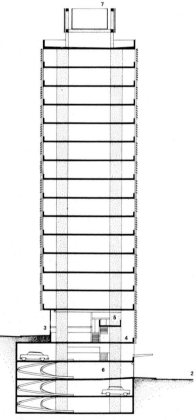

Erdgeschoß / Ground floor / Rez-de-chaussée:
1 Eingangshalle / Entrance lobby / Hall d'entrée
2 Ausstellungsraum / Showroom / Hall d'exposition
3 Zwischengeschoßdecke / Mezzanine floor canopy / Dalle entresol

Normalgeschoß / Typical floor / Etage type:
1 Empfang / Reception / Réception

2 Sekretariat / Secretaries / Secrétariat
3 Büro / Office / Bureau
4 Einzelbüros / Individual offices / Bureaux individuels
5 Sitzungszimmer / Board room / Salle de réunion
6 Zimmer des Geschäftsleiters / Manager's room / Bureau directorial
7 Direktionseßzimmer / Directorial dining room / Salle à manger directoriale
8 Küche / Kitchen / Cuisine

Typisches Kellergeschoß / Typical basement / Etage souterrain type:
1 Rampe abwärts / Ramp down / Rampe de descente
2 Rampe aufwärts / Ramp up / Rampe de montée

Schnitt / Section / Coupe:
1 Macquarie Street
2 Circular Quai
3 Eingang / Entrance / Entrée
4 Ausstellungsraum / Showroom / Hall

d'exposition
5 Zwischengeschoß / Mezzanine floor / Entresol
6 Garage
7 Kühlraum, Liftmotoren, Ventilatoren / Refrigeration, lift motors, ventilators / Chambre froide, moteurs, ventilateurs

Photo: Lend Lease House, Ostseite / East side / Vue de l'est

Unity Apartment House
Harumi, Tokyo, Japan (1958)
Kunio Mayekawa, Tokyo

kann beliebig unterteilt werden. Der Versuch, mit der vorge-schlagenen Konstruktion einen neuen Weg im japanischen Hochhausbau zu finden, ist außerordentlich interessant.

Height: 112 ft. The highest residential building so far in Japan, Unity, is part of a completely new development area. The staircase core is carried on the earthquake-proof walls which are at right angles to the long front. Between these walls the space is completely fluid and can be divided up as necessary. The attempt to find by this form of construction a new approach in Japanese highrise building is interesting.

Bauhöhe: 31 m. Das höchste Wohnhaus, «Unity», das bisher in Japan gebaut wurde, ist Teil eines vollständig neuen Sied-lungsraumes. Der Treppenhauskern befindet sich jeweils an den erdbebensicheren Mauern, die senkrecht zur Längsfassade stehen. Zwischen diesen Mauern ist der Raum völlig frei und

Hauteur: 31 m. La tour d'habitation «Unity», partie d'un nou-veau quartier, est la plus haute maison-tour construite jus-qu'ici au Japon. La cage d'escalier est adossée aux murs offrant le plus de sécurité en cas de tremblements de terre, situés per-pendiculairement à la façade longitudinale. Entre ces murs l'espace est libre et peut être subdivisé à volonté. La construc-tion représente un essai intéressant dans la recherche d'une voie nouvelle au Japon.

2., 4., 5., 7., 8., 10. Geschoß, Wohnungen Typ A / Floors, flats type A / Etage, appartements type A

3., 6., 9. Geschoß, Wohnungen Typ B / Floors, flats type B / Etage, appartements type B

Erdgeschoß, Wohnungen Typ C / Ground floor, flats type C / Rez-de-chaussée, appartements type C

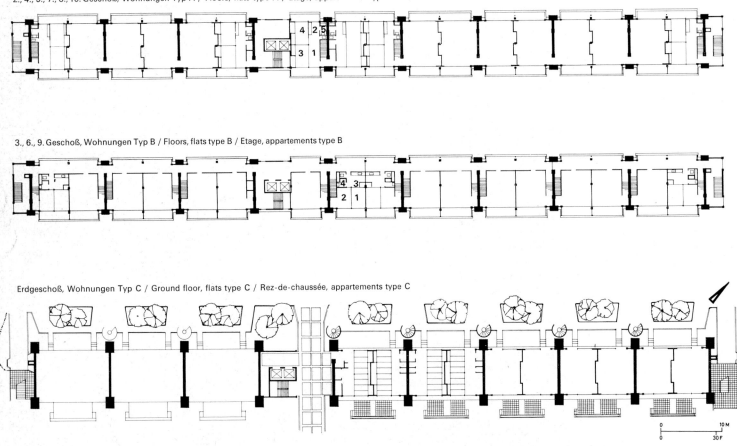

2., 4., 5., 7., 8., 10. Geschoß, Wohnungen Typ A / Storeys, flats type A / Etage, ap-partements type A:
1 Eßplatz / Dining area / Coin à manger
2 Küche / Kitchen / Cuisine
3 Wohnraum / Living room / Salle de séjour

4 Schlafzimmer / Bedroom / Chambre à coucher
5 Bad / Bathroom / Bains

3., 6., 9. Geschoß, Wohnungen Typ B / Storeys, flats type B / Etage, appartements type B:

1 Wohnraum / Living room / Salle de séjour
2 Schlafraum / Bedroom / Chambre à coucher
3 Küche / Kitchen / Cuisine
4 Bad, WC / Bath, WC / Bains, toilettes

Schnitt 1:300 / Section / Coupe: Wohnungen Typ A, B, C / Flats type A, B, C / Appartements type A, B, C

Photo: Ansicht von Südwesten / View from the south-west / Vue du sud-ouest

Schnitt / Section / Coupe 1 : 300

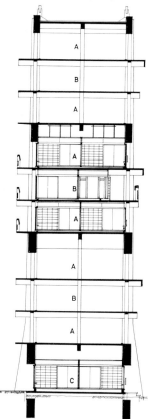

L'Unité d'habitation
Marseilles, France (1947–1952)
Le Corbusier

Bauhöhe: 56 m. Die berühmte «Unité» von Le Corbusier in Marseille ist bis heute die konsequenteste Durchbildung einer Wohnhochhaus-Einheit. Eine auf Betonpfeilern liegende Kragplatte, die über dem freien Erdgeschoß liegt, trägt einen Betonskelettbau.

Die verschiedenen Wohntypen sind über «innere» Straßen zu erreichen. Es bestehen 23 verschiedene Wohneinheiten, die zumeist zweigeschossig sind. Im 7. und 8. Geschoß befinden sich eine Einkaufsstraße mit Restaurant, Snackbar und Läden. Auf dem Dachgeschoß sind außer den technischen Installationen, Turnhalle, Kindergarten, Schwimmbassin und Spielplätze eingerichtet.

Besonders hervorzuheben sind die großen Wohnungsloggias für jede Wohneinheit.

Height: 184 ft. The famous 'Unité' by Le Corbusier in Marseilles forms the most influential highrise unit yet created. A cantilevered slab on concrete piers above the open ground floor carries a concrete skeleton building.

The different types of flats can be reached by interior roads. There are twenty-three different living units mostly on two floors. On the seventh and eighth floor there is a shopping street with restaurant, snack bar, and shops. On the roof in addition to the technical installations are gymnasium, nursery school, swimming pool and playing fields. Large living balconies are provided for each unit.

Hauteur: 56 m. L'«Unité» projetée par Le Corbusier à Marseille reste la réalisation la plus accomplie des unités d'habitation. Le squelette de béton repose sur une dalle bisautée située au-dessus du sol et supportée par des piliers de béton. Les divers logements sont accessibles par des routes intérieures. On compte 23 unités d'habitation diverses, la plupart aménagées sur deux étages. Une rue groupe aux 7e et 8e étages restaurant, snack-bar et magasins. Au dernier étage, les services techniques, la salle de gymnastique, le jardin d'enfants, la piscine et des emplacements de jeux.

Chaque unité d'habitation est pourvue d'une grande loggia.

Schnitt durch Wohnung / Section through flat / Coupe transversale appartement

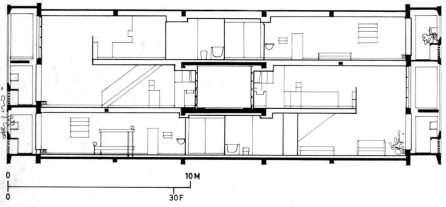

0   10 M
0   30 F

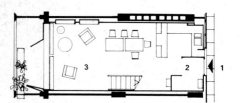

Maisonnettewohnungen für Familien mit 2–4 Kindern / Maisonnettes for families with 2–4 children / Appartements-villas pour familles de 2 à 4 enfants

Schnitt / Section / Coupe

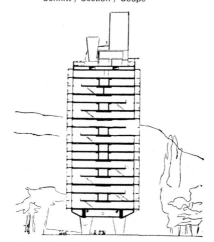

Maisonnettewohnungen für Familien mit 2–4 Kindern / Maisonnette-apartments for families with 2–4 children / Appartements-villas pour familles de 2 à 4 enfants:

1 Innenstraße / Internal street / Rue intérieure
2 Eingang / Entrance / Entrée
3 Wohnraum / Living room / Salle de séjour
4 Elternschlafzimmer / Parents' bedroom / Chambre à coucher des parents
5 Dusche für Kinder / Children's shower / Douche pour les enfants
6 Kinderzimmer / Children / Chambres des enfants
7 Luftraum, Wohnraum / Living room / Aération, Séjour

Normalgeschoß / Typical floor / Etage type

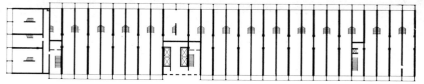

Geschoß mit Innenstraße / Floor with internal street / Etage avec rue intérieure

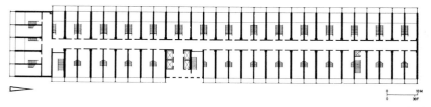

Photo: Ansicht von Norden / View from the north / Vue du nord

Engineering Building, Leicester University
Leicester, England (1960–1963)
James Stirling and James Gowan, London

Die Konstruktion besteht aus einem Stahlskelettbau, der mit gefärbtem Glas, Backstein und Keramik verkleidet ist.

Height: 120 ft. This college for two hundred and fifty students, situated in the University Park, is divided into three parts. The main hall can be used for a variety of purposes. The two towers of six and ten floors respectively contain laboratories, administration and auditorium. In front of the towers the service installations and the water tank provide massive formal elements. The construction is a steel skeleton clad with coloured glass, brick and ceramic tiles.

Bauhöhe: 36,5 m. Die für 250 Studenten im Universitätspark gebaute Hochschule ist in drei Bezirke unterteilt. Die Haupthalle kann für die verschiedensten Anlässe verwendet werden. Laboratorien, Verwaltungsbüro und Auditorium sind in den beiden Türmen von sechs und zehn Etagen untergebracht. Die technische Installation und ein Wasserbehälter stehen als massive plastische Körper vor den Türmen.

Hauteur: 36,5 m. Construite dans le parc de l'Université et d'une capacité de 250 étudiants, l'école se subdivise en trois secteurs. Le hall principal peut répondre aux nécessités les plus diverses. Laboratoires, bureaux de l'administration et auditoires occupent les deux tours de six et dix étages. Devant les tours, deux éléments plastiques massifs abritent les services techniques et un réservoir d'eau.
La construction est un squelette d'acier revêtu de verre teinté, briques et céramique.

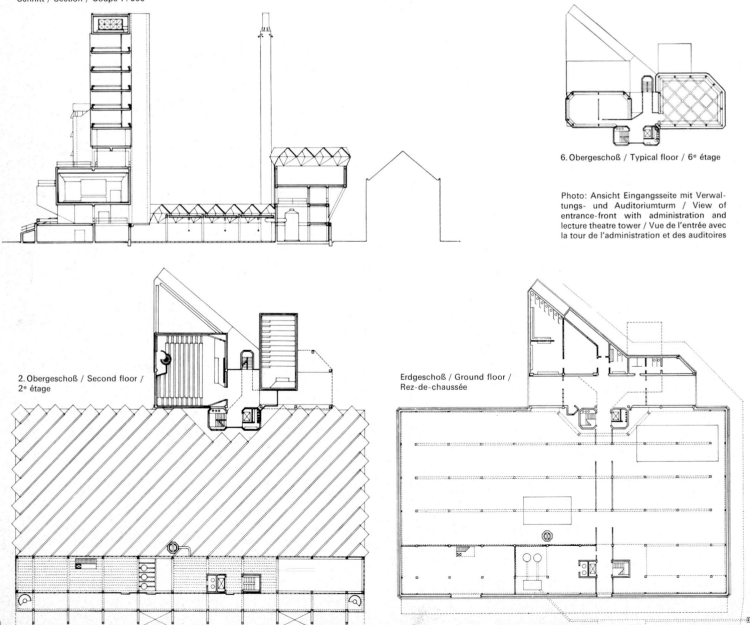

Schnitt / Section / Coupe 1 : 600

6. Obergeschoß / Typical floor / 6e étage

Photo: Ansicht Eingangsseite mit Verwaltungs- und Auditoriumturm / View of entrance-front with administration and lecture theatre tower / Vue de l'entrée avec la tour de l'administration et des auditoires

2. Obergeschoß / Second floor / 2e étage

Erdgeschoß / Ground floor / Rez-de-chaussée

Cluster Block
Bethnal Green, London
Denys Lasdun and Partners
London

On the outskirts of London, in a part which was heavily damaged in the last world war, a highrise building with an unusual ground plan has been constructed. Around a central tower, which contains the vertical circulation, four towers have been built which contain fourteen maisonnettes each and two flats. The units are arranged in such a way that all rooms are exposed to sunlight. The central tower has alternative floors for communication to the maisonnettes, the playing areas and spaces for drying laundry. The building consists of prefabricated units.

In einem Außenquartier Londons, welches während des Zweiten Weltkrieges stark zerstört wurde, ist ein Hochhaus mit einer ungewöhnlichen Grundrißlösung gebaut worden. Vier Türme, die je 14 Maisonnettewohnungen enthalten, sind um einen Zentralturm gebaut, der die Vertikalverbindungen enthält.
Die Wohnungen sind so angeordnet, daß alle Zimmer täglich Sonnenlicht bekommen. Im Zentralturm wechseln eine Etage für Verkehrswege zu den Maisonnettes und eine für Spielplätze und Möglichkeit zum Wäschetrocknen ab.
Der Bau wurde aus vorgefertigten Elementen errichtet.

Erigée à la périphérie de Londres, dans un quartier fortement détruit pendant la 2e Guerre mondiale, «Bethnal Green» représente une solution inhabituelle. Quatre tours, comprenant chacune 14 appartements-villas, sont construites autour d'une tour centrale assurant les liaisons verticales.
Les appartements sont disposés de telle manière que chaque chambre puisse être journellement ensoleillée. Dans la tour centrale, un étage de communication alterne avec un étage d'emplacements de jeu et de séchoirs.
La construction est réalisée en éléments préfabriqués.

1., 3., 8., 10., 12., 14. Obergeschoß (Wohngeschoß der Maisonnettewohnungen) / Upper floor (living floor of maisonnettes) / Etage (étage de jour des appartements-villas)

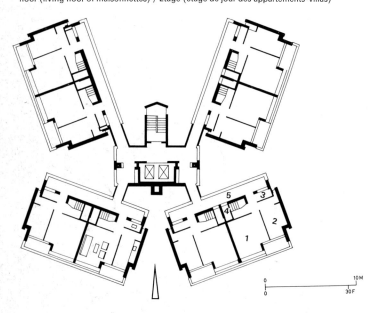

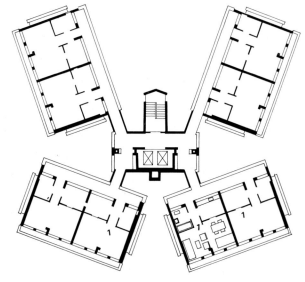

5. Obergeschoß / Fifth floor / 5e étage

2., 4., 7., 9., 11., 13., 15. Obergeschoß (Schlafgeschoß der Maisonnettewohnungen) / Upper floor (bedroom-floors of maisonnettes) / Etage (étage de nuit des appartements-villas)

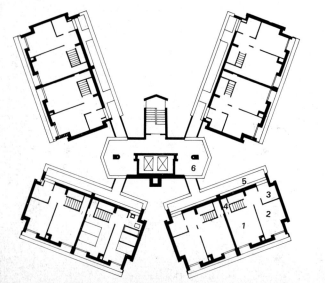

1., 3., 8., 10., 12., 14. Obergeschoß (Wohngeschoß der Maisonnettewohnungen) / Upper storey (residential floor containing maisonnettes) / Etage (étage de jour des appartements-villas):
1 Wohnraum / Living room / Salle de séjour
2 Wohnküche / Dining-kitchen / Cuisine-séjour
3 WC
4 Nottreppe / Fire escape / Escalier de secours
5 Laubengang / Access balcony / Balcon d'accès

2., 4., 7., 11., 13., 15. Obergeschoß (Schlafgeschoß der Maisonnettewohnungen) / Upper storeys (Bedroom-storey of mai-

sonnettes)/ Etage (étage de nuit des appartements-villas):
1 Elternzimmer / Parents' bedroom / Chambre des parents
2 Kinderzimmer / Children / Chambre des enfants
3 Bad / Bathroom / Bains
4 Nottreppe / Fire escape / Escalier de secours
5 Laubengang / Access balcony / Balcon d'accès
6 Trockenraum / Drying space / Séchoir

5. Obergeschoß / Fifth storey / 5e étage:
1 Ein-Zimmer-Wohnungen / 1-room flats / Appartements de 1 pièce

Photo: Ansicht von Norden / View from the
north / Vue du nord

Velasca Tower
Milan, Italy (1956–1957)
Belgiojoso, Peressutti and Rogers, Milan

Bauhöhe: 99 m. In der Nähe des Domes von Mailand steht der Torre Velasca auf einem kleinen Platz, allseitig von Hauptstraßen umgeben.

In den beiden unteren Geschossen befinden sich Läden, es folgen Büros, Räume für Dienstpersonal, dann im auskragenden Teil 2½- bis 3½-Zimmer-Wohnungen und Maisonnettes in der 25. und 26. Etage. Es wird hier ein Versuch gemacht, das Leben der Bewohner mit den verschiedenen Lebensbereichen in einem Haus unterzubringen.

Die Konstruktion besteht aus dynamischen Rohbetonsäulen und aus einem «Turm im Turm», der die vertikalen Verbindungen und Installationen enthält.

Height: 325 ft. The Velasca Tower stands on a small square near the Duomo at Milan surrounded by main streets.

In the two lower floors there are shops, offices and rooms for service personnel. In the overhanging part there are two and three-room flats and on the twenty-fifth and twenty-sixth floors, maisonnettes. An attempt has been made here to contain the various activities of the inhabitants in one building. The construction consists of rough concrete columns and of a tower within the tower which contains the vertical circulation and the service installations.

Hauteur: 99 m. La Tour Velasca est située à proximité du Dôme de Milan sur une petite place circonscrite par des routes principales.

Les deux étages inférieurs abritent des magasins, des bureaux et des locaux pour le personnel de service, la partie en surplomb des appartements de 2½ à 3½ pièces et des appartements-villas au 25e et 26e étage. On a tenté ici d'intégrer dans une seule maison les diverses sphères d'activité humaine.

La construction est constituée de piliers de béton brut dynamiques et d'une «tour dans la tour» abritant les liaisons verticales et les services techniques.

Typisches Wohngeschoß / Typical living floor / Etage d'habitation type

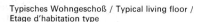

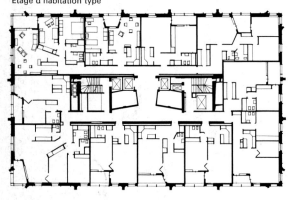

Typisches Bürogeschoß / Typical office-floor / Etage de bureaux type

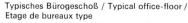

Schnitt 1 : 1000 / Section / Coupe

Erdgeschoß / Ground floor / Rez-de-chaussée

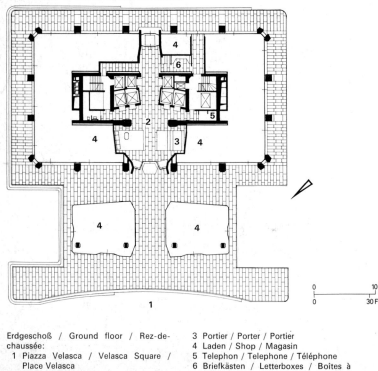

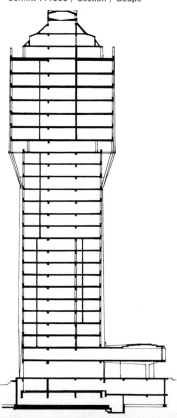

Erdgeschoß / Ground floor / Rez-de-chaussée:
1 Piazza Velasca / Velasca Square / Place Velasca
2 Halle / Lobby / Hall
3 Portier / Porter / Portier
4 Laden / Shop / Magasin
5 Telephon / Telephone / Téléphone
6 Briefkästen / Letterboxes / Boîtes à lettres

Photo: Ansicht von Südosten / View from
the south-east / Vue du sud-est

Pirelli Building
Milan, Italy (1957–1961)
Studio Ponti, Fornaroli, Rosselli, Studio Valtolina
and Dell'Orto, engineers, Milan

die Untergeschosse enthalten Garagen, Werkstätten und einen großen Vortragssaal.

Height: 417 ft. The building stands in the centre of Milan, an elegant two-point slab, and dominates the station square. The basements reach a depth of 37 ft. 6 in. The construction of the building consists of four solid triangular points and four massive pylon walls which get slimmer towards the top. This arrangement allows for maximum freedom of internal planning. The two-storey building and the basement floors contain garages, workshops and a large lecture hall.

Bauhöhe: 127 m. Das Gebäude steht im Zentrum von Mailand und dominiert als elegante Zweispitzscheibe den Bahnhofplatz. Die Kellergeschosse reichen 11,50 m in die Tiefe. Die statische Konstruktion des Bauwerkes besteht aus vier steifen Dreieckspitzen und vier massiven, nach oben sich verjüngenden Pfeilerwänden. Diese Anordnung gestattet größtmögliche Freiheit der inneren Aufteilung. Der zweistöckige Flachbau und

Hauteur: 127 m. Située au centre de Milan, l'élégante construction domine la place de la gare. La hauteur des étages souterrains est de 11,50 m. Statique, l'édifice est constitué de quatre pointes triangulaires rigides et de quatre parois-piliers massives se réduisant vers le haut. Cette ordonnance permet une distribution intérieure très libre. La construction basse de deux étages et les étages souterrains abritent des garages, des ateliers et une grande salle de conférences.

Erdgeschoß / Ground floor / Rez-de-chaussée

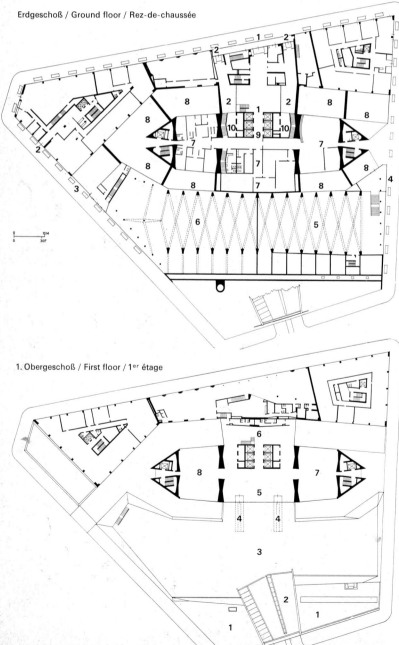

1. Obergeschoß / First floor / 1er étage

Normalgeschoß / Typical floor / Etage type

Erdgeschoß / Ground floor / Rez-de-chaussée:
1 Eingang Angestellte / Staff entrance / Entrée des employés
2 Eingänge Direktion / Directors entrance / Entrée de la direction
3 Privateingang / Private entrance / Entrée privée
4 Eingang zum Auditorium / Entrance to lecture theatre / Entrée vers auditoire
5 Luftraum Auditorium / Space above auditorium / Aération auditoire
6 Luftraum Rechenzentrum / Space above Computer room / Aération centre de calcul
7 Büro / Office / Bureau
8 Kantine / Canteen / Cantines

1. Obergeschoß / Upper floor / 1er étage
1 Grünfläche / Lawn / Pelouse
2 Rampe / Ramp / Rampe
3 Zufahrt für Autos / Drive / Accès voitures
4 Vordach / Porch / Auvent
5 Eingangshalle / Entrance lobby / Hall d'entrée
6 Wartehalle / Waiting hall / Salle d'attente
7 Besprechungsraum / Conference room / Salle de réunion
8 Kasse / Cashdesk / Caisse

Normalgeschoß / Typical floor / Etage type:
1 Büros / Offices / Bureaux
2 Garderobe / Cloakroom / Vestiaire
3 Feuertreppe / Fire escape / Escalier de secours

Photo: Die charakteristische Seitenansicht des Pirelli-Hochhauses / Pirelli Building; side view / Vue latérale caractéristique de la tour

110

Schnitt / Section / Coupe 1 : 2000

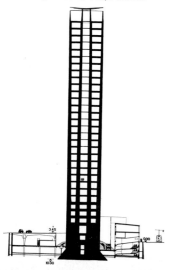

Torres Blancas
Madrid, Spain (1964–1966)
F. J. Saenz de Oiza, Madrid

Height: 197 ft. The two highrise towers, Torres Blancas, are situated on the Barajas Madrid motorway. These residential blocks are 197 feet high and each contains 160 units of one to eight room flats. In the basement there are garages for 80% of the flats. In addition there are a crèche and a chapel on the ground floor; restaurant, cafés and swimming pool on the two top floors. Stairs and lifts are in the central core. An extensive garden-terrace system gives a special character to the highrise towers so that they can be described as a vertical garden city.

Bauhöhe: 60 m. Die beiden Wohntürme «Torres Blancas» stehen an der Autobahn von Barajas nach Madrid. Die Wohntürme enthalten je 160 Wohneinheiten von Einzimmer- bis Achtzimmerwohnungen. Im Untergeschoß befinden sich für 80% der Wohnungen Garagen. Hinzu kommen Kindergarten und Hauskapelle im Erdgeschoß, Restaurants, Cafés und Schwimmbad in den beiden obersten Geschossen. Die Erschließung erfolgt im mittleren Kern durch Treppen und Aufzüge. Charakterisiert werden die Wohntürme durch ein großzügiges Gartenterrassensystem, so daß man von einer «vertikalen Gartenstadt» sprechen kann.

Hauteur: 60 m. Les deux tours d'habitation «Torres Blancas» sont situées le long de l'autoroute reliant Barajas à Madrid. D'une hauteur de 60 m, elles comptent chacune 160 appartements de un à huit pièces. Le sous-sol abrite des garages pour 80% des appartements. Le jardin d'enfants et la chapelle de la maison se trouvent au rez-de-chaussée, des restaurants, cafés et la piscine aux deux derniers étages. Escaliers et ascenseurs sont au centre des bâtiments. Caractéristique des tours, un imposant système de jardins-terrasses donne à l'ensemble un caractère de «cité-jardin verticale».

Wohngeschoß der großen zweigeschossigen Wohnungen / Large 2-storey maisonnettes, residential floor / Etage de jour des grands appartements à deux niveaux

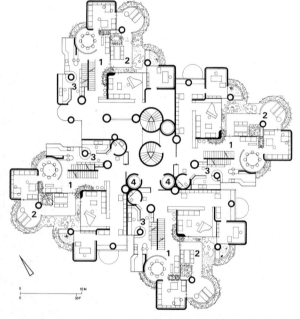

Schlafgeschoß der zweigeschossigen Wohnungen / Bedroom floor, 2-storey maisonnettes / Etage de nuit des appartements à deux niveaux

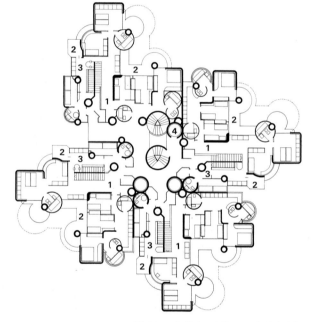

Photomontage der fertigen Wohntürme / Montage of completed residential towers / Montage photographique des tours d'habitation

Wohngeschoß der großen zweigeschossigen Wohnungen / Large 2-storey maisonnettes, living rooms storey / Etage de jour des grands appartements à deux niveaux
1 Wohnung, unteres Niveau mit Wohnräumen / Maisonnette, lower level with living quarters / Appartement, niveau inférieur des pièces de séjour
2 Überdeckte Terrasse, gleichzeitig Sonnenschutz für die Wohnräume / Covered terrace / Terrasse couverte fonctionnant comme pare-soleil
3 Service-Zone / Service area / Services
4 Aufzug / Lift / Ascenseur

Schlafgeschoß der zweigeschossigen Wohnungen / Bedroom floor, 2-storey maisonnettes / Etage de nuit des appartements à deux niveaux:
1 Wohnung, oberes Niveau mit Schlafräumen / Maisonnette, upper level with bedrooms / Appartement, niveau supérieur des chambres à coucher
2 Service-Balkon / Service balcony / Balcon de service
3 Service-Zone / Service area / Services
4 Aufzug / Lift / Ascenseur

Photo: Wohnhochhaus noch im Bau / The building under construction / Maison-tour d'habitation en construction

112

Reskustorni, Highrise Block
Tapiola, Finland (1960–1961)
Aarne Ervi, Helsinki

Height: 154 ft. The highrise tower Reskustorni is the centre and focal point of the garden city of Tapiola. It contains administration and general offices and on the top floor there is a restaurant with splendid views. There is a clear expression of the contrast between nature and architecture, between growth and planning. The building is open towards south, west and east, and if necessary can be protected from the sun by venetian blinds. There are no openings on the north side.
The construction is a skeleton of concrete. The façades are aluminium.

Bauhöhe: 47 m. Der Hochhausturm «Reskustorni» ist Zentrum und Akzent der Gartenstadt Tapiola. Er enthält Verwaltungs- und Büroräume sowie im obersten Geschoß ein Aussichtsrestaurant. Der Kontrast zwischen Natur und Architektur, zwischen Gewachsenem und Geplantem wird hier ganz besonders deutlich gemacht.
Die Konstruktion ist ein Skelett aus Ortbeton, die Fassaden bestehen aus Aluminium.

Hauteur: 47 m. La maison-tour «Reskustorni» est à la fois le centre et l'élément dominant de la cité-jardin de Tapiola. Elle abrite des services administratifs, des bureaux et au dernier étage un restaurant panoramique. Le contraste entre la nature et l'architecture apparaît ici dans toute sa force.
Complètement fermée au nord, la construction s'ouvre vers le sud, l'ouest et l'est où elle peut être protégée du soleil par des stores à lamelles.
Elle est constituée d'une ossature de béton et de façades d'aluminium.

Dachgeschoß mit Restaurant / Top floor with restaurant / Dernier étage et restaurant

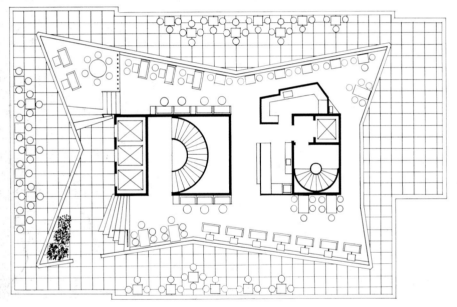

Bürogeschoß / Office floor / Etage de bureau

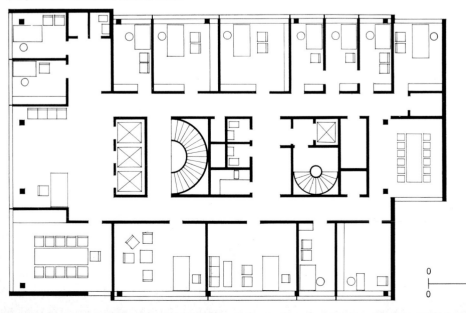

0   10 M
0   30 F

Ansicht Bürohochhaus Tapiola-Zentrum / Office tower Tapiola Centre / Vue de la maison-tour de bureaux

SAS Building
Copenhagen, Denmark (1956)
Aarne Jacobsen, Copenhagen

Glas und Aluminium versucht, das Gebäude so leicht und transparent wie möglich erscheinen zu lassen.

Height: 230 ft. The SAS building consists of two parts: the two-storey high section which contains the air terminal, travel bureaus, shops and reception hall and the twenty-two storey high hotel tower. It is situated in a central position on the main street of Copenhagen.

Glass and aluminium were used on the façade to make the building appear as light and transparent as possible so that its height would not dwarf the surrounding buildings.

Bauhöhe: 70 m. Gegliedert in zwei Baukörper, den zweige-schossigen Flachbau, der Air Terminal, Reisebüros, Geschäfte und eine Empfangshalle enthält, und den 22 geschossigen Hotelblock, steht das SAS-Gebäude in zentraler Lage an der Hauptstraße Kopenhagens.

Damit der Bau wegen seiner Höhe die umgebenden Bauten optisch nicht zu sehr erdrückt, wurde durch die Materialien

Hauteur: 70 m. Constitué de deux corps, l'un construction basse de deux étages comprenant Air terminal, bureaux de voyage, magasins et hall de réception, l'autre tour de 22 étages, le bâtiment «SAS» est situé au centre, sur la rue principale de Copenhague.

Afin que la construction, de par sa hauteur, n'écrase pas exagérément les bâtiments environnants, on a tenté de la faire apparaître aussi légère et transparente que possible en recourant au verre et à l'aluminium.

Erdgeschoß / Ground floor / Rez-de-chaussée

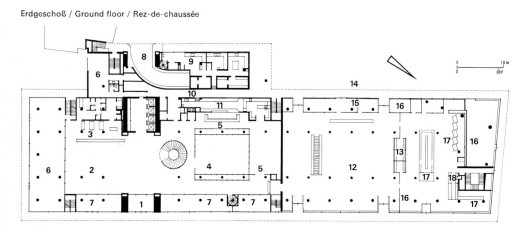

Normalgeschoß Hotel / Typical hotel floor / Etage type hôtel

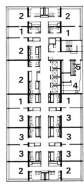

1. Obergeschoß / First floor / 1er étage

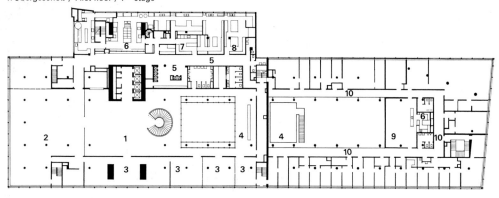

Erdgeschoß / Ground floor / Rez-de-chaussée:
1 Hoteleingang / Hotel entrance / Entrée de l'hôtel
2 Hotelhalle / Hotel lobby / Hall de l'hôtel
3 Reception / Reception / Réception
4 Wintergarten / Wintergarden / Jardin d'hiver
5 Snack-Bar / Snack bar / Snack-bar
6 Läden / Shops / Magasins
7 Kioske / Kiosks / Kiosques
8 Einfahrt zu den Garagen / Entrance to garages / Accès aux garages
9 Warenannahme / Goods entrance /

Réception marchandises
10 Gepäckkorridore / Service corridors / Corridors de service
11 Snack-Bar / Snack bar / Snack-bar
12 Air Terminal
13 Bank / Bank / Banque
14 Autobus-Haltestelle / Bus stop / Station d'autobus
15 Gepäck, Kundendienst / Luggage, Customer service / Bagages, service clientèle
16 Büros / Offices / Bureaux
17 Verschiedene Expeditionen / Dispatch / Expéditions
18 Kasse / Cash desk / Caisse

1. Obergeschoß / First floor / 1er étage
1 Vestibül / Vestibule / Vestibule
2 Restaurant
3 Gesellschaftsräume / Public rooms / Salles de réunion
4 Bar
5 Bedienung / Service / Service
6 Küche / Kitchen / Cuisine
7 Kaffeeküche / Coffee kitchen / Cuisine du café
8 Konditorei / Confectionary / Confiserie
9 Kantine / Canteen / Cantine
10 SAS-Büroräume / SAS offices / Bureaux de la SAS

Normalgeschoß Hotel / Typical hotel floor / Etage type hôtel:
1 Einbettzimmer / Single room / Chambre à un lit
2 Zweibettzimmer / Double room / Chambre à deux lits
3 Dem Zweck entsprechend veränderliche Zimmer / Convertible room / Chambre transformable suivant les besoins
4 Bedienungsraum / Service room / Office
5 Bedienungslift / Service lift / Ascenseur de service

Photo: SAS-Hotel von Süden / From the south / Vue du sud

Neue Vahr, Residential Block
Bremen, Germany (1959–1960)
Alvar Aalto, Helsinki

Bauhöhe: 61,5 m. Das 22 geschossige Wohnhochhaus, das das Zentrum der «Neuen Vahr» in Bremen bildet, öffnet sich wie ein Fächer. Diese Idee bestimmte auch den Grundriß. Alle Wohnungen verbreitern sich zum Licht und nehmen praktisch den ganzen Tag Sonne in sich auf. Es befinden sich lediglich Kleinwohnungen in diesem Gebäude. Der Bau ist ein Stahlbetongebäude mit vorgehängter Kunststeinfassade.

Height: 202 ft. The twenty-two storey high residential block which forms the centre of the Neue Vahr in Bremen opens out like a fan. This idea determined the plan. All the flats open out towards the light and enjoy sunshine practically all day. There are only small flats. The building is of reinforced concrete clad with artificial stone.

Hauteur: 61,5 m. Centre du quartier «Neue Vahr», la maison-tour de 22 étages s'ouvre en éventail. C'est l'idée de base du plan. Tous les appartements sont tournés vers la lumière et jouissent d'un ensoleillement quasi total. Le bâtiment ne compte que des petits appartements. La construction est en acier et béton avec une façade-rideau de pierres artificielles.

Erdgeschoß / Ground floor / Rez-de-chaussée

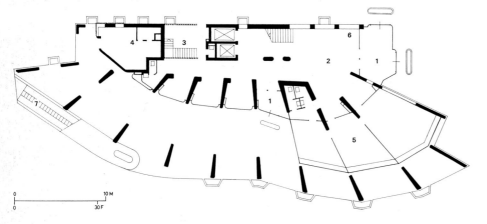

Normalgeschoß / Typical floor / Etage type

Erdgeschoß / Ground floor / Rez-de-chaussée:
1 Windfang / Wind screen / Pare-vent
2 Eingangshalle / Entrance lobby / Hall d'entrée
3 Außentreppe / Exterior stair / Escalier extérieur
4 Müllraum / Garbage / Déchets
5 Büro / Office / Bureau
6 Briefkasten / Letterbox / Boîte à lettres

7 Abfahrt zu Kellergarage / Entrance to underground garage / Accès aux garages souterrains

Normalgeschoß / Typical floor / Etage type:
1 Innentreppe / Interior stairs / Escalier intérieur
2 Außentreppe (von der Feuerpolizei verlangt) / Exterior stairs (required by the fire service) / Escalier extérieur (exigé par la police du feu)
3 Zweizimmerwohnung / 2-room flat / Appartement de deux pièces
4 Appartement mit Kleinküche (34,4 m²) / Flat with small kitchen (367 sq. ft) / Appartement avec cuisinette
5 Appartement mit Kleinküche (42,0 m²) / Flat with small kitchen (438 sq. ft) / Appartement avec cuisinette

6 Appartement mit Küche (59,5 m²) / Flat with kitchen (624 sq. ft) / Appartement avec cuisine

Photo: Alle Appartements liegen gegen Süden oder Südwesten / All apartments face south or south-west / Tous les appartements sont orientés vers le sud ou le sud-ouest

118

Finland House
Hamburg, Germany (1966)
Professor Helmut Hentrich and Hubert Petschnigg
engineers, Dusseldorf

The idea of a suspended highrise building has been inspired by the fly-over which is part of the town plan and which will be tangential to the Baufluchtlinie and also by the permission to project over the Baufluchtlinie. From the central core a square platform with 66 ft. long sides is cantilevered. The top floor contains the air-conditioning; from this floor are suspended a restaurant and eleven office floors. These are set at a sufficient height above railway lines and the projected fly-over which could otherwise form potential sources of disturbance.

Die von der Stadtplanung vorgesehene Hochstraße, die die Baufluchtlinie tangiert, und die Genehmigung, stützenfrei über die Baufluchtlinie auszukragen, führten zur Idee eines Hängehauses.

Um den zentralen Kern kragt nach allen Seiten eine quadratische Plattform von 20 m Seitenlänge aus. Im oberen Trägergeschoß ist die Klimaanlage untergebracht. An diesem Geschoß hängen ein Restaurant sowie 11 Bürogeschosse in ausreichender Höhe über den Störungsquellen Bahndamm und geplante Hochstraße.

L'idée d'une maison suspendue est née de la projection par le plan d'aménagement urbain d'une route surélevée, tangente à la limite du domaine public, et de l'autorisation de construire en surplomb au-dessus de ladite limite.

Une plate-forme quadrilatérale de 20 m de côté dépasse de toutes parts le noyau central. Les installations de climatisation se trouvent à l'étage porteur supérieur. Distribués en dessous de celui-ci, un restaurant et 11 étages de bureaux surplombent à une hauteur suffisante les sources de bruit, la voie ferrée et la route projetée.

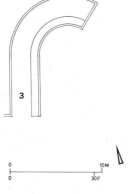

Erdgeschoß / Ground floor / Rez-de-chaussée

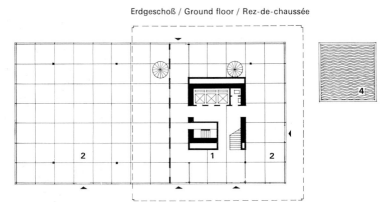

Dachgeschoß / Top floor / Dernier étage

Normalgeschoß für Büros / Typical office floor / Etage type de bureaux

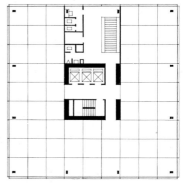

Schnitt / Section / Coupe 1 : 600

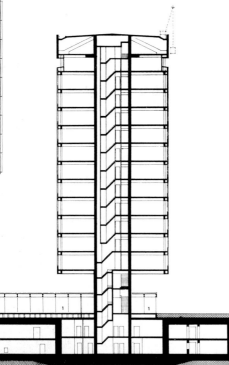

Dachgeschoß / Top storey / Dernier étage:
1 Restaurant
2 Küche / Kitchen / Cuisine

Erdgeschoß / Ground floor / Rez-de-chaussée:
1 Eingangshalle / Lobby / Hall d'entrée
2 Läden / Shops / Magasins
3 Abfahrtsrampe / Exit ramp / Rampe d'accès
4 Bassin / Fountain / Bassin

Photo: Ansicht des noch nicht ganz fertiggestellten Hängehochhauses / The cantilevered building under construction / Vue de la maison-tour suspendue en voie d'achèvement

Intercontinental Hotel
Frankfurt am Main, Germany
Apel and Beckert, Frankfurt am Main

Attikageschoß und den Aufbau der technischen Anlage zu einer in sich abgeschlossenen Einheit gestaltet. Für die 500 Hotelzimmer sind 163 Einstellplätze in Tiefgaragen vorgesehen.

Height: 218 ft. The Intercontinental Hotel is situated next to the main railway station on the river Main. The plan of the skeleton structure with its four rows of columns has been used to best advantage. The simple façade clad in natural stone forms a composite unit with the top floor and the service installations above. There are 163 parking places in underground garages for the 500 bedrooms.

Hauteur: 66,5 m. L'Hôtel Intercontinental se situe au bord du Main à proximité de la gare centrale. L'ossature et ses quatre séries de piliers permettent une mise en valeur optima du plan. Revêtue de pierre naturelle, la façade tire son caractère d'unité fermée de l'étage en attique et de la superstructure des services techniques. 163 parkings souterrains sont prévus pour les 500 chambres de l'hôtel.

Bauhöhe: 66,5 m. Das Hotel Intercontinental liegt am Ufer des Mains, in nächster Nähe des Hauptbahnhofes. Der Skelettbau mit vier Säulenreihen ist grundrißlich optimal ausgewertet. Die klare Fassade in Natursteinverkleidung wird durch das

Dachgeschoß / Top floor / Dernier étage

4.–19. Obergeschoß / Typical floor / Du 4e au 19e étage

1. Obergeschoß / First floor / 1er étage

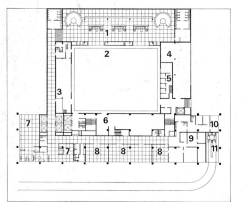

Erdgeschoß / Ground floor / Rez-de-chaussée

Erdgeschoß / Ground floor / Rez-de-chaussée:
1 Halle / Lobby / Hall
2 Läden / Shops / Magasins
3 Lounge / Lounge / Hall
4 Bar
5 Hotelspeisesaal / Hotel dining room / Salle à manger de l'hôtel
6 Reception / Reception / Réception
7 Café
8 Ballsaaleingang / Ballroom entrance / Entrée de la salle de bal
9 Terrasse / Terrace / Terrasse
10 Hauptküche / Main kitchen / Cuisine principale
11 Lager-, Kühlräume / Store- and refrigeration rooms / Entrepôts et chambre froide
12 Warenannahme / Goods entrance / Réception marchandises

13 Personalspeiseraum / Staff dining room / Salle à manger du personnel
14 Wirtschaftshof / Outdoor café / Cours du café
15 Garageeinfahrt / Entrance to garages / Entrée des garages
16 Garageausfahrt / Exit from garages / Sortie des garages

1. Obergeschoß / First floor / 1er étage:
1 Foyer
2 Ballsaal / Ballroom / Salle de bal
3 Lagerraum / Storerooms / Entrepôts
4 Ventilationsraum / Ventilation room / Ventilation
5 Film- und Simultananlagen / Screening room / Projection de films et traduction simultanée

6 Ballsaalküche / Ballroom kitchen / Cuisine de la salle de bal
7 Frisiersalon / Hairdressing salon / Salon de coiffure
8 Privatspeiseraum / Private dining room / Salle à manger privée
9 Büros Direktion / Administration offices / Bureaux de la direction
10 Arzt / Doctor / Médecin
11 Feuerleiter / Fire escape / Echelle de secours

4.–19. Obergeschoß / Upper floor / Du 4e au 19e étage:
1 Balkon / Balcony / Balcon
2 Wohnraum / Living room / Salle de séjour
3 Schlafraum / Bedroom / Chambre à coucher

4 Normalzimmer / Typical room / Chambre type

Dachgeschoß / Top floor / Dernier étage:
1 Privatspeiseraum / Private dining room / Salle à manger privée
2 Müllabwurf / Garbage / Déchets
3 Anrichte / Pantry / Table à manger
4 Kühlraum / Refrigeration room / Chambre froide
5 Tanzbar / Bar, dance floor / Dancing
6 Bar
7 Lounge / Lounge / Hall
8 Dachterrasse / Roof-terrace / Terrasse sur le toit

Photo: Hotel vom Main aus gesehen / Hotel, view from the Main / Vue du Main

Marl City Hall
Germany (1960–1967)
J. van den Broek and J. Bakema
Rotterdam

Bauhöhe: 55 m. Das im Bau befindliche Rathauszentrum von Marl soll der Mittelpunkt verschiedener Kleinstädte werden. Es besteht im Endzustand aus einem Sitzungstrakt, Zentralgebäude und vier Hängehochhäusern, in welchen sich die verschiedenen Verwaltungen befinden.

Der innere Betonturm der Hängehäuser enthält Aufzüge, Treppen und Installation. Auf diesem Betonkern ist ein Pilzkopf ausgebildet, an welchem die Spannbetonhängeglieder angebracht sind. Sie tragen die Geschoßdecken und somit auch die Fassaden. Da nur der Betonkern statische Funktionen hat, bleibt die übrige Grundrißfläche im Erdgeschoß frei.

Height: 180 ft. The town centre at Marl which is in course of construction is intended to become the centre of several small towns. It will consist finally of a council building, central buildings and four highrise buildings which will house the various administrative offices. The inner structural concrete tower contains lifts, stairs and service installations. On top of this core is a mushroom head to which the prestressed concrete's reinforcing rods are attached. These carry the load of all the floor slabs and consequently the façades as well. As the concrete core alone is structural, the rest of the ground-floor area is open.

Hauteur: 55 m. L'Hôtel de ville de Marl, en cours de construction, doit devenir le centre de plusieurs petites villes. Au stade final, il comprendra une aile de réunion, un bâtiment central et quatre maisons-tours suspendues abritant les diverses administrations.

Dans les maisons-tours, ascenseurs, escaliers et services techniques sont aménagés dans une tour de béton intérieure. Celle-ci se termine par un chapeau auquel sont fixés les éléments de béton précontraint porteurs des dalles et des façades. Seule la tour ayant des fonctions statiques, toute la surface au sol restante est libre.

Photo: Fertig erstellte Dezernatstürme, 1. Etappe des Rathauses / Completed towers, First stage of town hall / Tours des bureaux officiels, 1ʳᵉ étape de l'Hôtel de ville

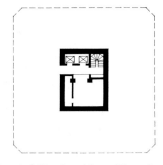

Erdgeschoß Bürotürme / Ground floor, office towers / Rez-de-chaussée des tours de bureaux 1 : 300

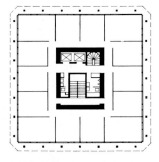

Normalgeschoß Bürotürme / Typical floor, office towers / Etage type des tours de bureaux

Rathaus, Gesamtausbau, Modellaufnahme von Süden gesehen / Town hall, total development, model photographed from the south / Hôtel de ville, stade final, maquette vue du sud

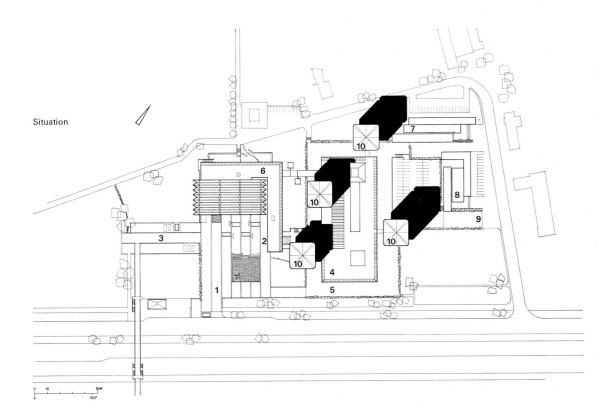

Situation

1 Vorplatz / Forecourt / Esplanade
2 Haupteingang Publikum / Main public entrance / Entrée principale du public
3 Parkplatz / Parking place / Parkings
4 Zentralgebäude / Central building /

Bâtiment central
5 Vertiefter Parkplatz / Underground parking / Parkings souterrains
6 Sitzungstrakt / Conference area / Alle de réunion
7 Stadtbücherei / City library / Biblio-

thèque municipale
8 Polizei / Police / Police
9 Einfahrt Parkgarage / Entrance to garage parking / Accès aux garages
10 Bürotürme / Office towers / Tours de bureaux

125

Le Lignon, Satellite Town
Geneva, Switzerland (1964–1968)
Addor and Juillard, Geneva

Height: 328 ft. The main tower is part of the satellite town Le Lignon which has been planned both as a town planning feature and a functional unit with accommodation for 10,000 people.

Apart from the flats which have been created by private initiative and public help there are schools, a church, park and shopping centre, post office and a bank. Like all flats in this town, those in the tower are orientated in two directions. The thirty floor high building contains a swimming pool, a skating rink and a solarium. The outer skin of the structure is a special tin cladding which has been used throughout the complex development.

Bauhöhe: 100 m. Die Satellitenstadt «Le Lignon», die als städtebauliche und funktionelle Einheit geplant ist, enthält Wohneinheiten für 10 000 Einwohner.

Neben den Wohnungen, die durch private Initiative und staatliche Hilfe entstanden sind, befinden sich in der Überbauung Schulen, Kirche, Gemeinschaftsanlagen, Einkaufszentren, Post und eine Bank. Wie alle Wohnungen in dieser «Stadt» sind die des Turmes nach zwei Seiten orientiert. Das 30stöckige Hochhaus enthält ein Schwimmbad, eine Eisbahn und ein Solarium.

Hauteur: 100 m. La cité-satellite «Le Lignon» est une unité urbanistique et fonctionnelle pour 10 000 habitants.

A part les logements, financés par l'initiative privée et l'aide de l'Etat, la cité comprend écoles, église, équipements communautaires, centres commerciaux, poste et banque. Comme tous les appartements de la cité, ceux de la tour sont orientés dans deux directions. Haute de 30 étages, la tour abrite une piscine, une patinoire et un solarium.

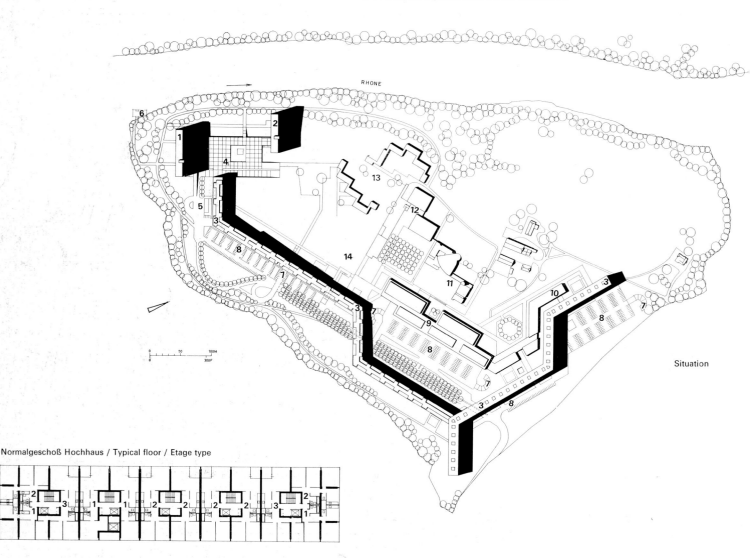

Situation

Normalgeschoß Hochhaus / Typical floor / Etage type

Zwischengeschoß Hochhaus / Mezzanine floor / Entresol

126

Situation:
1 Hochhaus mit 30 Geschossen / Highrise block with 30 storeys / Maisontour de 30 étages
2 Hochhaus mit 25 Geschossen / Highrise block with 25 storeys / Maisontour de 25 étages
3 Reihenwohnhäuser 12–17 Geschosse / Terraced blocks, 12–17 storeys / Maisons en ordre contigu de 12 à 17 étages
4 Platz / Square / Esplanade
5 Bus-Haltestelle / Bus stop / Station d'autobus
6 Bootssteg (Bootsdienst nach Genf) / Jetty (boat service to Geneva)/ Embarcadère (service de bateaux vers Genève)
7 Ein- und Ausfahrten in Kellergaragen / Entrance and exit to underground parking / Entrée et sortie des garages souterrains
8 Parkplätze / Parking / Parkings
9 Verkaufszentrum / Shopping centre / Centre commercial
10 Kulturelles Zentrum / Cultural centre / Centre culturel
11 Kirchen / Churches / Eglises
12 Sekundarschule / Secondary school / Ecole secondaire
13 Schulen / Schools / Ecoles
14 Sportplatz / Playing fields / Terrain de sports

Normalgeschoß Hochhaus / Typical floor / Etage type:
1 2½-Zimmer-Wohnung / 2½-room flat / Appartement de 2½ pièces
2 3½-Zimmer-Wohnung / 3½-room flat / Appartement de 3½ pièces
3 4½-Zimmer-Wohnung / 4½-room flat / Appartement de 4½ pièces

Zwischengeschoß Hochhaus / Mezzanine floor / Entresol:
1 2½-Zimmer-Wohnung / 2½-room flat / Appartement de 2½ pièces
2 3½-Zimmer-Wohnung / 3½-room flat / Appartement de 3½ pièces
3 5-Zimmer-Wohnung / 5-room flat / Appartement de 5 pièces
4 2-Zimmer-Wohnung / 2-room flat / Appartement de 2 pièces
5 Durchgänge zu Laubengang / Connection to access balconies / Couloirs vers balcons d'accès
6 Waschküchen / Laundry room / Buanderies
7 Trockenräume / Drying rooms / Séchoirs
8 Laubengang / Access balcony / Balcon d'accès

Photo: Ansicht des 30 geschossigen Hochhauses von der Rhone her / View of 30-storey block, seen from the Rhone / Vue du Rhône de la maison-tour de 30 étages

Nurses' Hostel
Zurich, Switzerland (1957–1959)
Jakob Zweifel, Zurich

Bauhöhe: 54 m. In unmittelbarer Nähe des Kantonsspitals sollte ein Gebäude für 250 Krankenschwestern gebaut werden. Das sehr knapp bemessene Terrain gestattete nur eine Hochhauslösung.
Jedes Geschoß umfaßt je zwei Gruppen zu sieben Schwesternzimmern, die nach Osten und Westen orientiert sind. Im Kern befinden sich die Treppen, Installations- und Nebenräume. Die tragenden Betonpfeiler an der Außenfassade, welche über die Dachterrasse hinweg die Pfeiler der anderen Fassadenseite horizontal verbinden, geben dem Bau eine elegante und zugleich kräftige Gliederung.

Height: 177 ft. A building to accommodate 250 nurses had to be built right next to the canton hospital. As space was very tight, a highrise structure was the only solution.
Every floor contains two groups of seven rooms each facing east and west. The core contains the stairs, service installations and subsidiary rooms. The building is given a strong form by the external concrete structural columns which are linked across the roof terrace with those on the other side.

Hauteur: 54 m. Destiné à loger 250 infirmières, le bâtiment devait se situer à proximité de l'hôpital cantonal. En raison de l'exiguïté du terrain, seule une maison-tour pouvait être envisagée.
Chaque étage comprend deux groupes de sept chambres orientées est—ouest. Escaliers, services techniques et locaux secondaires se trouvent au centre. Les piliers de béton porteurs de la façade extérieure reliés horizontalement par-dessus le toit-terrasse aux piliers de l'autre façade confèrent à la construction sa forte et élégante structure.

Längsschnitt / Section / Coupe longitudinale 1 : 600

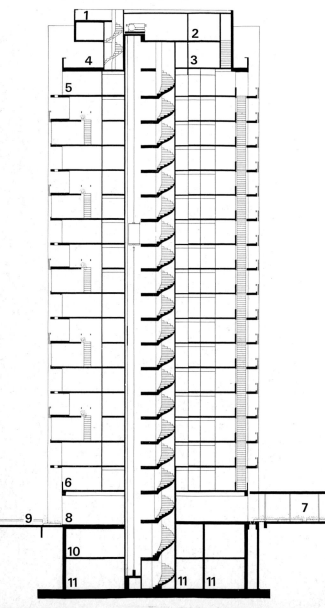

Obergeschosse / Upper floors / Etages supérieurs

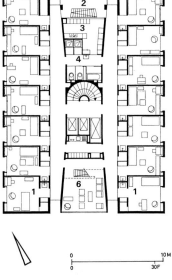

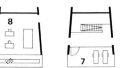

Erdgeschoß / Ground floor / Rez-de-chaussée

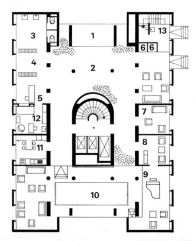

128

Längsschnitt 1:600 / Section / Coupe longitudinale:
1 Aussichtsterrasse / Terrace / Terrasse panoramique
2 Garderobe, Dusche / Cloakrooms, showers / Garde-robe, douches
3 Halle zu Dachgarten / Hall to roofgarden / Hall vers le jardin sur le toit
4 Liegehalle / Rest room / Salle de repos
5 Bastelraum / Hobby room / Salle de bricolage
6 Musikübungszimmer / Music room / Salle de musique
7 Haupteingang / Main entrance / Entrée principale
8 Halle für kleine Anlässe / Hall for small functions / Hall pour petites réceptions
9 Gartenterrasse / Garden terrace / Jardin-terrasse
10 Wäscheraum / Laundry room / Buanderie
11 Luftschutz / Air raid shelter / Protection aérienne

Obergeschosse / Upper floors / Etages supérieurs:
1 Schwesternzimmer / Nurses' room / Chambre d'infirmière
2 Feuertreppe / Fire exit / Escalier de secours
3 Putzraum / Room for cleaning materials / Salle de nettoyage
4 Bad, Duschen, WC / Bath, showers, WC's / Bains, douches, toilettes
5 Küche / Kitchen / Cuisine
6 Aufenthaltsraum / Lounge / Salle de séjour (3., 6., 9., 12., 15. Geschoß / storey / étage)
7 Loggia / Covered balcony / Loggia (4., 7., 10., 13., 16. Geschoß / storey / étage)
8 Näh- und Bügelzimmer / Sewing and ironing room / Salle de couture et de repassage

Erdgeschoß / Ground floor / Rez-de-chaussée:
1 Windfang / Draught lobby / Pare-vent
2 Eingangshalle / Entrance hall / Hall d'entrée
3 Garderobe / Cloakroom / Vestiaire
4 Post / Post / Bureau de poste
5 Hausmutter / Matron / Directrice
6 Telephon / Telephone / Téléphone
7 Besuchszimmer / Visitors' room / Chambre de visite
8 Besuch und Bibliothek / Visitors and library / Visite et bibliothèque
9 Bühne / Stage / Scène
10 Aufenthaltsraum / Lounge / Salle de séjour
11 Teeküche / Tea kitchen / Cuisinette
12 Pikettzimmer / Duty room / Chambre des infirmières de garde
13 Feuertreppe / Fire exit / Escalier de secours

Photo: Ansicht von Nordwesten / View from the north-west / Vue du nord-ouest

Highrise Residential Blocks, City Park
St. Gall, Switzerland (1959)
Otto Glaus and W. Schuchter, Zurich
Collaborator: R. Kauer

Height: 98 ft. The highrise development at City Park was an improvement of a built-up quarter of the town. The maximum amount of living accommodation had to be provided in the minimum amount of space.
The construction is on the box wall principle. Space dividing requirements are responsible for the way the glass façades are detailed.
The staircases had to be constructed on the outside to meet fire regulations.

Bauhöhe: 30 m. Die Hochhaussiedlung City Park entstand durch Sanierung eines alten Stadtquartiers. Auf engstem Raum mußte möglichst viel Wohnfläche neu geschaffen werden.
Die Konstruktion ist ein Schachtelwandprinzip in Massivbauweise. Die Auflösung der Fassaden in Glas ist aus raumsparenden Gründen motiviert. Das Treppenhaus mußte aus feuerpolizeilichen Gründen außerhalb des Gebäudes geführt werden.

Hauteur: 30 m. L'ensemble résidentiel «City Park» est un assainissement d'un ancien quartier de la ville. Sur un espace très exigu, il fallait obtenir autant de surface habitable que possible.
Le bâtiment est une construction massive réalisée selon le principe des murs-caissons. La décomposition des façades de verre est motivée par un souci d'économie de l'espace. La cage d'escalier a été aménagée à l'extérieur pour satisfaire les exigences de la police du feu.

Situation und 1. Obergeschoß / Ground and first floor / Situation et 1er étage

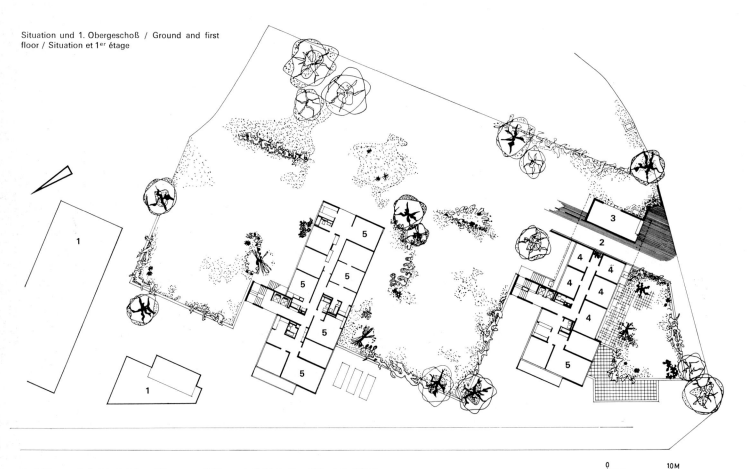

2.–8. Obergeschoß / Typical floor / Etage

Attikageschoß / Attic floor / Etage en attique

Situation und 1. Obergeschoß / Ground and first floor / Situation et 1er étage
1 2. Bauetappe / 2nd building stage / 2e étape de construction
2 Durchfahrt / Passage / Passage
3 Laden / Shop / Magasin
4 Büro / Office / Bureau
5 Wohnung / Flat / Appartement

2.–8. Obergeschoß / Typical storey / Etage:
1 Wohnung / Flat / Appartement

Attikageschoß / Attic storey / Etage en attique:
1 Einzimmerwohnung / 1-room flat / Appartement de 1 pièce
2 Maschinenraum / Machine room / Salle des machines

Photo: Hochhausgruppe von der Kantonsschule her / View from the canton school / Vue de l'école cantonale

Zur Palme, Highrise Block
Zurich, Switzerland (1960–1964)
Haefeli, Moser, Steiger, Zurich
Collaborator: A. Studer

Height: 164 ft. The highrise block Zur Palme stands in the centre of Zurich, surrounded by streets on all sides. The low shopping complex forms a strong contrast to the centrally-towering office block. Eight mushroom-shaped concrete piers support the concrete slab, on which the eleven-storey block stands. The exterior columns consisting of prefabricated concrete units are free-standing in front of the glass and aluminium façade. The ground-floor core contains stairs, lift and service installations.

Bauhöhe: 50 m. Das Hochhaus «Zur Palme» steht mitten in der City von Zürich und ist allseitig von Straßen umgeben.
Der flache Ladenkomplex steht in starkem Kontrast zu dem aus der Mitte herausragenden Bürohochhaus. Acht pilzförmige Betonstützen tragen eine Betonplatte, die windmühlenartig gegliedert ist und auf der der Hochhauskörper mit elf Etagen ruht. Die äußeren Tragstützen, die aus vorfabrizierten Betonelementen bestehen, sind frei vor die Glas-Aluminium-Fassade gestellt.
Der Grundrißkern enthält Treppen, Lift und Installation.

Hauteur: 50 m. Circonscrite de tous côtés par des routes, la maison-tour «Zur Palme» est située au centre de Zurich.
Le complexe de magasins contraste fortement avec la tour centrale. Huit piliers de béton en forme de champignon portent un sommier de béton, articulé à la manière d'un moulin à vent, point d'appui de la tour de onze étages. Les piliers extérieurs en éléments de béton préfabriqués sont détachés de la façade verre-aluminium.
Le centre est occupé par les escaliers, ascenseurs et services techniques.

Schnitt / Section / Coupe

Erdgeschoß / Ground floor / Rez-de-chaussée

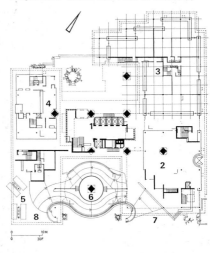

2.Obergeschoß / Upper floor / Etage

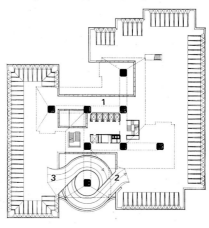

Normalgeschoß ohne Büroeinteilung / Typical floor without office partitions / Etage type sans distribution des bureaux

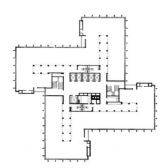

Erdgeschoß / Ground floor / Rez-de-chaussée:
1 Eingangshalle / Entrance lobby / Hall d'entrée
2 Restaurant
3 Läden / Shops / Magasins
4 Bank / Bank / Banque

5 Service-Station / Service station / Station service
6 Rampen zur Garage und zur Parkierungsterrasse / Ramp to garage and parking terrace / Rampes d'accès au garage et aux parkings de la terrasse

7 Einfahrt / Entrance / Entrée
8 Ausfahrt / Exit / Sortie

2. Obergeschoß / Upper floor / Etage:
1 Parkterrasse für 100 Wagen / Parking terrace for 100 cars / Terrasse de stationnement pour 100 voitures

2 Ausfahrt / Exit / Sortie
3 Abfahrt / Exit / Descente

Photo: Südost-Ansicht / South-east view / Vue du sud-est

132

Otto Glaus   Analysis   22 examples

Examples

Analyse von 22 Wohnhochhäusern
Analysis of 22 Highrise Apartment Houses
Analyse de 22 maisons-tours d'habitation

Ziel und Zweck:

1. Sammlung von typischem Vergleichsmaterial von architektonisch und grundrißlich guten Turm- und Scheibenhochhäusern, ausgehend von der geschlossenen Quadratform bis zur Auflösung der Fläche.
2. Auswertung der Flächen und Zahlenverhältnisse.
3. Sichtung des Gesamtprogrammes des Wohnhochhauses.

Bemerkungen:
Alle angegebenen Zahlenwerte sind reine Raumflächenmaße.
Halbe Zimmer beziehen sich auf den separaten Eßplatz im Wohnraum oder Korridor (2, 2½, 3, 3½ usw.). In der Auswertungstabelle werden sie zum entsprechenden ganzen Raum gezählt.
In den Tabellen konnten nicht alle Wohnungen aufgeführt werden, da teilweise zu viele, jedoch wenig differenzierte Varianten bestehen.
Zur Ermittlung einer einheitlichen Vergleichsordnung muß die Wohnung aufgeteilt werden in eine Zone des Aufenthaltes und in eine Zone der Nebenfunktionen (Nebenräume).
Die Durchschnittswerte sind nur zum Teil repräsentativ, da zu wenig gleichartige Wohnverhältnisse ermittelt werden konnten.
Korridore können im modernen Grundriß zur Aufenthaltszone werden.
Balkone und Loggias sind der Aufenthaltszone zugeordnete Freiflächen.

Auswertung:

a) Allgemeine Tendenzen
Das Wohnhochhaus zwingt zu neuen Grundrißkonzeptionen. Die Gründe dazu sind vor allem wirtschaftlicher Natur. Ein Treppenhaus muß möglichst viele Wohnungen erschließen. Gleichzeitig ist die Erhaltung der individuellen Familiengemeinschaft wesentliches Anliegen.
Die Wahrung der Individualität sowohl in der Gesamtanlage wie in der Einzelwohnung wird überall angestrebt.
Das Suchen nach einer betont introvertierten Wohnform ist im Wohnhochhaus, wo die unmittelbare Beziehung zum Boden fehlt, festzustellen.
Die insgesamt 1861 Wohnungen der 22 Hochhäuser verteilen sich wie folgt:
  718 Ein- bis Zweieinhalb-Zimmer-Wohnungen
1033 Drei- bis Viereinhalb-Zimmer-Wohnungen
  110 Wohnungen mit fünf und mehr Zimmern.
Aus diesen Zahlen läßt sich erkennen, daß beinahe zwei Drittel der Wohnungen für Familien mit Kindern geplant oder gebaut wurden.
Dem Kinderaufenthalt im Wohnhochhaus scheint noch nicht die genügende Aufmerksamkeit geschenkt zu werden.
Die Freizeitfläche zur Wohnung sowie jene im Hause für die Wohngemeinschaft und auch die Spielflächen im Rasen sind oft nicht genügend berücksichtigt.
Die Sichtung des allgemeinen Bauprogrammes zeigt, daß die Verhältnisse der Gesamtfläche oder Gesamtwohnungszahl zu Grünfläche oder Spielplatz, Parkierung usw. so sehr streuen, daß keine Auswertung möglich ist.
Vor allem sind Spielflächen und Freizeiträume teilweise ganz vernachlässigt.

b) Besondere Tendenzen im Wohnungsgrundriß
Wohnraum: Die großzügige, großräumige Wohnraumfläche wird allgemein angestrebt. Damit wird das Leben in der Familiengemeinschaft intensiviert.
Korridor, Halle: Korridore werden zur Erlangung des oben genannten Zieles wo möglich zur Wohnraumfläche integriert.
Balkone, Loggias: Große, vor Einblick und Wind geschützte Wohnungsfreiflächen werden angestrebt. Der ermittelte Durchschnittswert von 5 m² pro Zimmereinheit dürfte richtig sein.
Schlafzimmer: Im allgemeinen werden die Schlafzimmer zugunsten der Wohnraumfläche knapp bemessen. Kinderzimmer sollten im Hochhaus als Spiel-, Arbeits- und Aufenthaltsraum nicht zu klein sein.
Abstellflächen: Einbauschränke und Abstellräume werden für Hochhäuser zu klein geplant. 1,0 bis 1,5 m² pro Zimmereinheit wäre sicher das minimale Maß.

Goal and Purpose:

1. A collection of typical material for a comparison of tower and slab highrise buildings which are good in plan and in architectonic qualities, from the closed, square form to a loose, open plan.
2. Area and number analysis.
3. An overall view of the entire highrise apartment program.

Remarks:
All given values are net floor areas.
Half rooms refer to separate eating areas in the living area or in a corridor (2, 2½, 3, 3½, etc.). In the evaluation tables, they are counted in the corresponding whole room.
All apartments could not be enumerated in the tables since there are too many variations which are similar.
In order to have a unified basis for comparison, the apartments are divided into living zones and zones with auxiliary functions (auxiliary rooms).
The average values are only partly representative since the living conditions are rarely similar.
In modern plans, corridors can be in living zones.
Balconies and loggias are attached to the living zones as outdoor areas.

Evaluation:

a) General Trends
The highrise apartment house forces us to develop new plan concepts. The reasons for this are above all economic in nature. A stairwell must have access to as many apartments as possible. (Stairs, lift groups, etc., are expensive.)
Parallel to this is the desire to retain the individual family unit.
There is an attempt to maintain individuality in the total layout as well as in the individual dwelling.

The search for an expressly introverted dwelling form is to be seen in the highrise apartment house, where the direct relation to the ground is missing. The total of 1861 apartments in the 22 highrise buildings are divided as follows:

718 one to two and one half room apartments
1033 three to four and one half room apartments
110 apartments of five and more rooms.

From these figures it can be seen that practically two thirds of the apartments are planned or built for families with children.

It appears that as yet, not enough attention has been paid to child recreation areas in highrise apartment houses.

The recreation areas in the apartments as well as those in the building for the house members and play areas on the ground have not been sufficiently considered.

A glance at the general building program shows that the ratio of the total area or the total number of apartments to the green area or play area, parking, etc., is so varied that no evaluation is possible. For example, in some cases play areas and recreation rooms are completely neglected.

b) Particular Trends in Apartment Plans

Living area: Generally, living areas are large and spacious in order to intensify life in the family unit.

Corridor, Halls: As a furtherance of the above-mentioned goal, corridors are integrated into the living area wherever possible.

Balconies, Loggias: Outdoor living areas should be large and protected from wind and neighbors. The given average figure of 5 m² per room unit should be right.

Bedrooms: Generally, the bedrooms are made small in favour of the living areas. Children's rooms in highrise buildings are used as play, work, and recreation rooms, and should not be too small.

Storage areas: Built-in closets and storage rooms are generally too small in highrise buildings. 1.0 to 1.5 m² per room unit would surely be the minimum size.

Buts:

1. Réunir des documents types comparables sur des maisons-tours, du quadrilatère fermé aux surfaces décomposées, remarquables de par la qualité de leurs plans et de leur architecture.
2. Analyser les surfaces et les données chiffrées.
3. Etudier le programme général de la maison-tour d'habitation.

Observations:

Toutes les valeurs indiquées se rapportent à des surfaces nettes.

Sont considérés comme demi-pièces les coins à manger dans une salle de séjour et les corridors (2, 2½, 3, 3½, etc.). Dans les tableaux synoptiques, ils sont mentionnés avec la pièce entière à laquelle ils se rattachent. Tous les types d'appartement ne figurent pas dans les tableaux en raison

du nombre de variantes et du peu de différence qu'il y a entre elles. Afin de pouvoir comparer les divers renseignements, l'appartement a été divisé en aire de séjour et en aire des fonctions auxiliaires (pièces auxiliaires). Les conditions de logement étant rarement identiques, les valeurs moyennes ne sont que partiellement représentatives.

Les corridors peuvent faire partie, dans les plans modernes, de l'aire de séjour. Les surfaces des balcons et des loggias, pièces de plein air, s'ajoutent à l'aire de séjour.

Appréciation:

a) Tendances générales

La maison-tour impose, pour des raisons essentiellement économiques, une conception nouvelle des plans. Une cage d'escalier doit desservir autant d'appartements que possible. En outre, le maintien de la communauté familiale individuelle est un objectif important.

Partout la sauvegarde de l'individualité est recherchée aussi bien dans l'ensemble que dans l'appartement.

Dans la maison-tour d'habitation, où la liaison directe avec le sol fait défaut, on constate une recherche de vie fortement introvertie.

Les 1861 appartements des 22 maisons-tours se répartissent de la manière suivante:

718 appartements de 1 à 2½ pièces
1033 appartements de 3 à 4½ pièces
110 appartements de 5 pièces et plus.

Ces chiffres indiquent que près des deux tiers des appartements sont prévus pour des familles avec enfants.

Le séjour des enfants dans la maison-tour ne semble pas avoir reçu toute l'attention nécessaire.

Souvent l'espace affecté aux loisirs dans l'appartement, dans la maison et à l'extérieur est insuffisant.

L'examen du programme général de construction montre que les rapports entre la superficie totale ou le nombre total de logements et les surfaces vertes ou terrains de jeu, places de stationnement, etc. sont si disséminés qu'il est impossible de les apprécier. Les terrains de jeu et les salles de loisirs sont parfois totalement ignorés.

b) Tendances particulières du plan des appartements

Salle de séjour: On tend généralement vers une pièce de grandes dimensions permettant une intensification de la vie de famille.

Corridor, Hall: Dans le même but, les corridors sont si possible intégrés à l'aire de séjour.

Balcons, Loggias: On tend vers de grandes surfaces de plein air, protégées de la vue et du vent. La moyenne obtenue de 5 m² par pièce devrait être suffisante.

Chambre à coucher: En règle générale, les chambres à coucher sont de faibles dimensions en raison de l'importance du séjour. Les chambres d'enfant devraient être conçues, dans les maisons-tours, comme pièces de jeu, de travail et de séjour de bonnes dimensions.

Débarras: Dans les maisons-tours, les placards et les débarras sont trop petits. La surface minima par pièce devrait être de 1 à 1,5 m².

1
Blue Point Tower
Sydney

Harry Seidler, Sydney

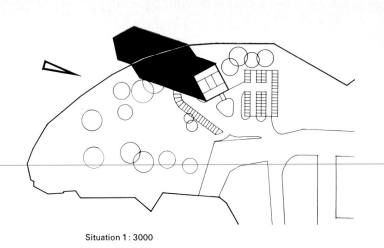

Situation 1 : 3000

Wohngeschoß 1 / Residential floor 1 / Etage d'habitation 1

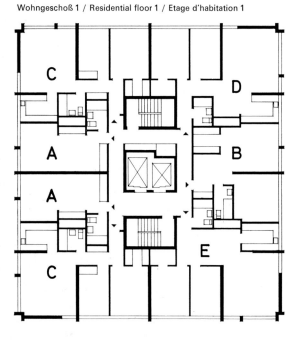

Wohngeschoß 2 / Residential floor 2 / Etage d'habitation 2

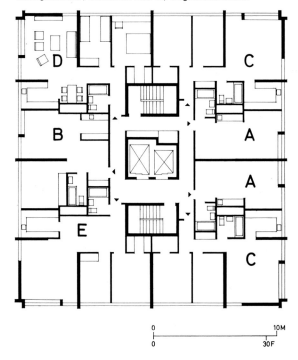

0   10M
0   30F

3-Zimmer-Wohnung Typ D, 1 : 100 / 3-room flat type D / Appartement de 3 pièces type D

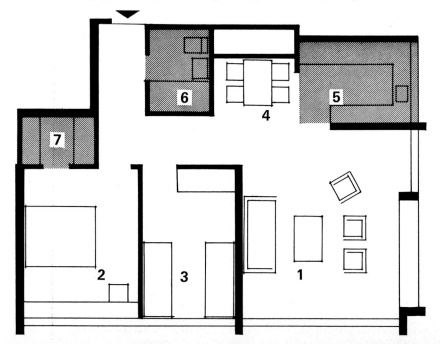

Wohnungstyp / Apartment type / Type de l'appartement		A	B	C	D	E
Zimmer pro Wohnung / Rooms per apartment / Chambres par appartement		1	2	3	3	3
Anzahl Wohnungen / Number of apartments / Nombre d'appartements		48	24	48	24	24
Aufenthaltsfläche einschließlich Korridore / Living area including corridors / Zone de séjour avec corridors	m²	24	37.9	49.6	55.5	60
Nebenraumfläche / Auxiliary rooms / Pièces auxiliaires	m²	5.2	•8.9	14.4	11.4	12.4
Fläche der Wohnung ohne Mauern und Treppenhaus / Area of apartment without walls and stairwell / Surface de l'appartement sans murs ni escaliers	m²	29.2	46.8	64	66.9	72.4
Aufenthaltsfläche der Wohnung / Living area / Zone de séjour	m²					
Wohnschlafzimmer / Living and bedroom / Chambre à coucher et de séjour		24				
Wohnraum / Living room / Séjour						21.5
Wohn- und Eßraum / Living and dining room / Séjour et salle à manger			24.5	22.5	28.1	
Eßraum, Halle / Dining room, hall / Salle à manger, hall						15.5
Elternschlafzimmer/Parents' room/Chambre des parents			13.4	12.4	12	12
Kinderzimmer / Children's room / Chambre d'enfant				8.9	10	10
Kinderzimmer / Children's room / Chambre d'enfant						
Andere Räume / Additional rooms / Chambres supplémentaires						
Interne Verkehrsfläche, Korridore / Internal circulation area, corridors / Circulation interne, corridors				5.8	5.4	1
Balkon / Balcony / Balcon						
Loggia						
Nebenraumfläche der Wohnung / Auxiliary rooms / Pièces auxiliaires	m²					
Küche / Kitchen / Cuisine			4.1	6.2	5.5	6.1
Kochnische / Kitchenette / Cuisinette		1.3				
WC						
Bad, Dusche / Bath, shower / Bain, douche		3.9	3.9	3.8	3.3	3.7
Dusche, 2. Bad / Shower, 2nd bath / Douche, 2e bain						
Einbauschränke / Built-in closets / Placards			0.9	1.8		
Abstellraum in der Wohnung / Storage area in apartment / Débarras dans l'appartement				2.6	2.6	2.6

Allgemeines / General information / Information générale

Baujahr / Year of construction / Année de construction	1961
Bauhöhe / Height of building / Hauteur du bâtiment	91 m
Geschoßzahl / Number of stories / Nombre d'étages	24
Anzahl Wohnungen / Number of apartments / Nombre d'appartements	168
Einzelhochhaus / Single highrise building / Maison-tour isolée	ja
Teil einer Gesamtbebauung / Part of a development / Partie d'un grand ensemble	nein
Frei finanzierter Wohnungsbau / Private housing / Construction de logements à financement libre	
Sozialer Wohnungsbau / Public housing / Construction de logements à caractère social	

Umgebung / Surroundings / Environs

Gesamtfläche des Areals / Total area / Superficie totale de l'aire	8 000 m²
Überbaute Fläche (einschließlich Garagen) / Built-upon area (including garages) / Emprise au sol (y compris les garages)	
Grünflächen / Garden area / Zones vertes	
Spielplatz / Playground / Place de jeu	
Parkplatzfläche / Parking area / Surface des places de stationnement	
Parkplätze / Parking / Places de stationnement	84
Garagen / Garages / Garages	84
Garagenfläche / Garage area / Surface des garages	

Verschiedene Nutzräume / Utility rooms / Chambres de service

Abstellräume / Storage / Débarras
Keller / Cellar / Caves
Velo- und Kinderwagenraum / Bicycles, baby carriages / Bicyclettes, Poussettes

Aufsicht / Controlled area / Zone contrôlée

Eingangspartie / Entrance area / Entrée
Hauswart (Sicht auf Eingang) / Janitor / Concierge

Kinderaufenthalt und Freizeit / Children's recreation and hobby area / Jeux et loisirs

Kindergarten / Nursery / Jardin d'enfants
Spielzimmer / Playroom / Salle de jeu
Bastelraum / Hobby room / Atelier de bricolage
Gedeckter Spielplatz / Covered play area / Place de jeu couverte
Terrassen / Terraces / Terrasses

Vertikalverbindungen / Vertical circulation / Circulation verticale

Haupttreppe / Main stairway / Escalier principal	2
Nottreppe / Emergency stairway / Escalier de secours	
Personenlift / Elevator / Ascenseur	1
Warenlift / Freight lift / Monte-charge	1

Andere Einrichtungen / Additional establishments / Autres aménagements

4 Läden / 4 shops / 4 magasins

3-Zimmer-Wohnung Typ D, 1:100 / 3-room flat type D / Appartement de 3 pièces type D:
1 Wohnraum / Living room / Salle de séjour
2 Elternschlafzimmer / Parents' bedroom / Chambre à coucher des parents
3 Kinderzimmer / Children / Chambre des enfants
4 Eßplatz / Dining area / Coin à manger
5 Küche / Kitchen / Cuisine
6 Bad / Bathroom / Bains
7 Kasten-Abstellraum / Boxroom / Débarras

Photo: Ansicht des Hochhauses gegen die Sydney Harbour Bridge / View of highrise block facing Sydney Harbour Bridge / Vue vers le Sydney Harbour Bridge

2
Alton Residential Estate
Roehampton, London

Hubert Bennett, London

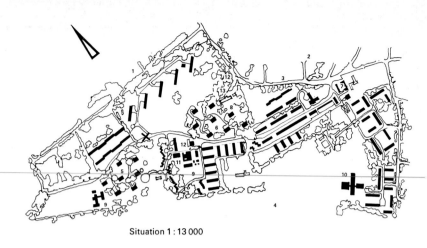

Situation 1 : 13 000

Erdgeschoß / Ground floor / Rez-de-chaussée

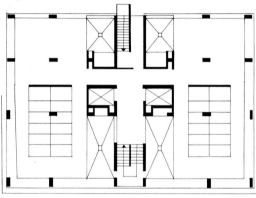

Normalgeschoß / Typical floor / Etage type

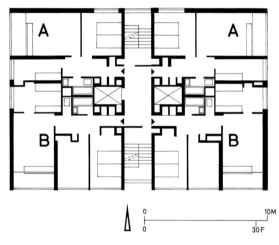

A   A

B   B

0   10M
0   30F

3-Zimmer-Wohnung Typ B, 1 : 100 / 3-room flat type B / Appartement de 3 pièces type B

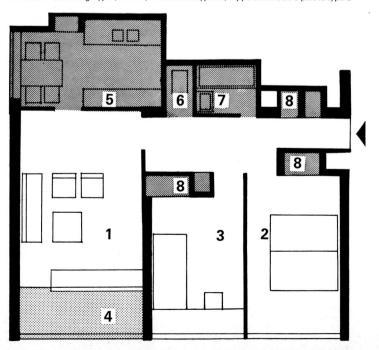

Wohnungstyp / Apartment type / Type de l'appartement		A	B
Zimmer pro Wohnung / Rooms per apartment / Chambres par appartement		2	3
Anzahl Wohnungen / Number of apartments / Nombre d'appartements		20	20
Aufenthaltsfläche einschließlich Korridore / Living area including corridors / Zone de séjour avec corridors	m²	31.8	41.3
Nebenraumfläche / Auxiliary rooms / Pièces auxiliaires	m²	11	11.9
Fläche der Wohnung ohne Mauern und Treppenhaus / Area of apartment without walls and stairwell / Surface de l'appartement sans murs ni escaliers	m²	42.8	53.2

Aufenthaltsfläche der Wohnung / Living area / Zone de séjour	m²		
Wohnschlafzimmer / Living and bedroom / Chambre à coucher et de séjour			
Wohnraum / Living room / Séjour			
Wohn- und Eßraum / Living and dining room / Séjour et salle à manger		15	15.2
Eßraum, Halle / Dining room, hall / Salle à manger, hall			
Elternschlafzimmer/Parents' room/Chambre des parents		10.5	10
Kinderzimmer / Children's room / Chambre d'enfant			9
Kinderzimmer / Children's room / Chambre d'enfant			
Andere Räume / Additional rooms / Chambres supplémentaires			
Interne Verkehrsfläche, Korridore / Internal circulation area, corridors / Circulation interne, corridors		6.3	7.1
Balkon / Balcony / Balcon			
Loggia		4	4

Nebenraumfläche der Wohnung / Auxiliary rooms / Pièces auxiliaires	m²		
Küche / Kitchen / Cuisine		6.5	7
Kochnische / Kitchenette / Cuisinette			
WC			1.1
Bad, Dusche / Bath, shower / Bain, douche		2.7	2
Dusche, 2. Bad / Shower, 2nd bath / Douche, 2e bain			
Einbauschränke / Built-in closets / Placards		1.8	1.8
Abstellraum in der Wohnung / Storage area in apartment / Débarras dans l'appartement			

Situation 1:13000:
1 Ostende des Roehampton-Parks / East end of Roehampton Park / Partie est de Roehampton Park
2 Roehampton-Dorf / Roehampton village / Village de Roehampton
3 Roehampton Lane
4 Richmond Park
5 Gruppe West mit 11-geschossigen Punkthäusern / West group of 11-storey highrise blocks / Groupe ouest de maisons-tours de 11 étages
6 Gruppe Ost mit 11-geschossigen Punkthäusern / East group of 11-storey highrise blocks / Groupe est de maisons-tours de 11 étages
7 Läden / Shops / Magasins
8 Kinderhort / Nursery / Crèche
9 Primarschule / Primary school / Ecole primaire
10 Sekundarschule / Secondary school / Ecole secondaire
11 Kirche / Church / Eglise
12 Gemeinschaftszentrum / Community Centre / Centre communautaire
13 Erholungszentrum / Recreation Centre / Centre de loisirs

3-Zimmer-Wohnung Typ B, 1:100 / 3-room flat type B / Appartement de 3 pièces type B:
1 Wohnraum / Living room / Salle de séjour
2 Elternschlafzimmer / Parents' bedroom / Chambre à coucher des parents
3 Kinderzimmer / Children / Chambre des enfants
4 Loggia / Covered balcony / Loggia
5 Wohnküche / Kitchen-living room / Cuisine-séjour
6 WC / WC / Toilettes
7 Bad / Bath / Bains
8 Einbauschränke / Fitted cupboards / Placards

Photo: 11-geschossiges Hochhaus aus der Westgruppe / 11-storey block in the west-group / Maison-tour de 11 étages du groupe ouest

Allgemeines / General information / Information générale

Baujahr / Year of construction / Année de construction	1959
Bauhöhe / Height of building / Hauteur du bâtiment	35 m
Geschoßzahl / Number of stories / Nombre d'étages	11
Anzahl Wohnungen / Number of apartments / Nombre d'appartements	40
Einzelhochhaus / Single highrise building / Maison-tour isolée	nein
Teil einer Gesamtbebauung / Part of a development / Partie d'un grand ensemble	ja
Frei finanzierter Wohnungsbau / Private housing / Construction de logements à financement libre	nein
Sozialer Wohnungsbau / Public housing / Construction de logements à caractère social	ja

Umgebung / Surroundings / Environs

Gesamtfläche des Areals / Total area / Superficie totale de l'aire	
Überbaute Fläche (einschließlich Garagen) / Built-upon area (including garages) / Emprise au sol (y compris les garages)	
Grünflächen / Garden area / Zones vertes	
Spielplatz / Playground / Place de jeu	o
Parkplatzfläche / Parking area / Surface des places de stationnement	
Parkplätze / Parking / Places de stationnement	
Garagen / Garages / Garages	
Garagenfläche / Garage area / Surface des garages	

Verschiedene Nutzräume / Utility rooms / Chambres de service

Abstellräume / Storage / Débarras	65.8 m²
Keller / Cellar / Caves	
Velo- und Kinderwagenraum / Bicycles, baby carriages / Bicyclettes, Poussettes	

Aufsicht / Controlled area / Zone contrôlée

Eingangspartie / Entrance area / Entrée	80 m²
Hauswart (Sicht auf Eingang) / Janitor / Concierge	nein

Kinderaufenthalt und Freizeit / Children's recreation and hobby area / Jeux et loisirs

Kindergarten / Nursery / Jardin d'enfants	o
Spielzimmer / Playroom / Salle de jeu	
Bastelraum / Hobby room / Atelier de bricolage	
Gedeckter Spielplatz / Covered play area / Place de jeu couverte	
Terrassen / Terraces / Terrasses	

Vertikalverbindungen / Vertical circulation / Circulation verticale

Haupttreppe / Main stairway / Escalier principal	2
Nottreppe / Emergency stairway / Escalier de secours	
Personenlift / Elevator / Ascenseur	2
Warenlift / Freight lift / Monte-charge	

Andere Einrichtungen / Additional establishments / Autres aménagements

o = in Gesamtbebauung vorhanden / existing in development / existant dans le grand ensemble

3
Tours de Lancy
Petit-Lancy, Geneva

J. M. Lamunière, Geneva

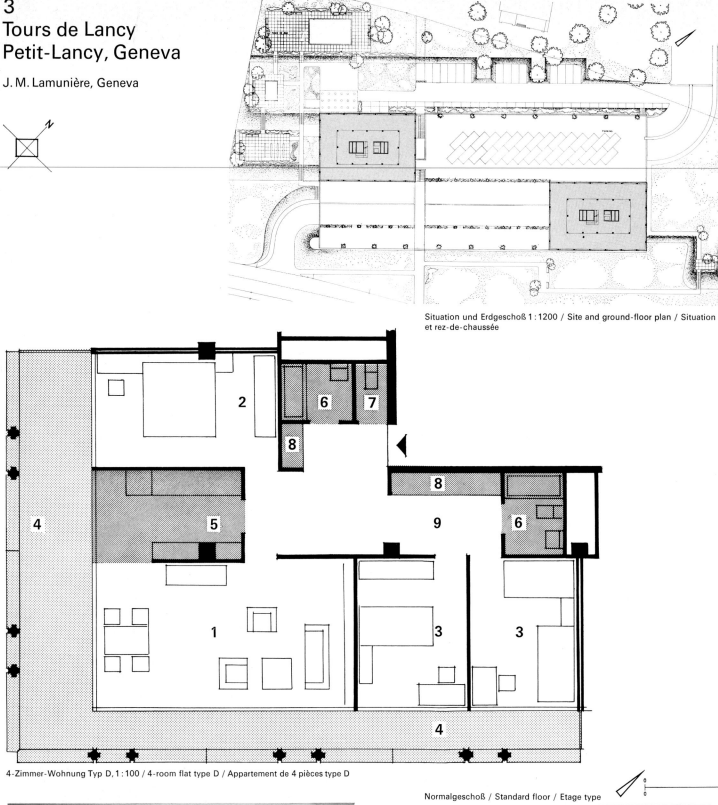

Situation und Erdgeschoß 1:1200 / Site and ground-floor plan / Situation et rez-de-chaussée

4-Zimmer-Wohnung Typ D, 1:100 / 4-room flat type D / Appartement de 4 pièces type D

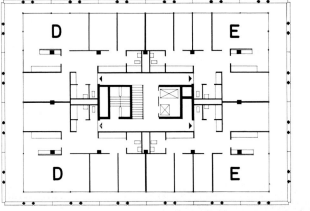

Normalgeschoß / Standard floor / Etage type

Wohnungstyp / Apartment type / Type de l'appartement		A	B	C	D	E
Zimmer pro Wohnung / Rooms per apartment / Chambres par agpartement		2	3	4	4	5
Anzahl Wohnungen / Number of apartments / Nombre d'appartements		46	46	46	6	6
Aufenthaltsfläche einschließlich Korridore / Living area including corridors / Zone de séjour avec corridors	m²	41.3	57.9	69.1	81.7	81.4
Nebenraumfläche / Auxiliary rooms / Pièces auxiliaires	m²	8.5	15.1	15.1	20	20
Fläche der Wohnung ohne Mauern und Treppenhaus / Area of apartment without walls and stairwell / Surface de l'appartement sans murs ni escaliers	m²	49.8	73	84.2	101.7	101.4

Aufenthaltsfläche der Wohnung / Living area / Zone de séjour	m²					
Wohnschlafzimmer / Living and bedroom / Chambre à coucher et de séjour						
Wohnraum / Living room / Séjour						
Wohn- und Eßraum / Living and dining room / Séjour et salle à manger		20.8	20.4	20.4	29.1	24.6
Eßraum, Halle / Dining room, hall / Salle à manger, hall						
Elternschlafzimmer/Parents' room/Chambre des parents		17	15.1	15.1	15.1	15.2
Kinderzimmer / Children's room / Chambre d'enfant			12.4	12.6	12.3	8.4
Kinderzimmer / Children's room / Chambre d'enfant				8	12.2	8
Andere Räume / Additional rooms / Chambres supplémentaires						12.2
Interne Verkehrsfläche, Korridore / Internal circulation area, corridors / Circulation interne, corridors		3.5	10	13	13	13
Balkon / Balcony / Balcon		8.2	29.2	31.3	34.3	34.3
Loggia						

Nebenraumfläche der Wohnung / Auxiliary rooms / Pièces auxiliaires	m²					
Küche / Kitchen / Cuisine		4	8.5	8.5	8.5	8.5
Kochnische / Kitchenette / Cuisinette						
WC			1.5	1.5	1.5	1.5
Bad, Dusche / Bath, shower / Bain, douche		3.2			4.3	4.3
Dusche, 2. Bad / Shower, 2nd bath / Douche, 2e bain			3.2	3.2	3.2	3.2
Einbauschränke / Built-in closets / Placards		1.3	1.9	1.9	2.5	2.5
Abstellraum in der Wohnung / Storage area in apartment / Débarras dans l'appartement						

Allgemeines / General information / Information générale

Baujahr / Year of construction / Année de construction	1964
Bauhöhe / Height of building / Hauteur du bâtiment	45 m
Geschoßzahl / Number of stories / Nombre d'étages	13+2
Anzahl Wohnungen / Number of apartments / Nombre d'appartements	150
Einzelhochhaus / Single highrise building / Maison-tour isolée	nein
Teil einer Gesamtbebauung / Part of a development / Partie d'un grand ensemble	ja
Frei finanzierter Wohnungsbau / Private housing / Construction de logements à financement libre	ja
Sozialer Wohnungsbau / Public housing / Construction de logements à caractère social	nein

Umgebung / Surroundings / Environs

Gesamtfläche des Areals / Total area / Superficie totale de l'aire	14 093 m²
Überbaute Fläche (einschließlich Garagen) / Built-upon area (including garages) / Emprise au sol (y compris les garages)	4 438 m²
Grünflächen / Garden area / Zones vertes	6 950 m²
Spielplatz / Playground / Place de jeu	246 m²
Parkplatzfläche / Parking area / Surface des places de stationnement	1 213 m²
Parkplätze / Parking / Places de stationnement	83
Garagen / Garages / Garages	81
Garagenfläche / Garage area / Surface des garages	2 850 m²

Verschiedene Nutzräume / Utility rooms / Chambres de service

Abstellräume / Storage / Débarras	
Keller / Cellar / Caves	493 m²
Velo- und Kinderwagenraum / Bicycles, baby carriages / Bicyclettes, Poussettes	100 m²

Aufsicht / Controlled area / Zone contrôlée

Eingangspartie / Entrance area / Entrée	320 m²
Hauswart (Sicht auf Eingang) / Janitor / Concierge	nein

Kinderaufenthalt und Freizeit / Children's recreation and hobby area / Jeux et loisirs

Kindergarten / Nursery / Jardin d'enfants	ja
Spielzimmer / Playroom / Salle de jeu	nein
Bastelraum / Hobby room / Atelier de bricolage	nein
Gedeckter Spielplatz / Covered play area / Place de jeu couverte	nein
Terrassen / Terraces / Terrasses	246 m²

Vertikalverbindungen / Vertical circulation / Circulation verticale

Haupttreppe / Main stairway / Escalier principal	1
Nottreppe / Emergency stairway / Escalier de secours	1
Personenlift / Elevator / Ascenseur	1
Warenlift / Freight lift / Monte-charge	1

Andere Einrichtungen / Additional establishments / Autres aménagements

Projektiert: Kaffeebar, Ausstellungshalle f. Autos, Bureaux / Planned: coffee bar, exhibition hall for cars, offices / Projeté: bar à café, hall d'exposition pour voitures, bureaux

4-Zimmer-Wohnung Typ D, 1:100 / 4-room flat type D / Appartement de 4 pièces type D:
1 Wohnraum / Living room / Salle de séjour
2 Elternschlafzimmer / Parents' bedroom/ Chambre à coucher des parents
3 Kinderzimmer / Children / Chambre des enfants
4 Balkon / Balcony / Balcon
5 Küche / Kitchen / Cuisine
6 Bad / Bathroom / Bains
7 WC / WC / Toilettes
8 Einbauschränke / Fitted cupboards / Placards
9 Vorplatz mit Schränken zu Kinderzimmern / Hall with cupboards for children's use / Vestibule avec armoires pour les chambres des enfants

Photo: Ansicht der beiden Wohnhochhäuser aus vorfabrizierten Fassadenelementen / View of both houses with prefabricated façade elements / Vue des deux maisons-tours avec éléments de façade préfabriqués

4
Highrise Block
Hansaviertel, Berlin

J. van den Broek and J. Bakema, Rotterdam

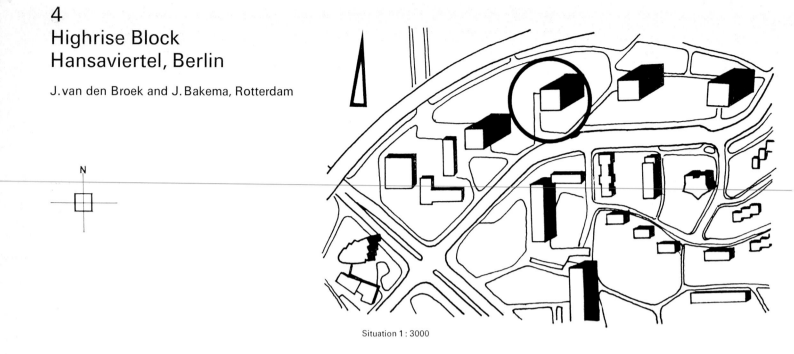

Situation 1 : 3000

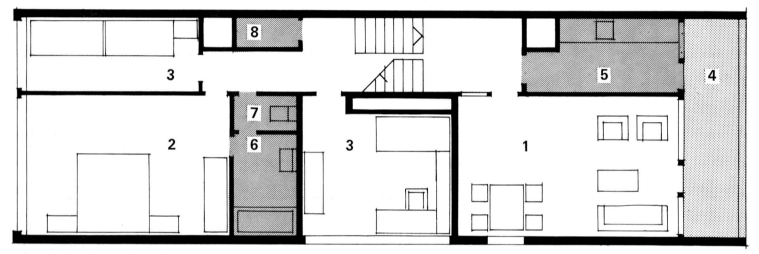

4-Zimmer-Wohnung Typ C, 1 : 100 / 4-room flat type C / Appartement de 4 pièces type C

Wohngeschoß mit durchgehendem Korridor und allgemeiner Sonnenterrasse / Residential floor with connecting corridor and public sundeck / Etage d'habitation avec corridor et solarium collectif

Wohngeschoß mit durchgehenden Wohnungen / Residential floor with duplex flats / Etage d'habitation avec appartements traversants

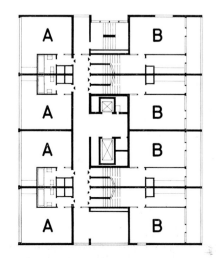

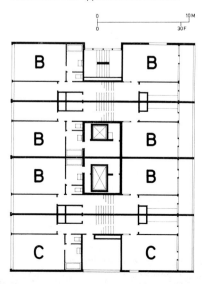

Wohnungstyp / Apartment type / Type de l'appartement		A	B	C
Zimmer pro Wohnung / Rooms per apartment / Chambres par appartement		1	3	4
Anzahl Wohnungen / Number of apartments / Nombre d'appartements		24	43	5
Aufenthaltsfläche einschließlich Korridore / Living area including corridors / Zone de séjour avec corridors	m²	25.8	65.7	79.3
Nebenraumfläche / Auxiliary rooms / Pièces auxiliaires	m²	7.4	15.1	15.1
Fläche der Wohnung ohne Mauern und Treppenhaus / Area of apartment without walls and stairwell / Surface de l'appartement sans murs ni escaliers	m²	33.2	80.8	94.4

Aufenthaltsfläche der Wohnung / Living area / Zone de séjour — m²

	A	B	C
Wohnschlafzimmer / Living and bedroom / Chambre à coucher et de séjour	24		
Wohnraum / Living room / Séjour			
Wohn- und Eßraum / Living and dining room / Séjour et salle à manger		22	22
Eßraum, Halle / Dining room, hall / Salle à manger, hall			
Elternschlafzimmer / Parents' room / Chambre des parents		20	20
Kinderzimmer / Children's room / Chambre d'enfant			9.4
Kinderzimmer / Children's room / Chambre d'enfant			9.4
Andere Räume / Additional rooms / Chambres supplémentaires			13.6
Interne Verkehrsfläche, Korridore / Internal circulation area, corridors / Circulation interne, corridors	1.8	14.3	14.3
Balkon / Balcony / Balcon			
Loggia		8.1	8.1

Nebenraumfläche der Wohnung / Auxiliary rooms / Pièces auxiliaires — m²

	A	B	C
Küche / Kitchen / Cuisine		7.4	7.4
Kochnische / Kitchenette / Cuisinette	3.4		
WC		1.5	1.5
Bad, Dusche / Bath, shower / Bain, douche	4	4.8	4.8
Dusche, 2. Bad / Shower, 2nd bath / Douche, 2e bain			
Einbauschränke / Built-in closets / Placards			
Abstellraum in der Wohnung / Storage area in apartment / Débarras dans l'appartement		1.4	1.4

Allgemeines / General information / Information générale

Baujahr / Year of construction / Année de construction	1957/58
Bauhöhe / Height of building / Hauteur du bâtiment	51 m
Geschoßzahl / Number of stories / Nombre d'étages	16+1
Anzahl Wohnungen / Number of apartments / Nombre d'appartements	72
Einzelhochhaus / Single highrise building / Maison-tour isolée	ja
Teil einer Gesamtbebauung / Part of a development / Partie d'un grand ensemble	nein
Frei finanzierter Wohnungsbau / Private housing / Construction de logements à financement libre	nein
Sozialer Wohnungsbau / Public housing / Construction de logements à caractère social	ja

Umgebung / Surroundings / Environs

Gesamtfläche des Areals / Total area / Superficie totale de l'aire	
Überbaute Fläche (einschließlich Garagen) / Built-upon area (including garages) / Emprise au sol (y compris les garages)	
Grünflächen / Garden area / Zones vertes	
Spielplatz / Playground / Place de jeu	
Parkplatzfläche / Parking area / Surface des places de stationnement	
Parkplätze / Parking / Places de stationnement	
Garagen / Garages / Garages	nein
Garagenfläche / Garage area / Surface des garages	

Verschiedene Nutzräume / Utility rooms / Chambres de service

Abstellräume / Storage / Débarras	
Keller / Cellar / Caves	138,6 m²
Velo- und Kinderwagenraum / Bicycles, baby carriages / Bicyclettes, Poussettes	38 m²

Aufsicht / Controlled area / Zone contrôlée

Eingangspartie / Entrance area / Entrée	79 m²
Hauswart (Sicht auf Eingang) / Janitor / Concierge	nein

Kinderaufenthalt und Freizeit / Children's recreation and hobby area / Jeux et loisirs

Kindergarten / Nursery / Jardin d'enfants	nein
Spielzimmer / Playroom / Salle de jeu	
Bastelraum / Hobby room / Atelier de bricolage	
Gedeckter Spielplatz / Covered play area / Place de jeu couverte	284 m²
Terrassen / Terraces / Terrasses	98 m²

Vertikalverbindungen / Vertical circulation / Circulation verticale

Haupttreppe / Main stairway / Escalier principal	1
Nottreppe / Emergency stairway / Escalier de secours	nein
Personenlift / Elevator / Ascenseur	1
Warenlift / Freight lift / Monte-charge	1

Andere Einrichtungen / Additional establishments / Autres aménagements

Schnitt 1:600 / Section / Coupe

4-Zimmer-Wohnung Typ C, 1:100 / 4-room flat type C / Appartement de 4 pièces type C:
1 Wohnraum / Living room / Salle de séjour
2 Elternschlafzimmer / Parents' bedroom / Chambre à coucher des parents
3 Kinderzimmer / Children / Chambre des enfants
4 Loggia / Covered balcony / Loggia
5 Küche / Kitchen / Cuisine
6 Bad / Bathroom / Bains
7 WC / WC / Toilettes
8 Abstellraum / Boxroom / Débarras

Schnitt 1:600 / Section / Coupe:
1 Erschließungskorridore / Access corridors / Couloirs de communication

Photo: Südwest-Ansicht / Southwest view / Vue du sud-ouest

5
Nyfag, Residential Block
Hardstrasse, Basle

Hans Peter Baur, Basle

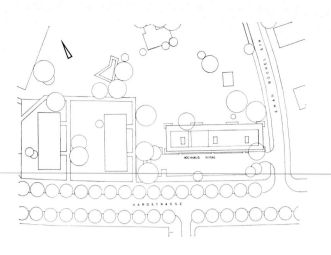

Situation 1 : 2000

4½-Zimmer-Wohnung Typ C, 1:100 / 4½-room flat type C / Appartement de 4½ pièces type C:
1 Wohnraum / Living room / Salle de séjour
2 Elternschlafzimmer / Parents' bedroom / Chambre à coucher des parents
3 Kinderzimmer / Children / Chambre des enfants
4 Eßplatz / Dining area / Coin à manger
5 Terrasse, Balkon / Terrace, Balcony / Terrasse, balcon
6 Küche / Kitchen / Cuisine
7 WC / WC / Toilettes
8 Bad / Bathroom / Bains
9 Abstellraum / Boxroom / Débarras

4 ½-Zimmer-Wohnung Typ C, 1 : 100 / 4 ½-room flat type C / Appartement de 4 ½ pièces type C

Photo: Ansicht von Südwesten / View from the south-west / Vue du sud-ouest

148

Dachgeschoß mit Atelierwohnung / Top
floor with studio flat / Dernier étage avec
appartement-atelier

Normalgeschoß 1 : 400 / Typical floor /
Etage type

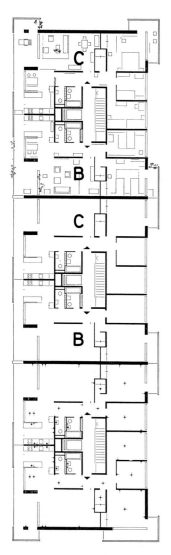

Wohnungstyp / Apartment type / Type de l'appartement		A	B	C
Zimmer pro Wohnung / Rooms per apartment / Chambres par appartement		2 ½	3 ½	4 ½
Anzahl Wohnungen / Number of apartments / Nombre d'appartements		1	24	24
Aufenthaltsfläche einschließlich Korridore / Living area including corridors / Zone de séjour avec corridors	m²	57.4	73.1	83.6
Nebenraumfläche / Auxiliary rooms / Pièces auxiliaires	m²	15.4	15.9	17
Fläche der Wohnung ohne Mauern und Treppenhaus / Area of apartment without walls and stairwell / Surface de l'appartement sans murs ni escaliers	m²	72.8	89.0	100.6

Aufenthaltsfläche der Wohnung / Living area / Zone de séjour	m²			
Wohnschlafzimmer / Living and bedroom / Chambre à coucher et de séjour				
Wohnraum / Living room / Séjour				
Wohn- und Eßraum / Living and dining room / Séjour et salle à manger		20.3	33.6	33.6
Eßraum, Halle / Dining room, hall / Salle à manger, hall				
Elternschlafzimmer/Parents' room/Chambre des parents		14	16.2	16.2
Kinderzimmer / Children's room / Chambre d'enfant			12.6	12.6
Kinderzimmer / Children's room / Chambre d'enfant				9.7
Andere Räume / Additional rooms / Chambres supplémentaires		13.8		
Interne Verkehrsfläche, Korridore / Internal circulation area, corridors / Circulation interne, corridors		9.3	10.7	11.5
Balkon / Balcony / Balcon		60	26.4	26.4
Loggia				

Nebenraumfläche der Wohnung / Auxiliary rooms / Pièces auxiliaires	m²			
Küche / Kitchen / Cuisine		7.6	8	8
Kochnische / Kitchenette / Cuisinette				
WC			1.7	1.7
Bad, Dusche / Bath, shower / Bain, douche		3.8	3.4	3.4
Dusche, 2. Bad / Shower, 2nd bath / Douche, 2e bain				
Einbauschränke / Built-in closets / Placards			1	1
Abstellraum in der Wohnung / Storage area in apartment / Débarras dans l'appartement		4	1.8	2.9

Allgemeines / General information / Information générale

Baujahr / Year of construction / Année de construction	1958/59
Bauhöhe / Height of building / Hauteur du bâtiment	29 m
Geschoßzahl / Number of stories / Nombre d'étages	10
Anzahl Wohnungen / Number of apartments / Nombre d'appartements	49
Einzelhochhaus / Single highrise building / Maison-tour isolée	ja
Teil einer Gesamtbebauung / Part of a development / Partie d'un grand ensemble	ja
Frei finanzierter Wohnungsbau / Private housing / Construction de logements à financement libre	ja
Sozialer Wohnungsbau / Public housing / Construction de logements à caractère social	nein

Umgebung / Surroundings / Environs

Gesamtfläche des Areals / Total area / Superficie totale de l'aire	2 400 m²
Überbaute Fläche (einschließlich Garagen) / Built-upon area (including garages) / Emprise au sol (y compris les garages)	713 m²
Grünflächen / Garden area / Zones vertes	1 000 m²
Spielplatz / Playground / Place de jeu	o
Parkplatzfläche / Parking area / Surface des places de stationnement	320 m²
Parkplätze / Parking / Places de stationnement	21
Garagen / Garages / Garages	o 30
Garagenfläche / Garage area / Surface des garages	600 m²

Verschiedene Nutzräume / Utility rooms / Chambres de service

Abstellräume / Storage / Débarras	80 m²
Keller / Cellar / Caves	500 m²
Velo- und Kinderwagenraum / Bicycles, baby carriages / Bicyclettes, Poussettes	60 m²

Aufsicht / Controlled area / Zone contrôlée

Eingangspartie / Entrance area / Entrée	135 m²
Hauswart (Sicht auf Eingang) / Janitor / Concierge	nein

Kinderaufenthalt und Freizeit / Children's recreation and hobby area / Jeux et loisirs

Kindergarten / Nursery / Jardin d'enfants	o
Spielzimmer / Playroom / Salle de jeu	nein
Bastelraum / Hobby room / Atelier de bricolage	nein
Gedeckter Spielplatz / Covered play area / Place de jeu couverte	577 m²
Terrassen / Terraces / Terrasses	540 m²

Vertikalverbindungen / Vertical circulation / Circulation verticale

Haupttreppe / Main stairway / Escalier principal	3
Nottreppe / Emergency stairway / Escalier de secours	
Personenlift / Elevator / Ascenseur	3
Warenlift / Freight lift / Monte-charge	

Andere Einrichtungen / Additional establishments / Autres aménagements

o = in Gesamtbebauung vorhanden / existing in development / existant dans le grand ensemble

6
Residential Highrise Block
Unter-Neusätz, Arbon
Switzerland

G. P. Dubois, Zurich

N

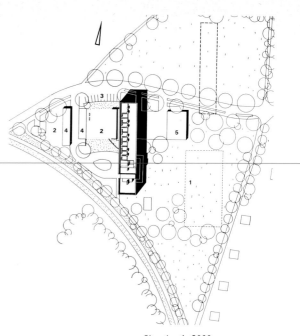

Situation 1 : 3000

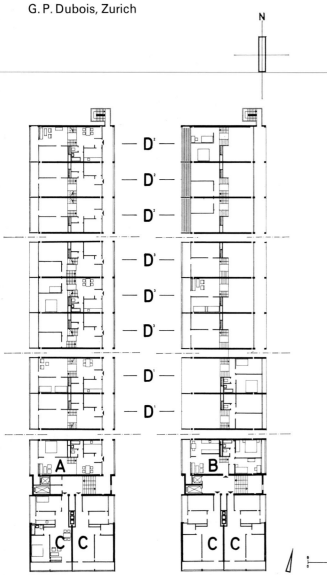

Wohngeschosse mit durchgehenden Wohnungen / Floors with
duplex flats / Etage d'habitation avec appartements traversants

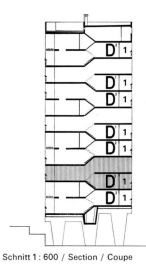

Schnitt 1 : 600 / Section / Coupe

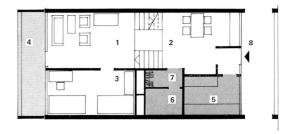

4 ½-Zimmer-Wohnung Typ D, 1 : 200 / 4 ½-room flat type D /
Appartement de 4 ½ pièces type D

Wohnungstyp / Apartment type / Type de l'appartement		A	B	C	D	D¹	D²
Zimmer pro Wohnung / Rooms per apartment / Chambres par appartement		2 ½	3	3	4 ½	4 ½	4 ½
Anzahl Wohnungen / Number of apartments / Nombre d'appartements		6	3	22	27	25	11
Aufenthaltsfläche einschließlich Korridore / Living area including corridors / Zone de séjour avec corridors	m²	42.4	45.4	57	63	63.3	63.3
Nebenraumfläche / Auxiliary rooms / Pièces auxiliaires	m²	10.8	11.4	11.2	13.6	13.6	13.6
Fläche der Wohnung ohne Mauern und Treppenhaus / Area of apartment without walls and stairwell / Surface de l'appartement sans murs ni escaliers	m²	53.2	56.8	68.2	76.6	76.9	76.9
Aufenthaltsfläche der Wohnung / Living area / Zone de séjour	m²						
Wohnschlafzimmer / Living and bedroom / Chambre à coucher et de séjour							
Wohnraum / Living room / Séjour							
Wohn- und Eßraum / Living and dining room / Séjour et salle à manger		26.2	19.2	23.7	25.8	25.8	25.8
Eßraum, Halle / Dining room, hall / Salle à manger, hall							
Elternschlafzimmer / Parents' room / Chambre des parents		12	12	12.2	12	13.6	13.6
Kinderzimmer / Children's room / Chambre d'enfant			10	9.8	11	11	11
Kinderzimmer / Children's room / Chambre d'enfant					10	8.7	8.7
Andere Räume / Additional rooms / Chambres supplémentaires							
Interne Verkehrsfläche, Korridore / Internal circulation area, corridors / Circulation interne, corridors		4.2	4.2	11.3	4.2	4.2	4.2
Balkon / Balcony / Balcon							
Loggia		7.5	7.5	7.5	7.5	7.5	7.5
Nebenraumfläche der Wohnung / Auxiliary rooms / Pièces auxiliaires	m²						
Küche / Kitchen / Cuisine		6	6.6	6	6	6	6
Kochnische / Kitchenette / Cuisinette							
WC		1	1		1	1	1
Bad, Dusche / Bath, shower / Bain, douche				3.2			
Dusche, 2. Bad / Shower, 2nd bath / Douche, 2e bain		2.8	2.8		2.8	2.8	2.8
Einbauschränke / Built-in closets / Placards				2	1	1	1
Abstellraum in der Wohnung / Storage area in apartment / Débarras dans l'appartement		1	1		2.8	2.8	2.8

Allgemeines / General information / Information générale

Baujahr / Year of construction / Année de construction	1959/60
Bauhöhe / Height of building / Hauteur du bâtiment	35 m
Geschoßzahl / Number of stories / Nombre d'étages	11
Anzahl Wohnungen / Number of apartments / Nombre d'appartements	95
Einzelhochhaus / Single highrise building / Maison-tour isolée	ja
Teil einer Gesamtbebauung / Part of a development / Partie d'un grand ensemble	ja
Frei finanzierter Wohnungsbau / Private housing / Construction de logements à financement libre	ja
Sozialer Wohnungsbau / Public housing / Construction de logements à caractère social	nein

Umgebung / Surroundings / Environs

Gesamtfläche des Areals / Total area / Superficie totale de l'aire	13 000 m²
Überbaute Fläche (einschließlich Garagen) / Built-upon area (including garages) / Emprise au sol (y compris les garages)	1 665 m²
Grünflächen / Garden area / Zones vertes	11 335 m²
Spielplatz / Playground / Place de jeu	
Parkplatzfläche / Parking area / Surface des places de stationnement	256 m²
Parkplätze / Parking / Places de stationnement	25
Garagen / Garages / Garages	20
Garagenfläche / Garage area / Surface des garages	312 m²

Verschiedene Nutzräume / Utility rooms / Chambres de service

Abstellräume / Storage / Débarras	
Keller / Cellar / Caves	576 m²
Velo- und Kinderwagenraum / Bicycles, baby carriages / Bicyclettes, Poussettes	345 m²

Aufsicht / Controlled area / Zone contrôlée

Eingangspartie / Entrance area / Entrée	90 m²
Hauswart (Sicht auf Eingang) / Janitor / Concierge	nein

Kinderaufenthalt und Freizeit / Children's recreation and hobby area / Jeux et loisirs

Kindergarten / Nursery / Jardin d'enfants	nein
Spielzimmer / Playroom / Salle de jeu	
Bastelraum / Hobby room / Atelier de bricolage	65.6 m²
Gedeckter Spielplatz / Covered play area / Place de jeu couverte	640 m²
Terrassen / Terraces / Terrasses	70 m²

Vertikalverbindungen / Vertical circulation / Circulation verticale

Haupttreppe / Main stairway / Escalier principal	1
Nottreppe / Emergency stairway / Escalier de secours	1
Personenlift / Elevator / Ascenseur	2
Warenlift / Freight lift / Monte-charge	

Andere Einrichtungen / Additional establishments / Autres aménagements

Situation 1 : 3000
1 Spielplatz 8600 m² / Playing field / Pelouse de jeu
2 Spielplatz für Kleinkinder / Infants playground / Terrain de jeu pour enfants
3 Parkplätze / Parking space / Parkings
4 Garagen / Garages
5 Fahrräder, Mopeds / Bicycles, mopeds / Bicyclettes, Bicyclettes à moteur

4½-Zimmer-Wohnung Typ D, 1:200 / 4½-room flat type D / Appartement de 4½ pièces type D:
1 Wohnraum / Living room / Salle de séjour
2 Eßzimmer / Dining room / Salle à manger
3 Kinderzimmer / Children / Chambre des enfants
4 Loggia / Covered balcony / Loggia
5 Küche / Kitchen / Cuisine
6 Abstellraum / Boxroom / Débarras
7 Garderobe / Dressing room / Garderobe
8 Verteilgänge / Corridors / Corridors de distribution
9 Elternschlafzimmer / Parents' bedroom / Chambre à coucher des parents
10 Kinderzimmer / Children / Chambre des enfants
11 WC / WC / Toilettes
12 Bad / Bathroom / Bains

Schnitt / Section / Coupe 1:600:
1 Verteilgänge / Corridors / Corridors de distribution

Photo: Ansicht von Westen / View from the west / Vue de l'ouest

Lochergut, Zurich
Competition project

Otto Glaus, Zurich

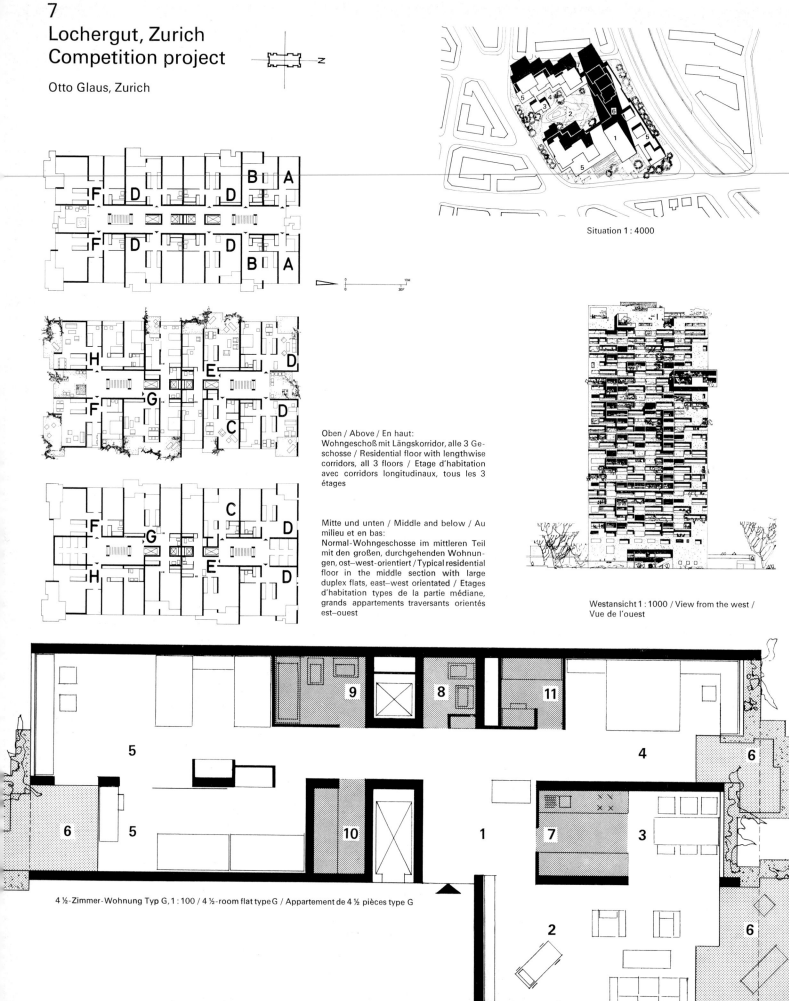

Situation 1 : 4000

Oben / Above / En haut:
Wohngeschoß mit Längskorridor, alle 3 Geschosse / Residential floor with lengthwise corridors, all 3 floors / Etage d'habitation avec corridors longitudinaux, tous les 3 étages

Mitte und unten / Middle and below / Au milieu et en bas:
Normal-Wohngeschosse im mittleren Teil mit den großen, durchgehenden Wohnungen, ost–west-orientiert / Typical residential floor in the middle section with large duplex flats, east–west orientated / Etages d'habitation types de la partie médiane, grands appartements traversants orientés est–ouest

Westansicht 1 : 1000 / View from the west / Vue de l'ouest

4 ½-Zimmer-Wohnung Typ G, 1 : 100 / 4 ½-room flat type G / Appartement de 4 ½ pièces type G

Wohnungstyp / Apartment type / Type de l'appartement		A	B	C	D	E	F	G	H
Zimmer pro Wohnung / Rooms per apartment / Chambres par appartement		1	1 ½	1 ½	2 ½	3 ½	3 ½	4 ½	4 ½
Anzahl Wohnungen / Number of apartments / Nombre d'appartements		18	18	18	70	17	35	17	17
Aufenthaltsfläche einschließlich Korridore / Living area including corridors / Zone de séjour avec corridors	m²	19.1	21.8	28.1	47.2	76.3	57.6	90.5	81.4
Nebenraumfläche / Auxiliary rooms / Pièces auxiliaires	m²	9.6	10.0	12.6	11.6	14.9	11.2	14.8	12.4
Fläche der Wohnung ohne Mauern und Treppenhaus / Area of apartment without walls and stairwell / Surface de l'appartement sans murs ni escaliers	m²	28.7	31.8	40.7	58.8	91.2	68.8	105.3	93.8

Aufenthaltsfläche der Wohnung / Living area / Zone de séjour	m²								
Wohnschlafzimmer / Living and bedroom / Chambre à coucher et de séjour		16	13.2	18.2					
Wohnraum / Living room / Séjour					18.6	18	20	17	19.5
Wohn- und Eßraum / Living and dining room / Séjour et salle à manger									
Eßraum, Halle / Dining room, hall / Salle à manger, hall			5.5	6.7	5.8	5.5	6.2	6.4	2.6
Elternschlafzimmer/Parents' room/Chambre des parents					16.5	20.4	13.4	17.8	16
Kinderzimmer / Children's room / Chambre d'enfant						17.2	9.2	21	16
Kinderzimmer / Children's room / Chambre d'enfant								12.4	9.2
Andere Räume / Additional rooms / Chambres supplémentaires									
Interne Verkehrsfläche, Korridore / Internal circulation area, corridors / Circulation interne, corridors		3.1	3.1	3.2	6.3	15.2	8.8	15.9	14.5
Balkon / Balcony / Balcon									
Loggia			5.7	5.5	8.8	17.7	24.1	34.3	14.5

Nebenraumfläche der Wohnung / Auxiliary rooms / Pièces auxiliaires	m²								
Küche / Kitchen / Cuisine		4.8	5.5	6.6	5.8	5.8	5.8	5.5	5.8
Kochnische / Kitchenette / Cuisinette									
WC						2.3		2.2	
Bad, Dusche / Bath, shower / Bain, douche		4	4	4	4	3.8	4	3.2	4
Dusche, 2. Bad / Shower, 2nd bath / Douche, 2ᵉ bain									
Einbauschränke / Built-in closets / Placards		0.8	0.5			0.7		1	2.6
Abstellraum in der Wohnung / Storage area in apartment / Débarras dans l'appartement				2	1.8	2.3	1.4	2.9	

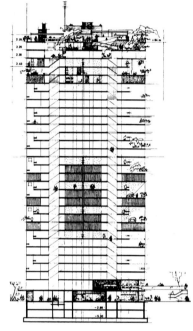

Längsschnitt 1 : 1000 / Longitudinal section / Coupe longitudinale

Situation 1 : 4000:
1 Hochhaus / Highrise block / Maison-tour
2 Spielwiese / Playing field / Pelouse de jeu
3 Kindergarten / Nursery school / Jardin d'enfants
4 Spielplatz für Kleinkinder / Infants' playground / Terrain de jeu pour les petits enfants
5 Läden / Shops / Magasins
6 Werkstätten / Studios / Ateliers
7 Garageeinfahrt, Tankstelle / Entrance to garage, petrol station / Accès aux garages, station service

4½-Zimmer-Wohnung Typ G, 1:100 / 4½-room flat type G / Appartement de 4½ pièces type G:
1 Eingang, Garderobe / Entrance, cloaks / Entrée, garde-robe
2 Wohnraum / Living room / Salle de séjour
3 Eßplatz / Dining room / Coin à manger
4 Elternschlafzimmer / Parents' bedroom / Chambre à coucher des parents
5 Kinderzimmer / Children / Chambre des enfants
6 Loggia / Covered balcony / Loggia
7 Küche / Kitchen / Cuisine
8 WC / WC / Toilettes
9 Bad / Bath / Bains
10 Abstellraum / Storeroom / Débarras
11 Schrankraum / Storage (closet) / Placards

Allgemeines / General information / Information générale

Baujahr / Year of construction / Année de construction	1960
Bauhöhe / Height of building / Hauteur du bâtiment	70 m
Geschoßzahl / Number of stories / Nombre d'étages	31
Anzahl Wohnungen / Number of apartments / Nombre d'appartements	210
Einzelhochhaus / Single highrise building / Maison-tour isolée	ja
Teil einer Gesamtbebauung / Part of a development / Partie d'un grand ensemble	ja
Frei finanzierter Wohnungsbau / Private housing / Construction de logements à financement libre	nein
Sozialer Wohnungsbau / Public housing / Construction de logements à caractère social	ja

Umgebung / Surroundings / Environs

Gesamtfläche des Areals / Total area / Superficie totale de l'aire	22 871 m²
Überbaute Fläche (einschließlich Garagen) / Built-upon area (including garages) / Emprise au sol (y compris les garages)	
Grünflächen / Garden area / Zones vertes	5 700 m²
Spielplatz / Playground / Place de jeu	420 m²
Parkplatzfläche / Parking area / Surface des places de stationnement	1 020 m²
Parkplätze / Parking / Places de stationnement	46
Garagen / Garages / Garages	327
Garagenfläche / Garage area / Surface des garages	9 810 m²

Verschiedene Nutzräume / Utility rooms / Chambres de service

Abstellräume / Storage / Débarras	480 m²
Keller / Cellar / Caves	ja
Velo- und Kinderwagenraum / Bicycles, baby carriages / Bicyclettes, Poussettes	ja

Aufsicht / Controlled area / Zone contrôlée

Eingangspartie / Entrance area / Entrée	200 m²
Hauswart (Sicht auf Eingang) / Janitor / Concierge	ja

Kinderaufenthalt und Freizeit / Children's recreation and hobby area / Jeux et loisirs

Kindergarten / Nursery / Jardin d'enfants	o
Spielzimmer / Playroom / Salle de jeu	200 m²
Bastelraum / Hobby room / Atelier de bricolage	80 m²
Gedeckter Spielplatz / Covered play area / Place de jeu couverte	285 m²
Terrassen / Terraces / Terrasses	280 m²

Vertikalverbindungen / Vertical circulation / Circulation verticale

Haupttreppe / Main stairway / Escalier principal	2
Nottreppe / Emergency stairway / Escalier de secours	
Personenlift / Elevator / Ascenseur	2
Warenlift / Freight lift / Monte-charge	2

Andere Einrichtungen / Additional establishments / Autres aménagements

Restaurant, Kiosk / Restaurant, kiosque / Restaurant, kiosque

o = in Gesamtbebauung vorhanden / existing in development / existant dans le grand ensemble

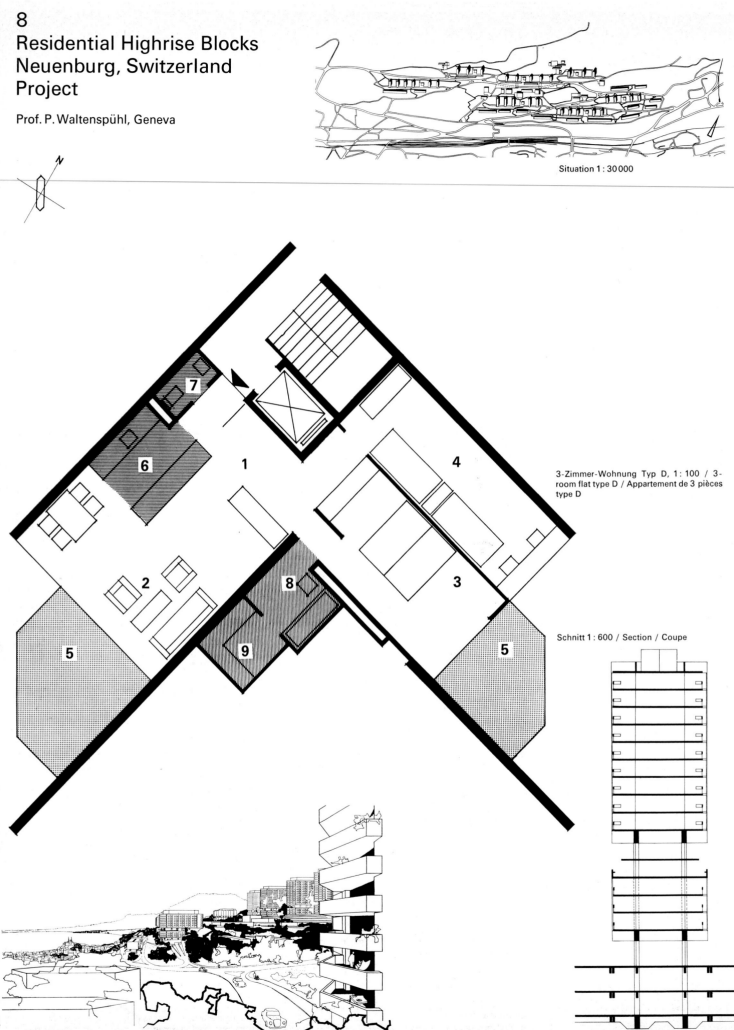

8
Residential Highrise Blocks
Neuenburg, Switzerland
Project

Prof. P. Waltenspühl, Geneva

Situation 1 : 30 000

3-Zimmer-Wohnung Typ D, 1 : 100 / 3-room flat type D / Appartement de 3 pièces type D

Schnitt 1 : 600 / Section / Coupe

Wohnungstyp / Apartment type / Type de l'appartement		A	B	C	D	E	F
Zimmer pro Wohnung / Rooms per apartment / Chambres par appartement		1	1	2	3	3	5
Anzahl Wohnungen / Number of apartments / Nombre d'appartements		6	18	24	30	30	12
Aufenthaltsfläche einschließlich Korridore / Living area including corridors / Zone de séjour avec corridors	m²	22.8	19.7	37.2	59.6	59.6	91.8
Nebenraumfläche / Auxiliary rooms / Pièces auxiliaires	m²	10.4	9.3	12.2	15.9	15.5	13.5
Fläche der Wohnung ohne Mauern und Treppenhaus / Area of apartment without walls and stairwell / Surface de l'appartement sans murs ni escaliers	m²	33.2	29	49.4	75.5	75.1	105.3

Aufenthaltsfläche der Wohnung / Living area / Zone de séjour	m²						
Wohnschlafzimmer / Living and bedroom / Chambre à coucher et de séjour		17.8	16.2				
Wohnraum / Living room / Séjour				18.3	20.5	22.2	24.4
Wohn- und Eßraum / Living and dining room / Séjour et salle à manger							
Eßraum, Halle / Dining room, hall / Salle à manger, hall							
Elternschlafzimmer / Parents' room / Chambre des parents				13.7	15	11.6	15.1
Kinderzimmer / Children's room / Chambre d'enfant					14.3	13.8	12
Kinderzimmer / Children's room / Chambre d'enfant							12
Andere Räume / Additional rooms / Chambres supplémentaires							11.6
Interne Verkehrsfläche, Korridore / Internal circulation area, corridors / Circulation interne, corridors		5	3.5	5.2	9.8	12	16.7
Balkon / Balcony / Balcon		9.9	9.9	10.6	18.8	18.8	9.4
Loggia							

Nebenraumfläche der Wohnung / Auxiliary rooms / Pièces auxiliaires	m²						
Küche / Kitchen / Cuisine		5.5		4.4	8.3	4.8	5.7
Kochnische / Kitchenette / Cuisinette			2.5				
WC					1.5	1.4	1.5
Bad, Dusche / Bath, shower / Bain, douche		3.8	3.8	3.9	2.7	2.5	3.2
Dusche, 2. Bad / Shower, 2nd bath / Douche, 2e bain							
Einbauschränke / Built-in closets / Placards		1.1	0.9	1	3.4	3.7	3.1
Abstellraum in der Wohnung / Storage area in apartment / Débarras dans l'appartement			2.1	2.9	3	3.1	

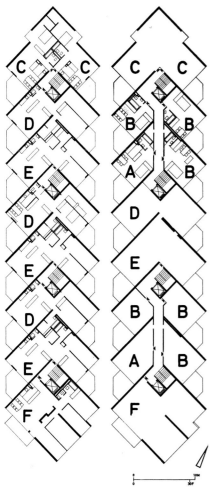

Links: Normalgeschoß / Left: Typical floor / A gauche: Etage type
Rechts: Zwischengeschoß mit kleinen Wohnungen / Right: Mezzanine with small flats / A droite: Entresol avec petits appartements

3-Zimmer-Wohnung Typ D, 1:100 / 3-room flat type D / Appartement de 3 pièces type D:
1 Garderobe / Cloaks / Garde-robe
2 Wohn-Eßraum / Living-dining room / Séjour, salle à manger
3 Elternschlafzimmer / Parents' bedroom / Chambre à coucher des parents
4 Kinderzimmer / Children / Chambre des enfants
5 Balkon / Balcony / Balcon
6 Küche / Kitchen / Cuisine
7 WC / WC / Toilettes
8 Bad / Bathroom / Bains
9 Abstellraum / Boxroom / Débarras

Skizze: Blick von der alten Stadt auf die neu geplanten Quartiere / View from the old town towards the newly planned quarters / Vue des quartiers projetés prise de la vieille ville

Allgemeines / General information / Information générale

Baujahr / Year of construction / Année de construction	1964
Bauhöhe / Height of building / Hauteur du bâtiment	48 m
Geschoßzahl / Number of stories / Nombre d'étages	15
Anzahl Wohnungen / Number of apartments / Nombre d'appartements	120
Einzelhochhaus / Single highrise building / Maison-tour isolée	nein
Teil einer Gesamtbebauung / Part of a development / Partie d'un grand ensemble	ja
Frei finanzierter Wohnungsbau / Private housing / Construction de logements à financement libre	ja
Sozialer Wohnungsbau / Public housing / Construction de logements à caractère social	ja

Umgebung / Surroundings / Environs

Gesamtfläche des Areals / Total area / Superficie totale de l'aire	5 220 m²
Überbaute Fläche (einschließlich Garagen) / Built-upon area (including garages) / Emprise au sol (y compris les garages)	2 652 m²
Grünflächen / Garden area / Zones vertes	2 645 m²
Spielplatz / Playground / Place de jeu	884 m²
Parkplatzfläche / Parking area / Surface des places de stationnement	
Parkplätze / Parking / Places de stationnement	o
Garagen / Garages / Garages	140
Garagenfläche / Garage area / Surface des garages	3 352 m²

Verschiedene Nutzräume / Utility rooms / Chambres de service

Abstellräume / Storage / Débarras	
Keller / Cellar / Caves	1 080 m²
Velo- und Kinderwagenraum / Bicycles, baby carriages / Bicyclettes, Poussettes	177 m²

Aufsicht / Controlled area / Zone contrôlée

Eingangspartie / Entrance area / Entrée	320 m²
Hauswart (Sicht auf Eingang) / Janitor / Concierge	nein

Kinderaufenthalt und Freizeit / Children's recreation and hobby area / Jeux et loisirs

Kindergarten / Nursery / Jardin d'enfants	o
Spielzimmer / Playroom / Salle de jeu	nein
Bastelraum / Hobby room / Atelier de bricolage	nein
Gedeckter Spielplatz / Covered play area / Place de jeu couverte	265 m²
Terrassen / Terraces / Terrasses	530 m²

Vertikalverbindungen / Vertical circulation / Circulation verticale

Haupttreppe / Main stairway / Escalier principal	4
Nottreppe / Emergency stairway / Escalier de secours	
Personenlift / Elevator / Ascenseur	4
Warenlift / Freight lift / Monte-charge	

Andere Einrichtungen / Additional establishments / Autres aménagements

Verwaltungsräume 628 m², Läden 190 m² / Administration space 628 m², Shops 190 m² / Locaux administratifs 628 m², Magasins 190 m²

o = in Gesamtbebauung vorhanden / existing in development / existant dans le grand ensemble

9
Highrise Block
Standstrasse, Berne

Zimmermann, Lienhard and Strasser, Berne

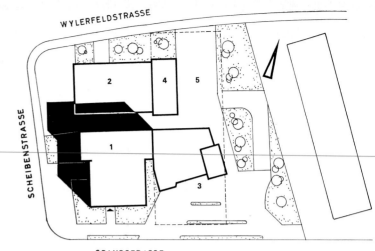

Situation 1 : 1000

Normalgeschoß / Standard floor / Etage type

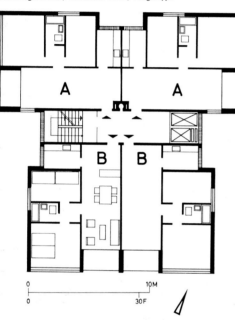

0   10M
0   30F

Dachgeschoß / Top storey / Dernier étage

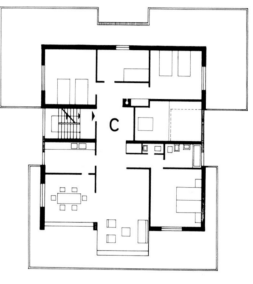

3-Zimmer-Wohnung Typ B, 1 : 100 / 3-room
flat type B / Appartement de 3 pièces type B

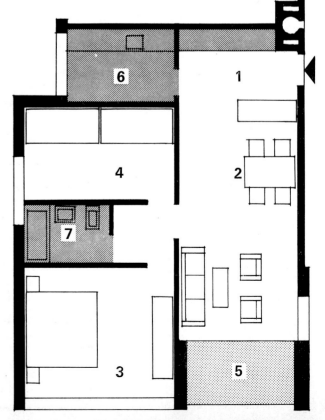

Wohnungstyp / Apartment type / Type de l'appartement		A	B	C
Zimmer pro Wohnung / Rooms per apartment / Chambres par appartement			3	3	6
Anzahl Wohnungen / Number of apartments / Nombre d'appartements		22	22	1
Aufenthaltsfläche einschließlich Korridore / Living area including corridors / Zone de séjour avec corridors	m²	52.6	52.6	134.1
Nebenraumfläche / Auxiliary rooms / Pièces auxiliaires	m²	10.9	10.9	22.7
Fläche der Wohnung ohne Mauern und Treppenhaus / Area of apartment without walls and stairwell / Surface de l'appartement sans murs ni escaliers	m²	63.5	63.5	156.8

Aufenthaltsfläche der Wohnung / Living area / Zone de séjour	m²			
Wohnschlafzimmer / Living and bedroom / Chambre à coucher et de séjour				
Wohnraum / Living room / Séjour				28.6
Wohn- und Eßraum / Living and dining room / Séjour et salle à manger		19	19	
Eßraum, Halle / Dining room, hall / Salle à manger, hall				17.2
Elternschlafzimmer / Parents' room / Chambre des parents		14.3	14.3	19.1
Kinderzimmer / Children's room / Chambre d'enfant		9.3	9.3	19
Kinderzimmer / Children's room / Chambre d'enfant				16.7
Andere Räume / Additional rooms / Chambres supplémentaires				10.5
Interne Verkehrsfläche, Korridore / Internal circulation area, corridors / Circulation interne, corridors		10	10	23
Balkon / Balcony / Balcon				
Loggia		4.1	4.1	130

Nebenraumfläche der Wohnung / Auxiliary rooms / Pièces auxiliaires	m²			
Küche / Kitchen / Cuisine		6.3	6.3	10.6
Kochnische / Kitchenette / Cuisinette				
WC				1.5
Bad, Dusche / Bath, shower / Bain, douche		3.4	3.4	5.9
Dusche, 2. Bad / Shower, 2nd bath / Douche, 2e bain				
Einbauschränke / Built-in closets / Placards		1.2	1.2	3.7
Abstellraum in der Wohnung / Storage area in apartment / Débarras dans l'appartement				1

Allgemeines / General information / Information générale

Baujahr / Year of construction / Année de construction	1959/60
Bauhöhe / Height of building / Hauteur du bâtiment	36 m
Geschoßzahl / Number of stories / Nombre d'étages	13
Anzahl Wohnungen / Number of apartments / Nombre d'appartements	45
Einzelhochhaus / Single highrise building / Maison-tour isolée	nein
Teil einer Gesamtbebauung / Part of a development / Partie d'un grand ensemble	ja
Frei finanzierter Wohnungsbau / Private housing / Construction de logements à financement libre	ja
Sozialer Wohnungsbau / Public housing / Construction de logements à caractère social	nein

Umgebung / Surroundings / Environs

Gesamtfläche des Areals / Total area / Superficie totale de l'aire	3 900 m²
Überbaute Fläche (einschließlich Garagen) / Built-upon area (including garages) / Emprise au sol (y compris les garages)	1 012 m²
Grünflächen / Garden area / Zones vertes	970 m²
Spielplatz / Playground / Place de jeu	nein
Parkplatzfläche / Parking area / Surface des places de stationnement	180 m²
Parkplätze / Parking / Places de stationnement	10
Garagen / Garages / Garages	61
Garagenfläche / Garage area / Surface des garages	1 218 m²

Verschiedene Nutzräume / Utility rooms / Chambres de service

Abstellräume / Storage / Débarras	231 m²
Keller / Cellar / Caves	240 m²
Velo- und Kinderwagenraum / Bicycles, baby carriages / Bicyclettes, Poussettes	110 m²

Aufsicht / Controlled area / Zone contrôlée

Eingangspartie / Entrance area / Entrée	nein
Hauswart (Sicht auf Eingang) / Janitor / Concierge	nein

Kinderaufenthalt und Freizeit / Children's recreation and hobby area / Jeux et loisirs

Kindergarten / Nursery / Jardin d'enfants	nein
Spielzimmer / Playroom / Salle de jeu	nein
Bastelraum / Hobby room / Atelier de bricolage	nein
Gedeckter Spielplatz / Covered play area / Place de jeu couverte	143 m²
Terrassen / Terraces / Terrasses	nein

Vertikalverbindungen / Vertical circulation / Circulation verticale

Haupttreppe / Main stairway / Escalier principal	1
Nottreppe / Emergency stairway / Escalier de secours	nein
Personenlift / Elevator / Ascenseur	2
Warenlift / Freight lift / Monte-charge	

Andere Einrichtungen / Additional establishments / Autres aménagements

Parterre-Anbau mit Restaurant und Auto-Servicestation / Ground-floor annex with restaurant and car service station / Annexe avec restaurant et station service

Situation 1:1000:
1 Hochhaus / Highrise block / Maison-tour
2 Restaurant
3 Service-Station / Service station / Station service
4 Garagetrakt / Garage space / Aile garages
5 Einstellhalle / Parking space / Halle parkings

3-Zimmer-Wohnung Typ B, 1:100 / 3-room flat type B / Appartement de 3 pièces type B:
1 Eingang, Garderobe / Entrance, cloaks / Entrée, garde-robe
2 Wohnraum / Living room / Salle de séjour
3 Elternschlafzimmer / Parents' bedroom / Chambre à coucher des parents
4 Kinderzimmer / Children / Chambre des enfants
5 Loggia / Covered balcony / Loggia
6 Küche / Kitchen / Cuisine
7 Bad / Bath / Bains

Photo: Ansicht von Südwesten / View from the south-west / Vue du sud-ouest

10
La Gradelle, Highrise Block
Geneva

J. Hentsch, Geneva

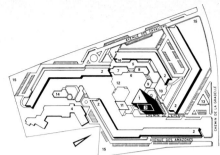

Situation 1 : 2000

1.–8. Geschoß / Storey / Etage

0   10M
0   30F

9.–16. Geschoß / Storey / Etage

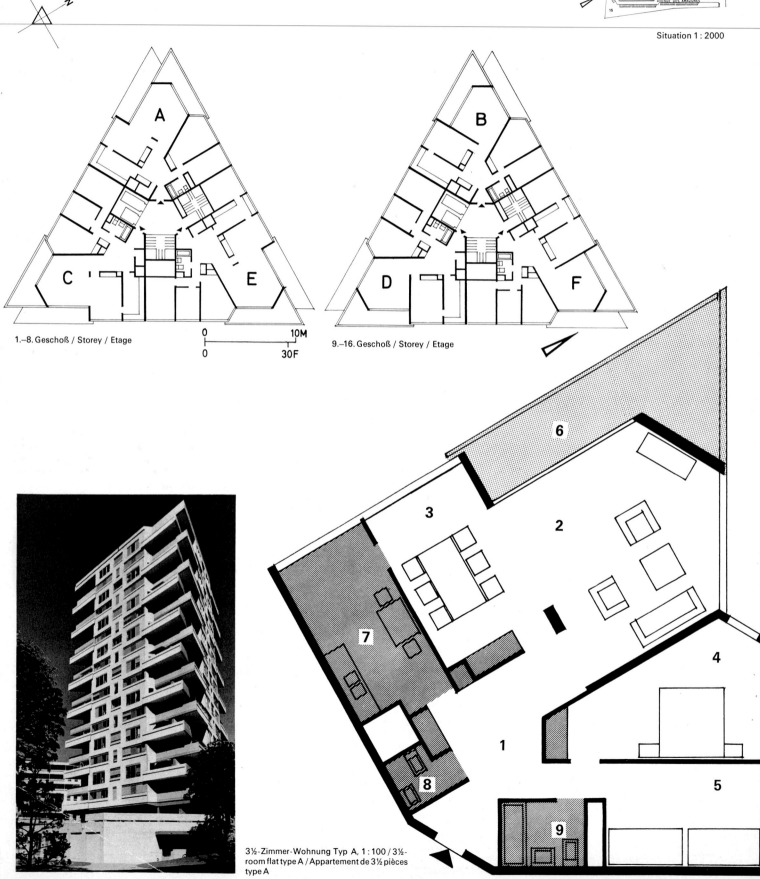

3½-Zimmer-Wohnung Typ A, 1:100 / 3½-room flat type A / Appartement de 3½ pièces type A

Wohnungstyp / Apartment type / Type de l'appartement		A	B	C	D	E	F
Zimmer pro Wohnung / Rooms per apartment / Chambres par appartement		3½	4	4½	5	5½	6
Anzahl Wohnungen / Number of apartments / Nombre d'appartements		8	8	8	8	8	8
Aufenthaltsfläche einschließlich Korridore / Living area including corridors / Zone de séjour avec corridors	m²	81.4	81.4	95.8	95.8	108.5	108.5
Nebenraumfläche / Auxiliary rooms / Pièces auxiliaires	m²	21.1	20.6	21.1	21.1	21.4	21.4
Fläche der Wohnung ohne Mauern und Treppenhaus / Area of apartment without walls and stairwell / Surface de l'appartement sans murs ni escaliers	m²	102.5	102.0	116.9	116.9	129.9	129.9

Aufenthaltsfläche der Wohnung / Living area / Zone de séjour	m²						
Wohnschlafzimmer / Living and bedroom / Chambre à coucher et de séjour							
Wohnraum / Living room / Séjour			27.6		27.6		27.6
Wohn- und Eßraum / Living and dining room / Séjour et salle à manger		42.4		42.9		42.9	
Eßraum, Halle / Dining room, hall / Salle à manger, hall			14.8		15.3		15.3
Elternschlafzimmer/Parents' room/Chambre des parents		15.7	15.7	14.7	14.7	14.7	14.7
Kinderzimmer / Children's room / Chambre d'enfant		12.3	12.3	14.3	14.3	14.3	14.3
Kinderzimmer / Children's room / Chambre d'enfant				10	10	10	10
Andere Räume / Additional rooms / Chambres supplémentaires						12.7	12.7
Interne Verkehrsfläche, Korridore / Internal circulation area, corridors / Circulation interne, corridors		11	11	13.9	13.9	13.9	13.9
Balkon / Balcony / Balcon		17.3	17.3	17.3	17.3	17.3	17.3
Loggia							

Nebenraumfläche der Wohnung / Auxiliary rooms / Pièces auxiliaires	m²						
Küche / Kitchen / Cuisine		12.7	12.2	12.2	12.2	12.2	12.2
Kochnische / Kitchenette / Cuisinette							
WC		2.2	2.2	1.6	1.6	1.9	1.9
Bad, Dusche / Bath, shower / Bain, douche		3.9	3.9	4.3	4.3	4.3	4.3
Dusche, 2. Bad / Shower, 2nd bath / Douche, 2e bain							
Einbauschränke / Built-in closets / Placards		2.3	2.3	3	3	3	3
Abstellraum in der Wohnung / Storage area in apartment / Débarras dans l'appartement							

Situation 1:2000:
1 Hochhaus / Highrise block / Maison-tour
2 Reihen-Wohnhäuser / Terrace houses / Maisons d'habitation en ordre contigu
3 Heizung / Heating / Chauffage
4 Schule / School / Ecole
5 Geschäftsstraße / Shopping street / Rue commerçante
6 Gemeinschaftszentrum / Public square / Centre communautaire
7 Einkaufszentrum / Supermarket / Centre commercial
8 Restaurant
9 Bibliothek / Library / Bibliothèque
10 Kirche / Church / Eglise
11 Kirche / Temple
12 Gemeinschaftsräume / Public rooms / Salles communautaires
13 Service-Station / Service station / Station service
14 Schwimmbad / Swimming bath / Piscine
15 Kinderspielplatz / Playground / Terrain de jeu
16 Boutiquen / Shops / Boutiques

3½-Zimmer-Wohnung Typ A, 1:100 / 3½-room flat type A / Appartement de 3½ pièces type A:
1 Eingang, Garderobe / Entrance, cloaks / Entrée, garde-robe
2 Wohnraum / Living room / Salle de séjour
3 Eßplatz / Dining area / Coin à manger
4 Elternschlafzimmer / Parents' bedroom/ Chambre à coucher des parents
5 Kinderzimmer / Children / Chambre des enfants
6 Balkon / Balcony / Balcon
7 Küche / Kitchen / Cuisine
8 WC / WC / Toilettes
9 Bad / Bathroom / Bains

Photo: Ansicht des 16 geschossigen Hochhauses / View of the 16-storey building / Vue de la maison-tour de 16 étages

Allgemeines / General information / Information générale

Baujahr / Year of construction / Année de construction	1964/65
Bauhöhe / Height of building / Hauteur du bâtiment	48 m
Geschoßzahl / Number of stories / Nombre d'étages	16+1
Anzahl Wohnungen / Number of apartments / Nombre d'appartements	48
Einzelhochhaus / Single highrise building / Maison-tour isolée	ja
Teil einer Gesamtbebauung / Part of a development / Partie d'un grand ensemble	ja
Frei finanzierter Wohnungsbau / Private housing / Construction de logements à financement libre	nein
Sozialer Wohnungsbau / Public housing / Construction de logements à caractère social	ja

Umgebung / Surroundings / Environs

Gesamtfläche des Areals / Total area / Superficie totale de l'aire	3 600 m²
Überbaute Fläche (einschließlich Garagen) / Built-upon area (including garages) / Emprise au sol (y compris les garages)	
Grünflächen / Garden area / Zones vertes	2 000 m²
Spielplatz / Playground / Place de jeu	o
Parkplatzfläche / Parking area / Surface des places de stationnement	
Parkplätze / Parking / Places de stationnement	o
Garagen / Garages / Garages	45
Garagenfläche / Garage area / Surface des garages	

Verschiedene Nutzräume / Utility rooms / Chambres de service

Abstellräume / Storage / Débarras	
Keller / Cellar / Caves	
Velo- und Kinderwagenraum / Bicycles, baby carriages / Bicyclettes, Poussettes	

Aufsicht / Controlled area / Zone contrôlée

Eingangspartie / Entrance area / Entrée	50 m²
Hauswart (Sicht auf Eingang) / Janitor / Concierge	nein

Kinderaufenthalt und Freizeit / Children's recreation and hobby area / Jeux et loisirs

Kindergarten / Nursery / Jardin d'enfants	o
Spielzimmer / Playroom / Salle de jeu	nein
Bastelraum / Hobby room / Atelier de bricolage	o
Gedeckter Spielplatz / Covered play area / Place de jeu couverte	nein
Terrassen / Terraces / Terrasses	nein

Vertikalverbindungen / Vertical circulation / Circulation verticale

Haupttreppe / Main stairway / Escalier principal	1
Nottreppe / Emergency stairway / Escalier de secours	1
Personenlift / Elevator / Ascenseur	1
Warenlift / Freight lift / Monte-charge	1

Andere Einrichtungen / Additional establishments / Autres aménagements

o = in Gesamtbebauung vorhanden / existing in development / existant dans le grand ensemble

Residential Highrise Blocks Zollikerberg, Zurich

Andreas Eichhorn, Zurich

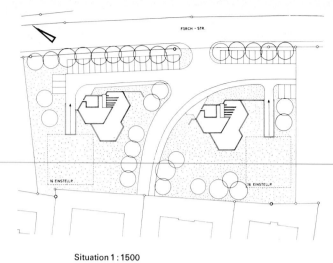

Situation 1 : 1500

Normalgeschoß / Typical floor / Etage type

Zweitoberstes Wohngeschoß, Wohnräume der Maisonnette-Wohnung / Last but one residential floor, living rooms of maisonnette / Avant-dernier étage d'habitation, salles de séjour de l'appartement-villa

Dachgeschoß, oberes Niveau der Maisonnette-Wohnung mit Dachgarten / Top storey, top floor of maisonnette with roof garden / Dernier étage, niveau supérieur de l'appartement-villa avec jardin sur le toit

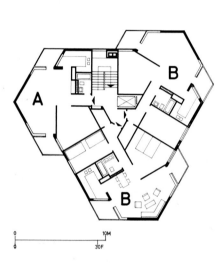

3-Zimmer-Wohnung Typ B, 1 : 100 / 3-room flat type B / Appartement de 3 pièces type B

Modellphoto / Model / Photo de maquette

Wohnungstyp / Apartment type / Type de l'appartement		A	B	C
Zimmer pro Wohnung / Rooms per apartment / Chambres par appartement		2	3	5
Anzahl Wohnungen / Number of apartments / Nombre d'appartements		16	36	2
Aufenthaltsfläche einschließlich Korridore / Living area including corridors / Zone de séjour avec corridors	m²	41.8	58.5	83
Nebenraumfläche / Auxiliary rooms / Pièces auxiliaires	m²	10	12.7	13.7
Fläche der Wohnung ohne Mauern und Treppenhaus / Area of apartment without walls and stairwell / Surface de l'appartement sans murs ni escaliers	m²	51.8	71.2	96.7

Aufenthaltsfläche der Wohnung / Living area / Zone de séjour — m²

	A	B	C
Wohnschlafzimmer / Living and bedroom / Chambre à coucher et de séjour			
Wohnraum / Living room / Séjour			
Wohn- und Eßraum / Living and dining room / Séjour et salle à manger	21.8	21.8	21.8
Eßraum, Halle / Dining room, hall / Salle à manger, hall			
Elternschlafzimmer/Parents' room/Chambre des parents	15.2	15.2	15.2
Kinderzimmer / Children's room / Chambre d'enfant		12.4	12.4
Kinderzimmer / Children's room / Chambre d'enfant			9.6
Andere Räume / Additional rooms / Chambres supplémentaires			19.2
Interne Verkehrsfläche, Korridore / Internal circulation area, corridors / Circulation interne, corridors	4.8	9.1	4.8
Balkon / Balcony / Balcon	4.2	4.2	29.9
Loggia			

Nebenraumfläche der Wohnung / Auxiliary rooms / Pièces auxiliaires — m²

	A	B	C
Küche / Kitchen / Cuisine	6	6	6
Kochnische / Kitchenette / Cuisinette			
WC			
Bad, Dusche / Bath, shower / Bain, douche	3.5	3.5	3.5
Dusche, 2. Bad / Shower, 2nd bath / Douche, 2e bain			
Einbauschränke / Built-in closets / Placards	0.5	1	2
Abstellraum in der Wohnung / Storage area in apartment / Débarras dans l'appartement		2.2	2.2

Allgemeines / General information / Information générale

Baujahr / Year of construction / Année de construction	
Bauhöhe / Height of building / Hauteur du bâtiment	29 m
Geschoßzahl / Number of stories / Nombre d'étages	10+1
Anzahl Wohnungen / Number of apartments / Nombre d'appartements	54
Einzelhochhaus / Single highrise building / Maison-tour isolée	nein
Teil einer Gesamtbebauung / Part of a development / Partie d'un grand ensemble	ja
Frei finanzierter Wohnungsbau / Private housing / Construction de logements à financement libre	ja
Sozialer Wohnungsbau / Public housing / Construction de logements à caractère social	nein

Umgebung / Surroundings / Environs

Gesamtfläche des Areals / Total area / Superficie totale de l'aire	6 380 m²
Überbaute Fläche (einschließlich Garagen) / Built-upon area (including garages) / Emprise au sol (y compris les garages)	1 380 m²
Grünflächen / Garden area / Zones vertes	3 956 m²
Spielplatz / Playground / Place de jeu	nein
Parkplatzfläche / Parking area / Surface des places de stationnement	510 m²
Parkplätze / Parking / Places de stationnement	37
Garagen / Garages / Garages	32
Garagenfläche / Garage area / Surface des garages	788 m²

Verschiedene Nutzräume / Utility rooms / Chambres de service

Abstellräume / Storage / Débarras	170 m²
Keller / Cellar / Caves	55 m²
Velo- und Kinderwagenraum / Bicycles, baby carriages / Bicyclettes, Poussettes	12 m²

Aufsicht / Controlled area / Zone contrôlée

Eingangspartie / Entrance area / Entrée	10 m²
Hauswart (Sicht auf Eingang) / Janitor / Concierge	nein

Kinderaufenthalt und Freizeit / Children's recreation and hobby area / Jeux et loisirs

Kindergarten / Nursery / Jardin d'enfants	nein
Spielzimmer / Playroom / Salle de jeu	nein
Bastelraum / Hobby room / Atelier de bricolage	nein
Gedeckter Spielplatz / Covered play area / Place de jeu couverte	nein
Terrassen / Terraces / Terrasses	169 m²

Vertikalverbindungen / Vertical circulation / Circulation verticale

Haupttreppe / Main stairway / Escalier principal	1
Nottreppe / Emergency stairway / Escalier de secours	nein
Personenlift / Elevator / Ascenseur	1
Warenlift / Freight lift / Monte-charge	

Andere Einrichtungen / Additional establishments / Autres aménagements

3-Zimmer-Wohnung Typ B, 1:100 / 3-room flat type B / Appartement de 3 pièces type B:
1 Wohn-Eßraum / Living-dining room / Séjour, salle à manger
2 Elternschlafzimmer / Parents' bedroom / Chambre à coucher des parents
3 Kinderzimmer / Children / Chambre des enfants
4 Balkon / Balcony / Balcon
5 Küche / Kitchen / Cuisine
6 Bad / Bath / Bains
7 Abstellraum / Boxroom / Débarras

12
Highrise Block
Hechtliacker, Basle

Otto and Walter Senn, Basle

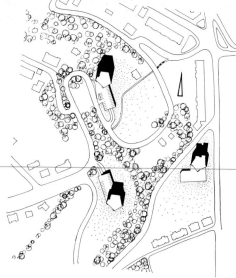

Situation 1 : 6000

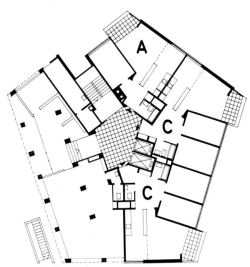

Erdgeschoß / Ground floor / Rez-de-chaussée

0   10M
0   30F

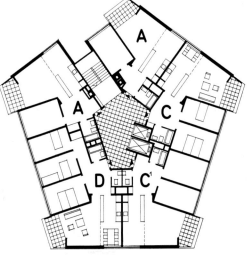

Normalgeschoß / Typical floor / Etage type

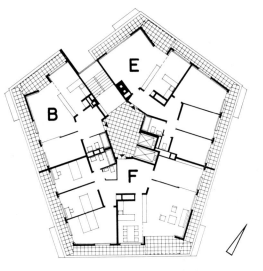

Dachgeschoß / Top floor / Dernier étage

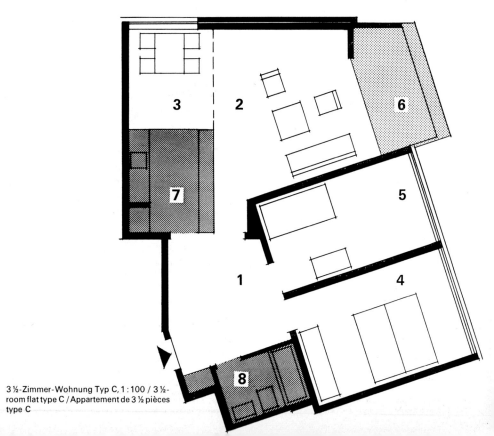

3 ½-Zimmer-Wohnung Typ C, 1 : 100 / 3 ½-
room flat type C / Appartement de 3 ½ pièces
type C

Wohnungstyp / Apartment type / Type de l'appartement		A	B	C	C¹	D	E	F
Zimmer pro Wohnung / Rooms per apartment / Chambres par appartement		2 ½	2 ½	3 ½	3 ½	4 ½	4 ½	5 ½
Anzahl Wohnungen / Number of apartments / Nombre d'appartements		31	1	16	16	15	1	1
Aufenthaltsfläche einschließlich Korridore / Living area including corridors / Zone de séjour avec corridors	m²	41	42.4	56.5	56.5	71.1	81.4	101
Nebenraumfläche / Auxiliary rooms / Pièces auxiliaires	m²	11.2	10.8	11	12.3	11.6	10.9	11.7
Fläche der Wohnung ohne Mauern und Treppenhaus / Area of apartment without walls and stairwell / Surface de l'appartement sans murs ni escaliers	m²	52.2	53.2	67.5	68.8	82.7	92.3	112.7

Aufenthaltsfläche der Wohnung / Living area / Zone de séjour	m²							
Wohnschlafzimmer / Living and bedroom / Chambre à coucher et de séjour								
Wohnraum / Living room / Séjour								
Wohn- und Eßraum / Living and dining room / Séjour et salle à manger		21.8	24.4	21.8	21.8	21.8	29.1	29.1
Eßraum, Halle / Dining room, hall / Salle à manger, hall								
Elternschlafzimmer / Parents' room / Chambre des parents		13.2	11	13.2	13.2	13.2	18.9	18.9
Kinderzimmer / Children's room / Chambre d'enfant				11	11	11	10.8	10.8
Kinderzimmer / Children's room / Chambre d'enfant						11	10.8	10.8
Andere Räume / Additional rooms / Chambres supplémentaires								13
Interne Verkehrsfläche, Korridore / Internal circulation area, corridors / Circulation interne, corridors		6	7	10.5	10.5	14.1	11.8	18.4
Balkon / Balcony / Balcon			16.5				31	31.7
Loggia		7		7	7	7		

Nebenraumfläche der Wohnung / Auxiliary rooms / Pièces auxiliaires	m²							
Küche / Kitchen / Cuisine		6.7	6.2	6.7	6.7	6.7	5.6	5.6
Kochnische / Kitchenette / Cuisinette								
WC					1.9	1.9	1.5	1.6
Bad, Dusche / Bath, shower / Bain, douche		3.5	4.2	3.5	2.7	2.7	3.5	4.2
Dusche, 2. Bad / Shower, 2nd bath / Douche, 2e bain								
Einbauschränke / Built-in closets / Placards		1	0.4	0.8	1	0.3	0.3	0.3
Abstellraum in der Wohnung / Storage area in apartment / Débarras dans l'appartement								

Allgemeines / General information / Information générale

Baujahr / Year of construction / Année de construction	1962
Bauhöhe / Height of building / Hauteur du bâtiment	
Geschoßzahl / Number of stories / Nombre d'étages	16+1
Anzahl Wohnungen / Number of apartments / Nombre d'appartements	81
Einzelhochhaus / Single highrise building / Maison-tour isolée	nein
Teil einer Gesamtbebauung / Part of a development / Partie d'un grand ensemble	ja
Frei finanzierter Wohnungsbau / Private housing / Construction de logements à financement libre	
Sozialer Wohnungsbau / Public housing / Construction de logements à caractère social	

Umgebung / Surroundings / Environs

Gesamtfläche des Areals / Total area / Superficie totale de l'aire	
Überbaute Fläche (einschließlich Garagen) / Built-upon area (including garages) / Emprise au sol (y compris les garages)	
Grünflächen / Garden area / Zones vertes	ja
Spielplatz / Playground / Place de jeu	ja
Parkplatzfläche / Parking area / Surface des places de stationnement	
Parkplätze / Parking / Places de stationnement	25
Garagen / Garages / Garages	50
Garagenfläche / Garage area / Surface des garages	

Verschiedene Nutzräume / Utility rooms / Chambres de service

Abstellräume / Storage / Débarras

Keller / Cellar / Caves

Velo- und Kinderwagenraum / Bicycles, baby carriages / Bicyclettes, Poussettes

Aufsicht / Controlled area / Zone contrôlée

Eingangspartie / Entrance area / Entrée

Hauswart (Sicht auf Eingang) / Janitor / Concierge

Kinderaufenthalt und Freizeit / Children's recreation and hobby area / Jeux et loisirs

Kindergarten / Nursery / Jardin d'enfants

Spielzimmer / Playroom / Salle de jeu

Bastelraum / Hobby room / Atelier de bricolage

Gedeckter Spielplatz / Covered play area / Place de jeu couverte

Terrassen / Terraces / Terrasses

Vertikalverbindungen / Vertical circulation / Circulation verticale

Haupttreppe / Main stairway / Escalier principal	1
Nottreppe / Emergency stairway / Escalier de secours	nein
Personenlift / Elevator / Ascenseur	1
Warenlift / Freight lift / Monte-charge	1

Andere Einrichtungen / Additional establishments / Autres aménagements

3½-Zimmer-Wohnung Typ C, 1 : 100 / 3½-room flat type C / Appartement de 3½ pièces type C:
1 Eingang / Entrance / Entrée
2 Wohnraum / Living room / Salle de séjour
3 Eßplatz / Dining area / Coin à manger
4 Elternschlafzimmer / Parents' bedroom / Chambre à coucher des parents
5 Kinderzimmer / Nursery / Chambre des enfants
6 Loggia / Covered balcony / Loggia
7 Küche / Kitchen / Cuisine
8 Bad / Bath / Bains

Photo: Ansicht von Südosten / View from the south-east / Vue du sud-est

13
Housing Development
Biel-Mett, Switzerland

Walter Niehus, Zurich
Collaborators: G. Albisetti, B. Davi,
E. Schriever

N

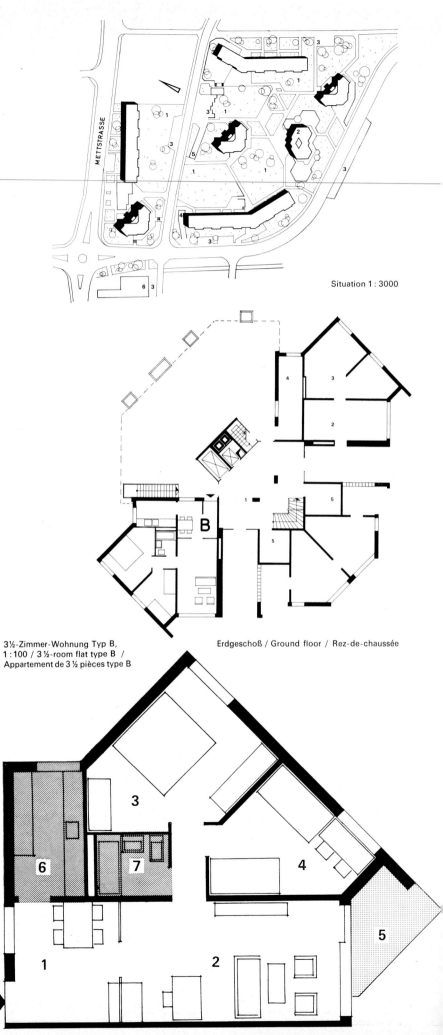

Situation 1 : 3000

Normalgeschoß / Typical floor / Etage type

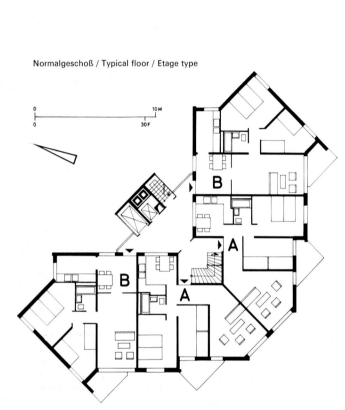

0   10 M
0   30 F

3½-Zimmer-Wohnung Typ B,
1 : 100 / 3 ½-room flat type B /
Appartement de 3 ½ pièces type B

Erdgeschoß / Ground floor / Rez-de-chaussée

Wohnungstyp / Apartment type / Type de l'appartement		A	B
Zimmer pro Wohnung / Rooms per apartment / Chambres par appartement		3	3 ½
Anzahl Wohnungen / Number of apartments / Nombre d'appartements		30	31
Aufenthaltsfläche einschließlich Korridore / Living area including corridors / Zone de séjour avec corridors	m²	46.7	52.9
Nebenraumfläche / Auxiliary rooms / Pièces auxiliaires	m²	13.5	10.6
Fläche der Wohnung ohne Mauern und Treppenhaus / Area of apartment without walls and stairwell / Surface de l'appartement sans murs ni escaliers	m²	60.2	63.5

Aufenthaltsfläche der Wohnung / Living area / Zone de séjour	m²		
Wohnschlafzimmer / Living and bedroom / Chambre à coucher et de séjour			
Wohnraum / Living room / Séjour		17.5	18.6
Wohn- und Eßraum / Living and dining room / Séjour et salle à manger			
Eßraum, Halle / Dining room, hall / Salle à manger, hall		4.7	9
Elternschlafzimmer / Parents' room / Chambre des parents		13.2	13
Kinderzimmer / Children's room / Chambre d'enfant		10.2	10.4
Kinderzimmer / Children's room / Chambre d'enfant			
Andere Räume / Additional rooms / Chambres supplémentaires			
Interne Verkehrsfläche, Korridore / Internal circulation area, corridors / Circulation interne, corridors		1.1	1.9
Balkon / Balcony / Balcon		4.5	4.3
Loggia			

Nebenraumfläche der Wohnung / Auxiliary rooms / Pièces auxiliaires	m²		
Küche / Kitchen / Cuisine		8.7	6.5
Kochnische / Kitchenette / Cuisinette			
WC			
Bad, Dusche / Bath, shower / Bain, douche		3.1	3.2
Dusche, 2. Bad / Shower, 2nd bath / Douche, 2e bain			
Einbauschränke / Built-in closets / Placards		1.7	0.9
Abstellraum in der Wohnung / Storage area in apartment / Débarras dans l'appartement			

Situation 1 : 3000
1 Spielplätze / Playing fields / Terrains de jeu
2 Kindergarten / Nursery school / Jardin d'enfants
3 Parkplätze / Parking spaces / Parkings
4 Garageeinfahrt / Garage entry / Entrée des garages
5 Garageausfahrt / Garage exit / Sortie des garages
6 Läden / Shops / Magasins

Erdgeschoß / Ground floor / Rez-de-chaussée:
1 Eingangshalle / Entrance hall / Hall d'entrée
2 Werkstatt / Workshop / Atelier
3 Kinder-Aufenthaltsraum / Day nursery / Salle de séjour pour les enfants
4 Zählertableau / Checklist / Tableau compteurs
5 Kinderwagen / Prams / Poussettes

3½-Zimmer-Wohnung Typ B, 1:100 / 3½-room flat type B / Appartement de 3½ pièces type B:
1 Eßplatz / Dining room / Coin à manger
2 Wohnraum / Living room / Salle de séjour
3 Elternschlafzimmer / Parents' bedroom / Chambre à coucher des parents
4 Kinderzimmer / Children / Chambre des enfants
5 Balkon / Balcony / Balcon
6 Küche / Kitchen / Cuisine
7 Bad / Bathroom / Bains

Photo: Blick von Süden, im Vordergrund Kindergarten / View from the south; in the foreground nursery school / Vue du sud, au premier plan le jardin d'enfants

Allgemeines / General information / Information générale

Baujahr / Year of construction / Année de construction	1960/63
Bauhöhe / Height of building / Hauteur du bâtiment	43 m
Geschoßzahl / Number of stories / Nombre d'étages	16
Anzahl Wohnungen / Number of apartments / Nombre d'appartements	61
Einzelhochhaus / Single highrise building / Maison-tour isolée	nein
Teil einer Gesamtbebauung / Part of a development / Partie d'un grand ensemble	ja
Frei finanzierter Wohnungsbau / Private housing / Construction de logements à financement libre	ja
Sozialer Wohnungsbau / Public housing / Construction de logements à caractère social	nein

Umgebung / Surroundings / Environs

Gesamtfläche des Areals / Total area / Superficie totale de l'aire	4 700 m²
Überbaute Fläche (einschließlich Garagen) / Built-upon area (including garages) / Emprise au sol (y compris les garages)	350 m²
Grünflächen / Garden area / Zones vertes	3 900 m²
Spielplatz / Playground / Place de jeu	200 m²
Parkplatzfläche / Parking area / Surface des places de stationnement	
Parkplätze / Parking / Places de stationnement	10
Garagen / Garages / Garage	14
Garagenfläche / Garage area / Surface des garages	420 m²

Verschiedene Nutzräume / Utility rooms / Chambres de service

Abstellräume / Storage / Débarras	nein
Keller / Cellar / Caves	122 m²
Velo- und Kinderwagenraum / Bicycles, baby carriages / Bicyclettes, Poussettes	50 m²

Aufsicht / Controlled area / Zone contrôlée

Eingangspartie / Entrance area / Entrée	44 m²
Hauswart (Sicht auf Eingang) / Janitor / Concierge	ja

Kinderaufenthalt und Freizeit / Children's recreation and hobby area / Jeux et loisirs

Kindergarten / Nursery / Jardin d'enfants	o
Spielzimmer / Playroom / Salle de jeu	
Bastelraum / Hobby room / Atelier de bricolage	30 m²
Gedeckter Spielplatz / Covered play area / Place de jeu couverte	
Terrassen / Terraces / Terrasses	nein

Vertikalverbindungen / Vertical circulation / Circulation verticale

Haupttreppe / Main stairway / Escalier principal	1
Nottreppe / Emergency stairway / Escalier de secours	1
Personenlift / Elevator / Ascenseur	1
Warenlift / Freight lift / Monte-charge	1

Andere Einrichtungen / Additional establishments / Autres aménagements

o = in Gesamtbebauung vorhanden / existing in development / existant dans le grand ensemble

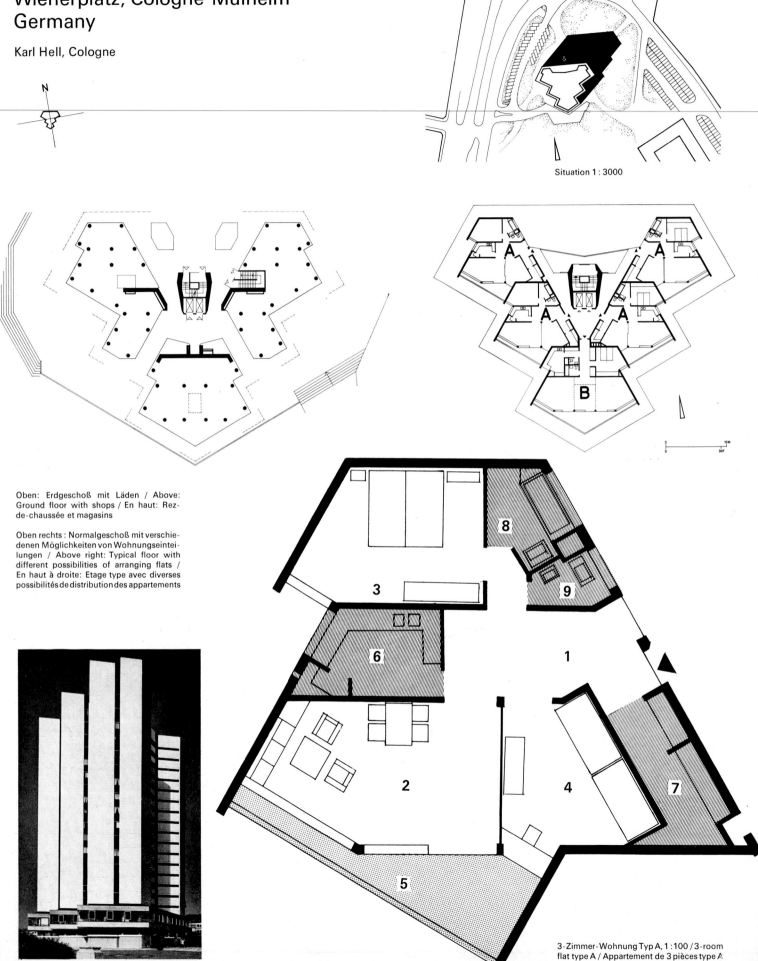

14
Highrise Block
Wienerplatz, Cologne-Mulheim
Germany

Karl Hell, Cologne

N

Situation 1 : 3000

Oben: Erdgeschoß mit Läden / Above: Ground floor with shops / En haut: Rez-de-chaussée et magasins

Oben rechts : Normalgeschoß mit verschiedenen Möglichkeiten von Wohnungseinteilungen / Above right: Typical floor with different possibilities of arranging flats / En haut à droite: Etage type avec diverses possibilités de distribution des appartements

3-Zimmer-Wohnung Typ A, 1 :100 / 3-room flat type A / Appartement de 3 pièces type A

Wohnungstyp / Apartment type / Type de l'appartement		A	B	B^1	B^2
Zimmer pro Wohnung / Rooms per apartment / Chambres par appartement		3 (2½)	2	(3½)	(4)
Anzahl Wohnungen / Number of apartments / Nombre d'appartements		64	16		
Aufenthaltsfläche einschließlich Korridore / Living area including corridors / Zone de séjour avec corridors	m^2	65.8	105.2	105.2	105.2
Nebenraumfläche / Auxiliary rooms / Pièces auxiliaires	m^2	21.2	23.1	23.1	23.1
Fläche der Wohnung ohne Mauern und Treppenhaus / Area of apartment without walls and stairwell / Surface de l'appartement sans murs ni escaliers	m^2	87	128.3	128.3	128.3

Aufenthaltsfläche der Wohnung / Living area / Zone de séjour	m^2				
Wohnschlafzimmer / Living and bedroom / Chambre à coucher et de séjour					
Wohnraum / Living room / Séjour				45	28
Wohn- und Eßraum / Living and dining room / Séjour et salle à manger		21.6	73		
Eßraum, Halle / Dining room, hall / Salle à manger, hall				28	14
Elternschlafzimmer / Parents' room / Chambre des parents		16.2	19.6	19.6	28
Kinderzimmer / Children's room / Chambre d'enfant		11.1			19.6
Kinderzimmer / Children's room / Chambre d'enfant					
Andere Räume / Additional rooms / Chambres supplémentaires					
Interne Verkehrsfläche, Korridore / Internal circulation area, corridors / Circulation interne, corridors		16.9	12.6	12.6	15.6
Balkon / Balcony / Balcon					
Loggia		9.1	24.7	24.7	24.7

Nebenraumfläche der Wohnung / Auxiliary rooms / Pièces auxiliaires	m^2				
Küche / Kitchen / Cuisine		8.2	12.2	12.2	12.2
Kochnische / Kitchenette / Cuisinette					
WC		2.4	1.6	1.6	1.6
Bad, Dusche / Bath, shower / Bain, douche		4.6	4.3	4.3	4.3
Dusche, 2. Bad / Shower, 2nd bath / Douche, 2e bain					
Einbauschränke / Built-in closets / Placards		2	1.8	1.8	1.8
Abstellraum in der Wohnung / Storage area in apartment / Débarras dans l'appartement		4	3.2	3.2	3.2

Allgemeines / General information / Information générale

Baujahr / Year of construction / Année de construction	1960/61
Bauhöhe / Height of building / Hauteur du bâtiment	55 m
Geschoßzahl / Number of stories / Nombre d'étages	18
Anzahl Wohnungen / Number of apartments / Nombre d'appartements	80
Einzelhochhaus / Single highrise building / Maison-tour isolée	ja
Teil einer Gesamtbebauung / Part of a development / Partie d'un grand ensemble	nein
Frei finanzierter Wohnungsbau / Private housing / Construction de logements à financement libre	ja
Sozialer Wohnungsbau / Public housing / Construction de logements à caractère social	nein

Umgebung / Surroundings / Environs

Gesamtfläche des Areals / Total area / Superficie totale de l'aire	4 500 m^2
Überbaute Fläche (einschließlich Garagen) / Built-upon area (including garages) / Emprise au sol (y compris les garages)	2 618 m^2
Grünflächen / Garden area / Zones vertes	940 m^2
Spielplatz / Playground / Place de jeu	940 m^2
Parkplatzfläche / Parking area / Surface des places de stationnement	940 m^2
Parkplätze / Parking / Places de stationnement	32
Garagen / Garages / Garages	70
Garagenfläche / Garage area / Surface des garages	1 750 m^2

Verschiedene Nutzräume / Utility rooms / Chambres de service

Abstellräume / Storage / Débarras	400 m^2
Keller / Cellar / Caves	600 m^2
Velo- und Kinderwagenraum / Bicycles, baby carriages / Bicyclettes, Poussettes	25 m^2

Aufsicht / Controlled area / Zone contrôlée

Eingangspartie / Entrance area / Entrée	12 m^2
Hauswart (Sicht auf Eingang) / Janitor / Concierge	nein

Kinderaufenthalt und Freizeit / Children's recreation and hobby area / Jeux et loisirs

Kindergarten / Nursery / Jardin d'enfants	nein
Spielzimmer / Playroom / Salle de jeu	nein
Bastelraum / Hobby room / Atelier de bricolage	nein
Gedeckter Spielplatz / Covered play area / Place de jeu couverte	o
Terrassen / Terraces / Terrasses	nein

Vertikalverbindungen / Vertical circulation / Circulation verticale

Haupttreppe / Main stairway / Escalier principal	1
Nottreppe / Emergency stairway / Escalier de secours	1
Personenlift / Elevator / Ascenseur	2
Warenlift / Freight lift / Monte-charge	

Andere Einrichtungen / Additional establishments / Autres aménagements

Restaurant, 4 Läden, 1. Geschoß als Bürogeschoß / Restaurant, 4 shops, first floor offices / Restaurant, 4 magasins, premier étage bureaux

Bemerkungen / Notes / Observations

Die Wohnungen können verschieden unterteilt werden / The apartments can be changed into smaller or larger units / Les appartements peuvent être subdivisés de manière différente

Variationsmöglichkeiten von Wohnungen sind in Klammern gesetzt / Possible variations of flats are indicated in brackets / Les diverses variantes d'appartements sont indiquées entre parenthèses

o = in Gesamtbebauung vorhanden / existing in development / existant dans le grand ensemble

3-Zimmer-Wohnung Typ A, 1:100 / 3-room flat type A / Appartement de 3 pièces type A:
1 Eingang, Garderobe / Entrance, cloaks / Entrée, garde-robe
2 Wohn-Eßraum / Living-dining room / Séjour, salle à manger
3 Elternschlafzimmer / Parents' bedroom / Chambre à coucher des parents
4 Kinderzimmer / Children / Chambre des enfants
5 Loggia / Covered balcony / Loggia
6 Küche / Kitchen / Cuisine
7 Abstellraum, Schrankraum / Boxroom, storage / Débarras, armoires
8 Bad / Bathroom / Bains
9 WC / WC / Toilettes

Photo: Ansicht von Osten / View from the east / Vue de l'est

15
Highrise Block
Triemliplatz, Zurich

Rudolf and Esther Guyer, Zurich
Collaborator: U. Hilfiker

Situation 1 : 1500

Erdgeschoß / Ground floor / Rez-de-chaussée

Normalgeschoß / Typical floor / Etage type

Attikageschoß / Attics / Etage en attique

2-Zimmer-Wohnung Typ B, 1 : 100 / 2-room
flat type B / Appartement de 2 pièces type B

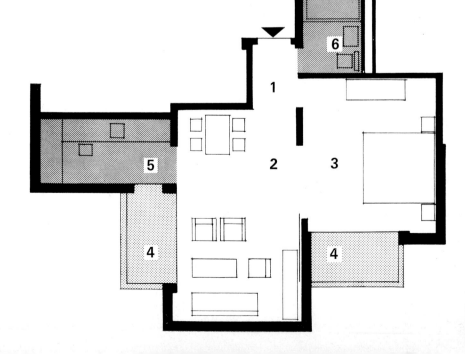

Wohnungstyp / Apartment type / Type de l'appartement		B	C	D
Zimmer pro Wohnung / Rooms per apartment / Chambres par appartement		2	3	5
Anzahl Wohnungen / Number of apartments / Nombre d'appartements		26	26	2
Aufenthaltsfläche einschließlich Korridore / Living area including corridors / Zone de séjour avec corridors	m²	36.8	52.1	87.9
Nebenraumfläche / Auxiliary rooms / Pièces auxiliaires	m²	9.8	10.6	16.4
Fläche der Wohnung ohne Mauern und Treppenhaus / Area of apartment without walls and stairwell / Surface de l'appartement sans murs ni escaliers	m²	46.6	62.7	104.3
Aufenthaltsfläche der Wohnung / Living area / Zone de séjour	m²			
Wohnschlafzimmer / Living and bedroom / Chambre à coucher et de séjour				
Wohnraum / Living room / Séjour				20
Wohn- und Eßraum / Living and dining room / Séjour et salle à manger		19.7	18.2	
Eßraum, Halle / Dining room, hall / Salle à manger, hall				17.7
Elternschlafzimmer / Parents' room / Chambre des parents		15	15.3	14.7
Kinderzimmer / Children's room / Chambre d'enfant			12.6	13.6
Kinderzimmer / Children's room / Chambre d'enfant				11.8
Andere Räume / Additional rooms / Chambres supplémentaires				
Interne Verkehrsfläche, Korridore / Internal circulation area, corridors / Circulation interne, corridors		2.1	6	10.1
Balkon / Balcony / Balcon				20.8
Loggia		6.2	8	14.2
Nebenraumfläche der Wohnung / Auxiliary rooms / Pièces auxiliaires	m²			
Küche / Kitchen / Cuisine		6.2	6.2	7.7
Kochnische / Kitchenette / Cuisinette				
WC				1.2
Bad, Dusche / Bath, shower / Bain, douche		3.6	3.6	3.9
Dusche, 2. Bad / Shower, 2nd bath / Douche, 2e bain				
Einbauschränke / Built-in closets / Placards			0.8	0.8
Abstellraum in der Wohnung / Storage area in apartment / Débarras dans l'appartement				2.8

Allgemeines / General information / Information générale

Baujahr / Year of construction / Année de construction	1963/66
Bauhöhe / Height of building / Hauteur du bâtiment	43.5 m
Geschoßzahl / Number of stories / Nombre d'étages	16
Anzahl Wohnungen / Number of apartments / Nombre d'appartements	55
Einzelhochhaus / Single highrise building / Maison-tour isolée	ja
Teil einer Gesamtbebauung / Part of a development / Partie d'un grand ensemble	ja
Frei finanzierter Wohnungsbau / Private housing / Construction de logements à financement libre	ja
Sozialer Wohnungsbau / Public housing / Construction de logements à caractère social	nein

Umgebung / Surroundings / Environs

Gesamtfläche des Areals / Total area / Superficie totale de l'aire	5 170 m²
Überbaute Fläche (einschließlich Garagen) / Built-upon area (including garages) / Emprise au sol (y compris les garages)	1 450 m²
Grünflächen / Garden area / Zones vertes	1 500 m²
Spielplatz / Playground / Place de jeu	550 m²
Parkplatzfläche / Parking area / Surface des places de stationnement	866 m²
Parkplätze / Parking / Places de stationnement	32
Garagen / Garages / Garages	19
Garagenfläche / Garage area / Surface des garages	477 m²

Verschiedene Nutzräume / Utility rooms / Chambres de service

Abstellräume / Storage / Débarras	
Keller / Cellar / Caves	230 m²
Velo- und Kinderwagenraum / Bicycles, baby carriages / Bicyclettes, Poussettes	42,5 m²

Aufsicht / Controlled area / Zone contrôlée

Eingangspartie / Entrance area / Entrée	50 m²
Hauswart (Sicht auf Eingang) / Janitor / Concierge	ja

Kinderaufenthalt und Freizeit / Children's recreation and hobby area / Jeux et loisirs

Kindergarten / Nursery / Jardin d'enfants	nein
Spielzimmer / Playroom / Salle de jeu	nein
Bastelraum / Hobby room / Atelier de bricolage	nein
Gedeckter Spielplatz / Covered play area / Place de jeu couverte	
Terrassen / Terraces / Terrasses	nein

Vertikalverbindungen / Vertical circulation / Circulation verticale

Haupttreppe / Main stairway / Escalier principal	1
Nottreppe / Emergency stairway / Escalier de secours	nein
Personenlift / Elevator / Ascenseur	1
Warenlift / Freight lift / Monte-charge	1

Andere Einrichtungen / Additional establishments / Autres aménagements

Restaurant, Zahnarztpraxis, Laden /
Restaurant, dentist's surgery, shop /
Restaurant, cabinet de dentiste, magasin

Situation 1:1500
1 Hochhaus / Highrise block / Maison-tour
2 Restaurant
3 Laden / Shop / Magasin
4 Garagen / Garages
5 Tankstelle / Petrol station / Station service

Erdgeschoß / Ground floor / Rez-de-chaussée:
1 Gedeckter Vorplatz / Covered precinct / Auvent
2 Hauswartwohnung / Porter's flat / Conciergerie
3 Zahnarztpraxis / Dental surgery / Cabinet de dentiste
4 Anlieferung Restaurant (1 Geschoß tiefer) / Delivery to restaurant (1 floor below) / Livraisons au restaurant (1 étage plus bas)

2-Zimmer-Wohnung Typ B, 1:100 / 2-room flat type B / Appartement de 2 pièces type B:
1 Eingang / Entrance / Entrée
2 Wohn-Eßraum / Living-dining room / Séjour, salle à manger
3 Elternschlafzimmer / Parents' bedroom / Chambre à coucher des parents
4 Loggia / Covered balcony / Loggia
5 Küche / Kitchen / Cuisine
6 Bad / Bathroom / Bains

Modellphoto, Ansicht von Südwesten / Model, view from the south-west / Photo de maquette, vue du sud-ouest

Housing Estate of the firm Brown, Boveri for immigrant workmen
Brisgi, Baden, Switzerland

D. Boller, Baden
Professor C. E. Geisendorf, Zurich
Collaborators: E. Walder, Zurich
R. and B. Winkler, Zurich

N

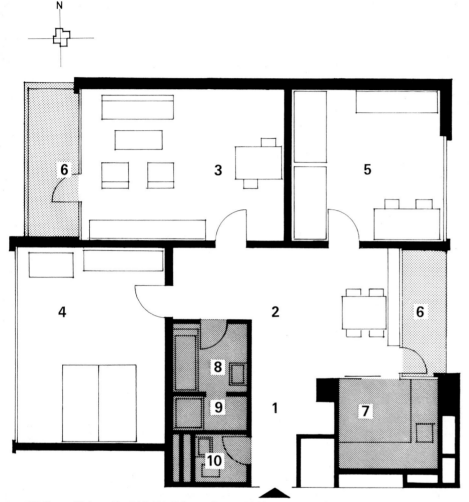

3 ½-Zimmer-Wohnung Typ D¹, 1 : 100 / 3 ½-room flat type D¹ / Appartement de 3 ½ pièces type D¹

0   10M
0   30F

3½-Zimmer-Wohnung Typ D¹, 1:100 / 3½-room flat type D¹ / Appartement de 3½ pièces type D¹:

1 Eingang, Garderobe / Entrance, cloaks / Entrée, garde-robe
2 Halle, Eßplatz / Hall, dining area / Hall, coin à manger
3 Wohnraum / Living room / Salle de séjour
4 Elternschlafzimmer / Parents' bedroom / Chambre à coucher des parents
5 Kinderzimmer / Children / Chambre des enfants
6 Loggia / Covered balcony / Loggia
7 Küche / Kitchen / Cuisine
8 Bad / Bathroom / Bains
9 Dusche / Shower / Douche
10 WC / WC / Toilettes

Photo: Ansicht des Hochhauses mit zum Teil vorfabrizierten Betonelementen / The block with partly prefabricated concrete elements / Vue de la maison-tour constituée partiellement d'éléments de béton préfabriqués

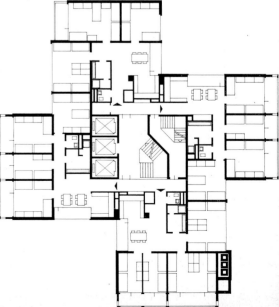

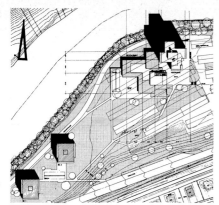

Situation 1:40 000

Wohnungstyp / Apartment type / Type de l'appartement		A	B	B[1]	C	D	D[1]	E
Zimmer pro Wohnung / Rooms per apartment / Chambres par appartement		1 ½	2 ½	2 ½	3 ½	3 ½	3 ½	4 ½
Anzahl Wohnungen / Number of apartments / Nombre d'appartements		36	18	18	36	1	1	2
Aufenthaltsfläche einschließlich Korridore / Living area including corridors / Zone de séjour avec corridors	m²	30.1	63	60	67.7	84.3	81.3	79.4
Nebenraumfläche / Auxiliary rooms / Pièces auxiliaires	m²	8.4	13.6	14.6	16.3	13.6	13.6	16.3
Fläche der Wohnung ohne Mauern und Treppenhaus / Area of apartment without walls and stairwell / Surface de l'appartement sans murs ni escaliers	m²	38.5	76.6	74.6	79	97.9	94.9	95.7
Aufenthaltsfläche der Wohnung / Living area / Zone de séjour	m²							
Wohnschlafzimmer / Living and bedroom / Chambre à coucher et de séjour		21.3						
Wohnraum / Living room / Séjour			21.3	22.6	15.9	21.3	22.6	15.9
Wohn- und Eßraum / Living and dining room / Séjour et salle à manger								
Eßraum, Halle / Dining room, hall / Salle à manger, hall		5.5	16.8	16.8	11.8	16.8	16.8	11.8
Elternschlafzimmer / Parents' room / Chambre des parents			21.3	17	15.9	21.3	21.3	15.9
Kinderzimmer / Children's room / Chambre d'enfant					10.5	21.3	17	16.7
Kinderzimmer / Children's room / Chambre d'enfant								10.5
Andere Räume / Additional rooms / Chambres supplémentaires								
Interne Verkehrsfläche, Korridore / Internal circulation area, corridors / Circulation interne, corridors		3.3	3.6	3.6	8.6	3.6	3.6	8.6
Balkon / Balcony / Balcon								
Loggia			14.6	10	19.4	14.6	10	19.4
Nebenraumfläche der Wohnung / Auxiliary rooms / Pièces auxiliaires	m²							
Küche / Kitchen / Cuisine		3.8	6.2	6.2	6.2	6.2	6.2	6.2
Kochnische / Kitchenette / Cuisinette								
WC			1.8	1.8	1.8	1.8	1.8	1.8
Bad, Dusche / Bath, shower / Bain, douche		3.6	5.6	5.6	6.7	5.6	5.6	6.7
Dusche, 2. Bad / Shower, 2nd bath / Douche, 2e bain								
Einbauschränke / Built-in closets / Placards		1		1	1.6			1.6
Abstellraum in der Wohnung / Storage area in apartment / Débarras dans l'appartement								

Allgemeines / General information / Information générale

Baujahr / Year of construction / Année de construction	1966/67
Bauhöhe / Height of building / Hauteur du bâtiment	60 m
Geschoßzahl / Number of stories / Nombre d'étages	19+2 DG
Anzahl Wohnungen / Number of apartments / Nombre d'appartements	112
Einzelhochhaus / Single highrise building / Maison-tour isolée	nein
Teil einer Gesamtbebauung / Part of a development / Partie d'un grand ensemble	ja
Frei finanzierter Wohnungsbau / Private housing / Construction de logements à financement libre	nein
Sozialer Wohnungsbau / Public housing / Construction de logements à caractère social	ja

Umgebung / Surroundings / Environs

Gesamtfläche des Areals / Total area / Superficie totale de l'aire	
Überbaute Fläche (einschließlich Garagen) / Built-upon area (including garages) / Emprise au sol (y compris les garages)	1200 m²
Grünflächen / Garden area / Zones vertes	570 m²
Spielplatz / Playground / Place de jeu	o
Parkplatzfläche / Parking area / Surface des places de stationnement	
Parkplätze / Parking / Places de stationnement	o
Garagen / Garages / Garages	o 220
Garagenfläche / Garage area / Surface des garages	

Verschiedene Nutzräume / Utility rooms / Chambres de service

Abstellräume / Storage / Débarras	
Keller / Cellar / Caves	ja
Velo- und Kinderwagenraum / Bicycles, baby carriages / Bicyclettes, Poussettes	

Aufsicht / Controlled area / Zone contrôlée

Eingangspartie / Entrance area / Entrée	
Hauswart (Sicht auf Eingang) / Janitor / Concierge	ja

Kinderaufenthalt und Freizeit / Children' srecreation and hobby area / Jeux et loisirs

Kindergarten / Nursery / Jardin d'enfants	
Spielzimmer / Playroom / Salle de jeu	
Bastelraum / Hobby room / Atelier de bricolage	
Gedeckter Spielplatz / Covered play area / Place de jeu couverte	o
Terrassen / Terraces / Terrasses	ja

Vertikalverbindungen / Circulation verticale / Vertical circulation

Haupttreppe / Main stairway / Escalier principal	1
Nottreppe / Emergency stairway / Escalier de secours	1
Personenlift / Elevator / Ascenseur	3
Warenlift / Freight lift / Monte-charge	

Andere Einrichtungen / Additional establishments / Autres aménagements

Restaurant, Bocciabahnen, Läden (2), Coiffeur / Restaurant, boccia, shops (2), hairdresser / Restaurant, pistes de boccia, magasins (2), salon de coiffure

Bemerkungen / Notes / Observations

Die Wohnungen wurden so geplant, daß jederzeit große oder kleine Familienwohnungen daraus gemacht werden können / The apartments were so planned that at any time they can be changed into smaller or larger units / Les appartements ont été ainsi conçus qu'il sera possible en tout temps d'en faire des logements pour familles petites ou grandes

o = in Gesamtbebauung vorhanden / existing in development / existant dans le grand ensemble

Oben: Wohngeschoß, in 5 kleine Wohnungen unterteilt, für Gastarbeiter mit Familien/ Above: Residential floor partitioned into 5 small flats for immigrant workmen with families / En haut: Etage d'habitation comprenant 5 petits appartements pour familles d'ouvriers étrangers

Mitte: Wohngeschoß, in 4 große Wohnungen unterteilt / Middle: Residential floor partitioned into 4 large flats / Au milieu: Etage d'habitation comprenant 4 grands appartements

Unten: Vorläufig wird das Hochhaus vor allem als Unterkunft für Gastarbeiter ohne Familie benutzt, kann aber je nach Bedarf geschoßweise in Wohnungen für Familien umgewandelt werden. / Below: For the time being the highrise building is mainly used to accommodate foreign labourers without family. It can however be transformed as necessary floor by floor into flats for families. / En bas: La maison-tour est occupée pour l'instant essentiellement par des travailleurs étrangers célibataires; elle peut toutefois être reconvertie étage par étage en logements familiaux

Highrise Blocks
Ivry-sur-Seine

G. Candilis, Paris

N

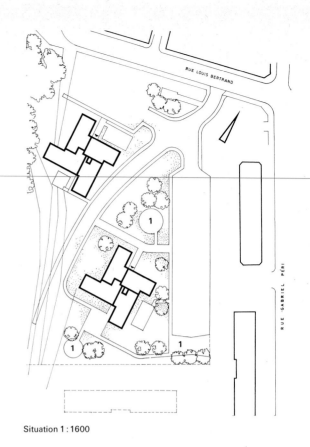

Situation 1 : 1600

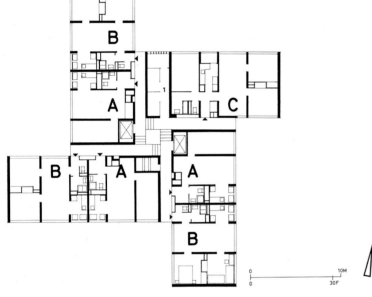

Normalgeschoß / Typical floor / Etage type

3-Zimmer-Wohnung Typ B, 1 : 100 / 3-room flat type B / Appartement de 3 pièces type B

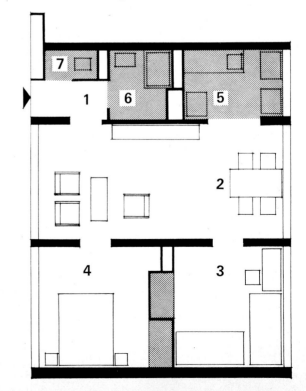

Wohnungstyp / Apartment type / Type de l'appartement		A	B	C
Zimmer pro Wohnung / Rooms per apartment / Chambres par appartement		2	3	4
Anzahl Wohnungen / Number of apartments / Nombre d'appartements		42	42	14
Aufenthaltsfläche einschließlich Korridore / Living area including corridors / Zone de séjour avec corridors	m²	32.3	40.5	55.4
Nebenraumfläche / Auxiliary rooms / Pièces auxiliaires	m²	10.7	13	14.4
Fläche der Wohnung ohne Mauern und Treppenhaus / Area of apartment without walls and stairwell / Surface de l'appartement sans murs ni escaliers	m²	43	53.5	69.8

Aufenthaltsfläche der Wohnung / Living area / Zone de séjour	m²			
Wohnschlafzimmer / Living and bedroom / Chambre à coucher et de séjour				
Wohnraum / Living room / Séjour				
Wohn- und Eßraum / Living and dining room / Séjour et salle à manger		17.8	18.3	20.1
Eßraum, Halle / Dining room, hall / Salle à manger, hall				
Elternschlafzimmer/Parents' room/Chambre des parents		12	10.1	12.5
Kinderzimmer / Children's room / Chambre d'enfant			9.9	10.1
Kinderzimmer / Children's room / Chambre d'enfant				9.9
Andere Räume / Additional rooms / Chambres supplémentaires				
Interne Verkehrsfläche, Korridore / Internal circulation area, corridors / Circulation interne, corridors		2.5	2.2	2.8
Balkon / Balcony / Balcon				
Loggia				

Nebenraumfläche der Wohnung / Auxiliary rooms / Pièces auxiliaires	m²			
Küche / Kitchen / Cuisine		4.8	4.8	6.4
Kochnische / Kitchenette / Cuisinette				
WC			1	1.1
Bad, Dusche / Bath, shower / Bain, douche		3.4	3.2	4.3
Dusche, 2. Bad / Shower, 2nd bath / Douche, 2e bain				
Einbauschränke / Built-in closets / Placards		2.5	4	2.6
Abstellraum in der Wohnung / Storage area in apartment / Débarras dans l'appartement				

Allgemeines / General information / Information générale

Baujahr / Year of construction / Année de construction	1960/61
Bauhöhe / Height of building / Hauteur du bâtiment	43 m
Geschoßzahl / Number of stories / Nombre d'étages	14
Anzahl Wohnungen / Number of apartments / Nombre d'appartements	98
Einzelhochhaus / Single highrise building / Maison-tour isolée	nein
Teil einer Gesamtbebauung / Part of a development / Partie d'un grand ensemble	ja
Frei finanzierter Wohnungsbau / Private housing / Construction de logements à financement libre	nein
Sozialer Wohnungsbau / Public housing / Construction de logements à caractère social	ja

Umgebung / Surroundings / Environs

Gesamtfläche des Areals / Total area / Superficie totale de l'aire	3 050 m²
Überbaute Fläche (einschließlich Garagen) / Built-upon area (including garages) / Emprise au sol (y compris les garages)	500 m²
Grünflächen / Garden area / Zones vertes	1 110 m²
Spielplatz / Playground / Place de jeu	ja
Parkplatzfläche / Parking area / Surface des places de stationnement	1 050 m²
Parkplätze / Parking / Places de stationnement	
Garagen / Garages / Garages	
Garagenfläche / Garage area / Surface des garages	

Verschiedene Nutzräume / Utility rooms / Chambres de service

Abstellräume / Storage / Débarras	
Keller / Cellar / Caves	276 m²
Velo- und Kinderwagenraum / Bicycles, baby carriages / Bicyclettes, Poussettes	32 m²

Aufsicht / Controlled area / Zone contrôlée

Eingangspartie / Entrance area / Entrée	20 m²
Hauswart (Sicht auf Eingang) / Janitor / Concierge	ja

Kinderaufenthalt und Freizeit / Children's recreation and hobby area / Jeux et loisirs

Kindergarten / Nursery / Jardin d'enfants	
Spielzimmer / Playroom / Salle de jeu	
Bastelraum / Hobby room / Atelier de bricolage	
Gedeckter Spielplatz / Covered play area / Place de jeu couverte	280 m²
Terrassen / Terraces / Terrasses	

Vertikalverbindungen / Vertical circulation / Circulation verticale

Haupttreppe / Main stairway / Escalier principal	1
Nottreppe / Emergency stairway / Escalier de secours	nein
Personenlift / Elevator / Ascenseur	2
Warenlift / Freight lift / Monte-charge	

Andere Einrichtungen / Additional establishments / Autres aménagements

Situation 1 : 1600
1 Kinderspielplätze / Playgrounds / Terrains de jeu

3-Zimmer-Wohnung Typ B, 1 : 100 / 3-room flat type B / Appartement de 3 pièces type B:
1 Eingang / Entrance / Entrée
2 Wohn-Eßraum / Living-dining room / Séjour, salle à manger
3 Kinderzimmer / Children / Chambre des enfants
4 Elternschlafzimmer / Parents' bedroom / Chambre à coucher des parents
5 Küche / Kitchen / Cuisine
6 Bad / Bath / Bains
7 WC / WC / Toilettes

Normalgeschoß / Typical floor / Etage type:
1 Trockenräume / Drying room / Séchoirs

Photo: Ansicht Hochhaus B / View of the highrise block B / Vue de la maison-tour B

18
Highrise Block
Milan

A. Rosselli,
Studio 'Ponti, Fornaroli, Rosselli', Milan

Erdgeschoß 1:550 / Ground floor / Rez-de-chaussée

A

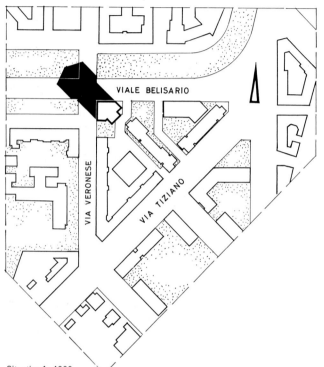

Situation 1 : 4000

1.–17. Geschoß / Floor / Etage

18. Geschoß / Floor / Etage

Modellphoto / Model / Photo de maquette

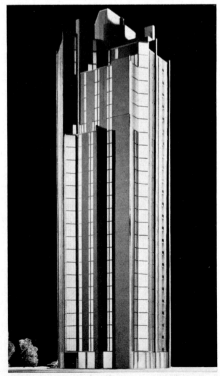

5-Zimmer-Wohnung Typ H, 1 : 200 / 5-room flat type H / Appartement de 5 pièces type H

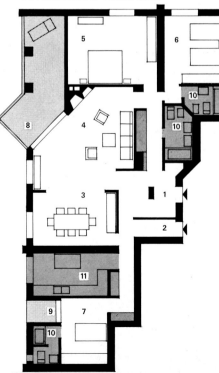

19.–22. Geschoß / Floor / Etage

23. Geschoß / Floor / Etage

24. Geschoß / Floor / Etage

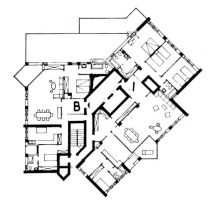

25. Geschoß / Floor / Etage

5-Zimmer-Wohnung Typ H, 1 : 200 / 5-room flat type H / Appartement de 5 pièces type H:

1 Eingang, Garderobe / Entrance, coats / Entrée, garde-robe
2 Service-Eingang / Service entrance / Entrée de service
3 Eßzimmer / Dining room / Salle à manger
4 Wohnraum / Living room / Salle de séjour
5 Elternschlafzimmer / Parents' bedroom / Chambre à coucher des parents
6 Kinderzimmer / Children / Chambre des enfants
7 Dienstenzimmer / Maid's room / Chambre de service
8 Loggia / Covered balcony / Loggia
9 Kleine Loggia, Dienstenzimmer / Small covered balcony, maid's room / Petite loggia, chambre de service
10 Bäder, WC, Dusche / Baths, WC, shower / Salles de bains, toilettes, douche
11 Küche / Kitchen / Cuisine

Wohnungstyp / Apartment type / Type de l'appartement	A	B	C	D	E	F	G	H	I	K
Zimmer pro Wohnung / Rooms per apartment / Chambres par appartement	2	3	4	4	4	5	5	5	6	6
Anzahl Wohnungen / Number of apartments / Nombre d'appartements	1	1	17	17	1	17	1	4	1	4
Aufenthaltsfläche einschließlich Korridore / Living area including corridors / Zone de séjour avec corridors m²	36.1	70.3	64.7	75.8	75.3	90	94.5	93.7	113.7	119.4
Nebenraumfläche / Auxiliary rooms / Pièces auxiliaires m²	5	21.9	21.5	19.5	24.5	23.2	21	22.2	34.4	34.9
Fläche der Wohnung ohne Mauern und Treppenhaus / Area of apartment without walls and stairwell / Surface de l'appartement sans murs ni escaliers m²	41.1	92.2	86.2	95.3	99.8	113	115.5	115.9	148.1	154.3

Aufenthaltsfläche der Wohnung / Living area / Zone de séjour m²

	A	B	C	D	E	F	G	H	I	K
Wohnschlafzimmer / Living and bedroom / Chambre à coucher et de séjour										
Wohnraum / Living room / Séjour					29	25	29.8	29	27.2	29.2
Wohn- und Eßraum / Living and dining room / Séjour et salle à manger	16.2	35	21	25						
Eßraum, Halle / Dining room, hall / Salle à manger, hall					14	11.2	11.2	11.2	14	12
Elternschlafzimmer / Parents' room / Chambre des parents	14	14.8	12.2	13.2	12.5	16.6	18.6	18.6	18	18
Kinderzimmer / Children's room / Chambre d'enfant		7.5	12.2	12	7.5	11	11.5	11.5	12	12
Kinderzimmer / Children's room / Chambre d'enfant									10	10
Andere Räume / Additional rooms / Chambres supplémentaires			5.6	8.4		7.6	7.5	7.5	7.5	11
Interne Verkehrsfläche, Korridore / Internal circulation area, corridors / Circulation interne, corridors	5.9	13	13.7	17.2	12.3	18.7	15.9	15.9	25	27.2
Balkon / Balcony / Balcon										
Loggia		7.2	5.6	6	28	5	20.4	13.8	6.4	6.4

Nebenraumfläche der Wohnung / Auxiliary rooms / Pièces auxiliaires m²

	A	B	C	D	E	F	G	H	I	K
Küche / Kitchen / Cuisine		8.8	8	8	8.8	8.8	8.8	8.8	12	10
Kochnische / Kitchenette / Cuisinette	2									
WC			3.3	3.1		1.2				
Bad, Dusche / Bath, shower / Bain, douche	3	5.9	4	4.6	6.3	4.6	3	4.2	4.3	4.3
Dusche, 2. Bad / Shower, 2nd bath / Douche, 2e bain		3	2.5		3	3	5.5	5.5	5.3	5.3
Einbauschränke / Built-in closets / Placards		4.2	3.7	3.8	6.4	5.6	3.7	3.7	7.8	7.8
Abstellraum in der Wohnung / Storage area in apartment / Débarras dans l'appartement									5	7.5

Allgemeines / General information / Information générale

Baujahr / Year of construction / Année de construction	Projekt
Bauhöhe / Height of building / Hauteur du bâtiment	86 m
Geschoßzahl / Number of stories / Nombre d'étages	26
Anzahl Wohnungen / Number of apartments / Nombre d'appartements	67
Einzelhochhaus / Single highrise building / Maison-tour isolée	ja
Teil einer Gesamtbebauung / Part of a development / Partie d'un grand ensemble	ja
Frei finanzierter Wohnungsbau / Private housing / Construction de logements à financement libre	ja
Sozialer Wohnungsbau / Public housing / Construction de logements à caractère social	nein

Umgebung / Surroundings / Environs

Gesamtfläche des Areals / Total area / Superficie totale de l'aire	
Überbaute Fläche (einschließlich Garagen) / Built-upon area (including garages) / Emprise au sol (y compris les garages)	530 m²
Grünflächen / Garden area / Zones vertes	nein
Spielplatz / Playground / Place de jeu	
Parkplatzfläche / Parking area / Surface des places de stationnement	
Parkplätze / Parking / Places de stationnement	
Garagen / Garages / Garages	
Garagenfläche / Garage area / Surface des garages	

Verschiedene Nutzräume / Utility rooms / Chambres de service

Abstellräume / Storage / Débarras	
Keller / Cellar / Caves	
Velo- und Kinderwagenraum / Bicycles, baby carriages / Bicyclettes, Poussettes	

Aufsicht / Controlled area / Zone contrôlée

Eingangspartie / Entrance area / Entrée	57 m²
Hauswart (Sicht auf Eingang) / Janitor / Concierge	ja

Kinderaufenthalt und Freizeit / Children's recreation and hobby area / Jeux et loisirs

Kindergarten / Nursery / Jardin d'enfants	nein
Spielzimmer / Playroom / Salle de jeu	nein
Bastelraum / Hobby room / Atelier de bricolage	nein
Gedeckter Spielplatz / Covered play area / Place de jeu couverte	
Terrassen / Terraces / Terrasses	nein

Vertikalverbindungen / Vertical circulation / Circulation verticale

Haupttreppe / Main stairway / Escalier principal	1
Nottreppe / Emergency stairway / Escalier de secours	1
Personenlift / Elevator / Ascenseur	2
Warenlift / Freight lift / Monte-charge	1

Andere Einrichtungen / Additional establishments / Autres aménagements

Im Erdgeschoß Büros / Ground floor offices / Au rez-de-chaussée des bureaux

19
Ile verte, Residential Block
Grenoble

R. H. Anger, Puccinelli, Pivot, Junillon
Paris and Grenoble

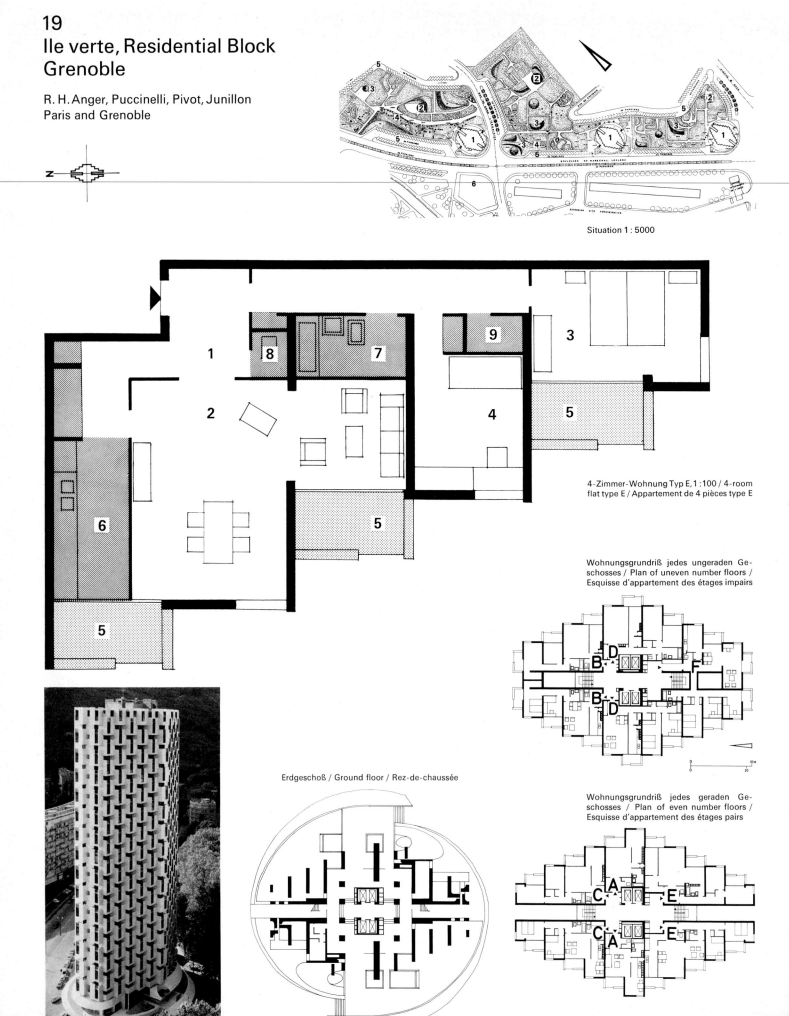

Situation 1 : 5000

4-Zimmer-Wohnung Typ E, 1 : 100 / 4-room
flat type E / Appartement de 4 pièces type E

Wohnungsgrundriß jedes ungeraden Ge-
schosses / Plan of uneven number floors /
Esquisse d'appartement des étages impairs

Erdgeschoß / Ground floor / Rez-de-chaussée

Wohnungsgrundriß jedes geraden Ge-
schosses / Plan of even number floors /
Esquisse d'appartement des étages pairs

176

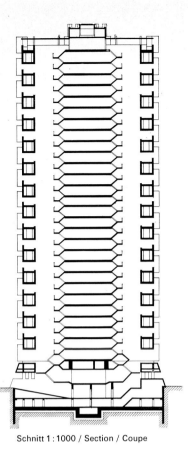

Schnitt 1 : 1000 / Section / Coupe

Wohnungstyp / Apartment type / Type de l'appartement		A	B	C	D	E	F
Zimmer pro Wohnung / Rooms per apartment / Chambres par appartement		2	3	3	3	4	4 ½
Anzahl Wohnungen / Number of apartments / Nombre d'appartements		28	28	28	28	28	14
Aufenthaltsfläche einschließlich Korridore / Living area including corridors / Zone de séjour avec corridors	m²	33.7	57.9	62	65	76.1	94.9
Nebenraumfläche / Auxiliary rooms / Pièces auxiliaires	m²	14.1	18.4	14.1	22.6	24.5	27.6
Fläche der Wohnung ohne Mauern und Treppenhaus / Area of apartment without walls and stairwell / Surface de l'appartement sans murs ni escaliers	m²	47.8	76.3	76.1	87.6	100.6	122.5

Aufenthaltsfläche der Wohnung / Living area / Zone de séjour	m²						
Wohnschlafzimmer / Living and bedroom / Chambre à coucher et de séjour		19.8					
Wohnraum / Living room / Séjour							
Wohn- und Eßraum / Living and dining room / Séjour et salle à manger			24.2	26.9	26.3	9.7	37.2
Eßraum, Halle / Dining room, hall / Salle à manger, hall		8.9				26.1	
Elternschlafzimmer / Parents' room / Chambre des parents			13.5	13.4	17.6	13.4	16.8
Kinderzimmer / Children's room / Chambre d'enfant			10.7	12.7	11.6	12.4	13
Kinderzimmer / Children's room / Chambre d'enfant							10.4
Andere Räume / Additional rooms / Chambres supplémentaires							
Interne Verkehrsfläche, Korridore / Internal circulation area, corridors / Circulation interne, corridors		5	9.5	9	9.5	14.5	17.5
Balkon / Balcony / Balcon		5	15	10	10	15	20
Loggia							

Nebenraumfläche der Wohnung / Auxiliary rooms / Pièces auxiliaires	m²						
Küche / Kitchen / Cuisine		5.7	8.3	5.5	11	13	14
Kochnische / Kitchenette / Cuisinette							
WC		1.2	1.3	1.4	1.2	1.1	1.3
Bad, Dusche / Bath, shower / Bain, douche		5.2	3.7	3.7	4	5	4.9
Dusche, 2. Bad / Shower, 2nd bath / Douche, 2e bain							1.9
Einbauschränke / Built-in closets / Placards		2	1.2	1.9	4.7	3.8	3.9
Abstellraum in der Wohnung / Storage area in apartment / Débarras dans l'appartement			3.9	1.6	1.7	1.6	1.6

Allgemeines / General information / Information générale

Baujahr / Year of construction / Année de construction	1964
Bauhöhe / Height of building / Hauteur du bâtiment	93 m
Geschoßzahl / Number of stories / Nombre d'étages	28
Anzahl Wohnungen / Number of apartments / Nombre d'appartements	154
Einzelhochhaus / Single highrise building / Maison-tour isolée	nein
Teil einer Gesamtbebauung / Part of a development / Partie d'un grand ensemble	ja
Frei finanzierter Wohnungsbau / Private housing / Construction de logements à financement libre	ja
Sozialer Wohnungsbau / Public housing / Construction de logements à caractère social	nein

Umgebung / Surroundings / Environs

Gesamtfläche des Areals / Total area / Superficie totale de l'aire	15 000 m²
Überbaute Fläche (einschließlich Garagen) / Built-upon area (including garages) / Emprise au sol (y compris les garages)	
Grünflächen / Garden area / Zones vertes	o
Spielplatz / Playground / Place de jeu	o
Parkplatzfläche / Parking area / Surface des places de stationnement	
Parkplätze / Parking / Places de stationnement	o
Garagen / Garages / Garages	
Garagenfläche / Garage area / Surface des garages	

Verschiedene Nutzräume / Utility rooms / Chambres de service

Abstellräume / Storage / Débarras	
Keller / Cellar / Caves	
Velo- und Kinderwagenraum / Bicycles, baby carriages / Bicyclettes, Poussettes	84 m²

Aufsicht / Controlled area / Zone contrôlée

Eingangspartie / Entrance area / Entrée	ja
Hauswart (Sicht auf Eingang) / Janitor / Concierge	ja

Kinderaufenthalt und Freizeit / Children's recreation and hobby area / Jeux et loisirs

Kindergarten / Nursery / Jardin d'enfants	nein
Spielzimmer / Playroom / Salle de jeu	nein
Bastelraum / Hobby room / Atelier de bricolage	nein
Gedeckter Spielplatz / Covered play area / Place de jeu couverte	nein
Terrassen / Terraces / Terrasses	663 m²

Vertikalverbindungen / Vertical circulation / Circulation verticale

Haupttreppe / Main stairway / Escalier principal	2
Nottreppe / Emergency stairway / Escalier de secours	
Personenlift / Elevator / Ascenseur	3
Warenlift / Freight lift / Monte-charge	

Andere Einrichtungen / Additional establishments / Autres aménagements

Situation 1 : 5000:
1 Hochhäuser / Highrise blocks / Maisons-tours
2 Bassin / Pool / Bassin
3 Erdbewegungen / Landscaping / Terrain aménagé
4 Bestehende Bäume / Existing trees / Arbres existants
5 Parkplätze / Parking space / Parkings
6 Einkaufszentrum / Shopping centre / Centre d'achats

4-Zimmer-Wohnung Typ E, 1 : 100 / 4-room flat type E / Appartement de 4 pièces type E:
1 Eingang, Garderobe / Entrance, cloaks / Entrée, garde-robe
2 Wohn-Eßraum / Living-dining room / Séjour, salle à manger
3 Elternschlafzimmer / Parents' bedroom / Chambre à coucher des parents
4 Kinderzimmer / Children / Chambre des enfants
5 Balkone / Balconies / Balcons
6 Küche / Kitchen / Cuisine
7 Bad / Bath / Bains
8 WC / WC / Toilettes
9 Abstellraum / Boxroom / Débarras

Photo: Ansicht des Hochhauses / View of the highrise block / Vue de la maison-tour

o = in Gesamtbebauung vorhanden / existing in development / existant dans le grand ensemble

20
Residential Highrise Block
Bietigheim, Baden-Württemberg
Germany

K. Weber and G. Hoffmann, Bietigheim

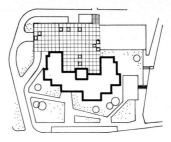

Situation 1 : 2000

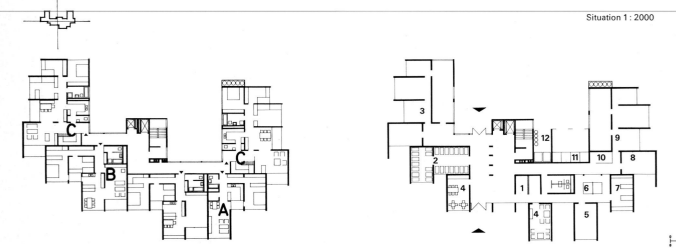

Normalgeschoß / Typical floor / Etage type

Erdgeschoß / Ground floor / Rez-de-chaussée

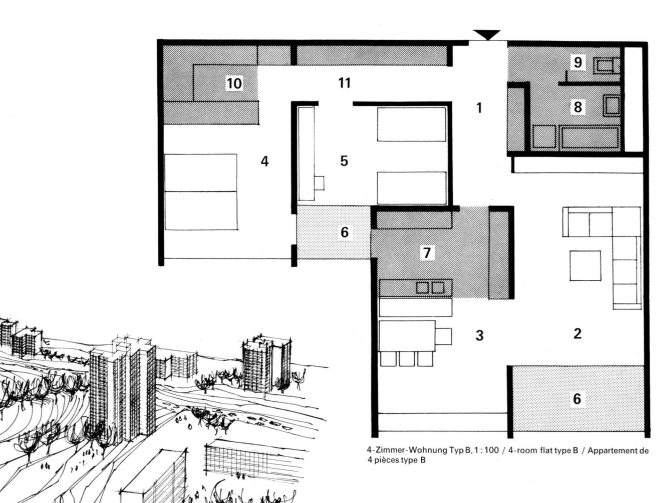

4-Zimmer-Wohnung Typ B, 1 : 100 / 4-room flat type B / Appartement de 4 pièces type B

Perspektive der Gesamtüberbauung / Perspective of total development / Perspective de l'ensemble

Wohnungstyp / Apartment type / Type de l'appartement		A	B	C
Zimmer pro Wohnung / Rooms per apartment / Chambres par appartement		2	4	5
Anzahl Wohnungen / Number of apartments / Nombre d'appartements		17	34	34
Aufenthaltsfläche einschließlich Korridore / Living area including corridors / Zone de séjour avec corridors	m²	49.3	72.2	95.9
Nebenraumfläche / Auxiliary rooms / Pièces auxiliaires	m²	15.4	21.6	23.9
Fläche der Wohnung ohne Mauern und Treppenhaus / Area of apartment without walls and stairwell / Surface de l'appartement sans murs ni escaliers	m²	64.7	93.8	119.8

Aufenthaltsfläche der Wohnung / Living area / Zone de séjour	m²			
Wohnschlafzimmer / Living and bedroom / Chambre à coucher et de séjour				
Wohnraum / Living room / Séjour			19.6	19.6
Wohn- und Eßraum / Living and dining room / Séjour et salle à manger		20.3		
Eßraum, Halle / Dining room, hall / Salle à manger, hall			12.3	15.9
Elternschlafzimmer/Parents' room/Chambre des parents		19.6	14.4	14.4
Kinderzimmer / Children's room / Chambre d'enfant			10.3	16.3
Kinderzimmer / Children's room / Chambre d'enfant				14.4
Andere Räume / Additional rooms / Chambres supplémentaires				
Interne Verkehrsfläche, Korridore / Internal circulation area, corridors / Circulation interne, corridors		9.4	15.9	15.3
Balkon / Balcony / Balcon				
Loggia		3	9.1	11.4

Nebenraumfläche der Wohnung / Auxiliary rooms / Pièces auxiliaires	m²			
Küche / Kitchen / Cuisine		6.3	8.1	8.1
Kochnische / Kitchenette / Cuisinette				
WC			1.5	1.8
Bad, Dusche / Bath, shower / Bain, douche		3.7	4.3	6.3
Dusche, 2. Bad / Shower, 2nd bath / Douche, 2e bain				
Einbauschränke / Built-in closets / Placards		3.2	4	1.3
Abstellraum in der Wohnung / Storage area in apartment / Débarras dans l'appartement		2.2	3.7	6.4

Erdgeschoß / Ground floor / Rez-de-chaussée:
1 Briefkästen / Letterboxes / Boîtes à lettres
2 Kinderwagen / Prams / Poussettes
3 Fahrräder, Mopeds / Bicycles, mopeds / Bicyclettes, bicyclettes à moteur
4 Aufenthaltsraum / Lounge / Salle de séjour
5 Spielzimmer / Playroom / Salle de jeu
6 Tischtennis / Tabletennis / Tennis de table
7 Bastelraum / Hobby room / Salle de bricolage
8 Waschküche / Laundry / Buanderie
9 Trockenräume / Drying / Séchoirs
10 Notstrom / Emergency electricity supply / Alimentation électrique de secours
11 Trafo / Transformer / Transformateur
12 Müllraum / Garbage / Déchets

4-Zimmer-Wohnung Typ B, 1:100 / 4-room flat type B / Appartement de 4 pièces type B:
1 Eingang, Garderobe / Entrance, cloaks / Entrée, garde-robe
2 Wohnraum / Living room / Salle de séjour
3 Eßplatz / Dining area / Coin à manger
4 Elternschlafzimmer / Parents' bedroom / Chambre à coucher des parents
5 Kinderzimmer / Children / Chambre des enfants
6 Loggia / Covered balcony / Loggia
7 Küche / Kitchen / Cuisine
8 Bad / Bath / Bains
9 WC / WC / Toilettes
10 Abstellraum / Boxroom / Débarras
11 Korridor mit Schränken / Corridor with built-in storage / Corridor avec placards

Allgemeines / General information / Information générale

Baujahr / Year of construction / Année de construction	1965/67
Bauhöhe / Height of building / Hauteur du bâtiment	55 m
Geschoßzahl / Number of stories / Nombre d'étages	21
Anzahl Wohnungen / Number of apartments / Nombre d'appartements	85
Einzelhochhaus / Single highrise building / Maison-tour isolée	ja
Teil einer Gesamtbebauung / Part of a development / Partie d'un grand ensemble	ja
Frei finanzierter Wohnungsbau / Private housing / Construction de logements à financement libre	ja
Sozialer Wohnungsbau / Public housing / Construction de logements à caractère social	nein

Umgebung / Surroundings / Environs

Gesamtfläche des Areals / Total area / Superficie totale de l'aire	14 000 m²
Überbaute Fläche (einschließlich Garagen) / Built-upon area (including garages) / Emprise au sol (y compris les garages)	1 620 m²
Grünflächen / Garden area / Zones vertes	11 000 m²
Spielplatz / Playground / Place de jeu	110 m²
Parkplatzfläche / Parking area / Surface des places de stationnement	
Parkplätze / Parking / Places de stationnement	○ 50
Garagen / Garages / Garages	84
Garagenfläche / Garage area / Surface des garages	1 662 m²

Verschiedene Nutzräume / Utility rooms / Chambres de service

Abstellräume / Storage / Débarras	
Keller / Cellar / Caves	1000 m²
Velo- und Kinderwagenraum / Bicycles, baby carriages / Bicyclettes, Poussettes	170 m²

Aufsicht / Controlled area / Zone contrôlée

Eingangspartie / Entrance area / Entrée	77 m²
Hauswart (Sicht auf Eingang) / Janitor / Concierge	nein

Kinderaufenthalt und Freizeit / Children's recreation and hobby area / Jeux et loisirs

Kindergarten / Nursery / Jardin d'enfants	nein
Spielzimmer / Playroom / Salle de jeu	
Bastelraum / Hobby room / Atelier de bricolage	65 m²
Gedeckter Spielplatz / Covered play area / Place de jeu couverte	
Terrassen / Terraces / Terrasses	nein

Vertikalverbindungen / Vertical circulation / Circulation verticale

Haupttreppe / Main stairway / Escalier principal	1
Nottreppe / Emergency stairway / Escalier de secours	1
Personenlift / Elevator / Ascenseur	2
Warenlift / Freight lift / Monte-charge	

Andere Einrichtungen / Additional establishments / Autres aménagements

Im Erdgeschoß in der Ausführung Bürofläche / Ground floor executed as office space / Au rez-de-chaussée des surfaces de bureaux en cours d'exécution

○ = in Gesamtbebauung vorhanden / existing in development / existant dans le grand ensemble

Highrise Block
Schönbühl, Lucerne

Highrise Block: Alvar Aalto, Helsinki
Supervision: K. Fleig, Zurich
Shopping Centre: Prof. A. Roth, Zurich
Local construction office: M. Wandeler, Lucerne

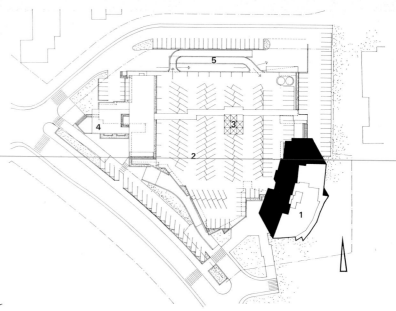

Situation Hochhaus und Einkaufszentrum 1:2000 / Site, highrise block and shopping centre / Situation maison-tour et centre commercial

Erdgeschoß / Ground floor / Rez-de-chaussée

Normalgeschoß / Typical floor / Etage type

Dachgeschoß mit 8-Zimmer-Wohnung / Top floor with 8-room flat / Dernier étage avec appartement de 8 pièces

2-Zimmer-Wohnung Typ C, 1:100 / 2-room flat type C / Appartement de 2 pièces type C

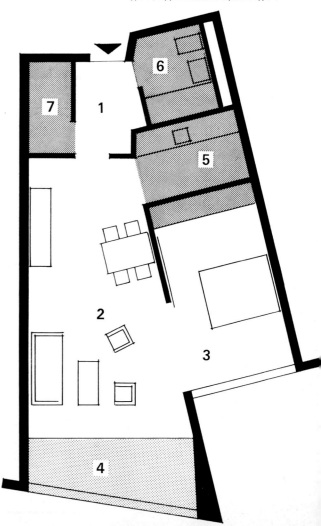

Wohnungstyp / Apartment type / Type de l'appartement		A	B	C	D	E	F	G
Zimmer pro Wohnung / Rooms per apartment / Chambres par appartement		1	1	2	3 ½	3 ½	5	8
Anzahl Wohnungen / Number of apartments / Nombre d'appartements		14	14	14	14	14	13	1
Aufenthaltsfläche einschließlich Korridore / Living area including corridors / Zone de séjour avec corridors	m²	26.5	28	37	73.5	78.5	120.5	395.6
Nebenraumfläche / Auxiliary rooms / Pièces auxiliaires	m²	10.5	10	12	18.1	19.3	19.5	51.2
Fläche der Wohnung ohne Mauern und Treppenhaus / Area of apartment without walls and stairwell / Surface de l'appartement sans murs ni escaliers	m²	37	38	49	91.6	97.8	140	446.8
Aufenthaltsfläche der Wohnung / Living area / Zone de séjour	m²							
Wohnschlafzimmer / Living and bedroom / Chambre à coucher et de séjour		26.5	28					
Wohnraum / Living room / Séjour							48	66.7
Wohn- und Eßraum / Living and dining room / Séjour et salle à manger				23	30.5	36		
Eßraum, Halle / Dining room, hall / Salle à manger, hall							14	28.5
Elternschlafzimmer/Parents' room/Chambre des parents				14	17.5	16.5	16	37.9
Kinderzimmer / Children's room / Chambre d'enfant					15	13	16	35
Kinderzimmer / Children's room / Chambre d'enfant							12	30
Andere Räume / Additional rooms / Chambres supplémentaires								101.7
Interne Verkehrsfläche, Korridore / Internal circulation area, corridors / Circulation interne, corridors					10.5	13	14.5	97
Balkon / Balcony / Balcon								
Loggia		3	3	6.5	8	9.5	19	136.7
Nebenraumfläche der Wohnung / Auxiliary rooms / Pièces auxiliaires	m²							
Küche / Kitchen / Cuisine					9.1	10	10	15
Kochnische / Kitchenette / Cuisinette		3.5	3.5	5				
WC					2	2	2	5.1
Bad, Dusche / Bath, shower / Bain, douche		4	4	4.5	4.5	4.3	4.5	17.9
Dusche, 2. Bad / Shower, 2nd bath / Douche, 2e bain								4
Einbauschränke / Built-in closets / Placards								16.7
Abstellraum in der Wohnung / Storage area in apartment / Débarras dans l'appartement		3	2.5	2.5	2.5	3	3	6.5

Situation Hochhaus und Einkaufszentrum 1:2000 / Site, highrise block and shopping centre / Situation maison-tour et centre commercial:

1 Hochhaus / Highrise block / Maison-tour
2 Dachparkierung (darunter Ladenzentrum) / Roof parking (shopping underneath) / Parkings sur le toit (en dessous centre commercial)
3 Vertikale Verbindung von der Dach- und Kellerparkierung zur Piazza, einer 2 geschossigen Halle mit Cafeteria am Kreuzpunkt der zwei Ladenstraßen / Vertical connection between roof and cellar parking with the Piazza, a 2-storey hall with cafeteria at the intersection of two shopping streets / Liaison verticale des parkings sur le toit et souterrains avec la piazza, halle sur deux niveaux avec cafétéria à la jonction des deux rues commerçantes
4 1. Geschoß Büros / First floor offices / 1er étage bureaux
2. Geschoß Zimmer für Ladenangestellte / Second floor staff rooms / 2e étage chambres pour employés des magasins
5 Ein- und Ausfahrtsrampen / Entrance and exit ramps / Rampes d'entrée et de sortie

Erdgeschoß / Ground floor / Rez-de-chaussée:
1 Eingangshalle / Entrance hall / Hall d'entrée
2 Eingang und Garderobe, Restaurant / Entrance and cloakroom, restaurant / Entrée et garde-robe, restaurant
3 Restaurant, Stübli / Restaurant, side rooms / Restaurant, petites salles
4 Küche / Kitchen / Cuisine
5 Büro / Office / Bureau
6 Fahrräder / Bicycles / Bicyclettes
7 Kinderwagen / Prams / Poussettes
8 Stuhlmagazin / Storage for chairs / Dépôt de chaises
9 Müll-Lift / Garbage shute / Vide-ordures

2-Zimmer-Wohnung Typ C, 1:100 / 2-room flat type C / Appartement de 2 pièces type C:
1 Eingang, Garderobe / Entrance, cloaks / Entrée, garde-robe
2 Wohn-Eßraum / Living-dining room / Séjour, salle à manger
3 Schlafzimmer / Bedroom / Chambre à coucher
4 Loggia / Covered balcony / Loggia
5 Küche / Kitchen / Cuisine
6 Bad / Bath / Bains
7 Abstellraum / Boxroom / Débarras

Modellphoto: Hochhaus mit Ladenzentrum / Model: highrise block with shopping centre / Photo de maquette: maison-tour et centre commercial

Allgemeines / General information / Information générale

Baujahr / Year of construction / Année de construction	1967
Bauhöhe / Height of building / Hauteur du bâtiment	49 m
Geschoßzahl / Number of stories / Nombre d'étages	15
Anzahl Wohnungen / Number of apartments / Nombre d'appartements	84
Einzelhochhaus / Single highrise building / Maison-tour isolée	ja
Teil einer Gesamtbebauung / Part of a development / Partie d'un grand ensemble	ja
Frei finanzierter Wohnungsbau / Private housing / Construction de logements à financement libre	ja
Sozialer Wohnungsbau / Public housing / Construction de logements à caractère social	nein

Umgebung / Surroundings / Environs

Gesamtfläche des Areals / Total area / Superficie totale de l'aire		14 000 m²
Überbaute Fläche (einschließlich Garagen) / Built-upon area (including garages) / Emprise au sol (y compris les garages)		6 800 m²
Grünflächen / Garden area / Zones vertes		1 800 m²
Spielplatz / Playground / Place de jeu		ja
Parkplatzfläche / Parking area / Surface des places de stationnement	o	6 400 m²
Parkplätze / Parking / Places de stationnement	o	230 m²
Garagen / Garages / Garages	o	100
Garagenfläche / Garage area / Surface des garages	o	2 600 m²

Verschiedene Nutzräume / Utility rooms / Chambres de service

Abstellräume / Storage / Débarras	
Keller / Cellar / Caves	250 m²
Velo- und Kinderwagenraum / Bicycles, baby carriages / Bicyclettes, Poussettes	50 m²

Aufsicht / Controlled area / Zone contrôlée

Eingangspartie / Entrance area / Entrée	90 m²
Hauswart (Sicht auf Eingang) / Janitor / Concierge	ja

Kinderaufenthalt und Freizeit / Children's recreation and hobby area / Jeux et loisirs

Kindergarten / Nursery / Jardin d'enfants	nein
Spielzimmer / Playroom / Salle de jeu	nein
Bastelraum / Hobby room / Atelier de bricolage	nein
Gedeckter Spielplatz / Covered play area / Place de jeu couverte	nein
Terrassen / Terraces / Terrasses	nein

Vertikalverbindungen / Vertical circulation / Circulation verticale

Haupttreppe / Main stairway / Escalier principal	1
Nottreppe / Emergency stairway / Escalier de secours	1
Personenlift / Elevator / Ascenseur	1
Warenlift / Freight lift / Monte-charge	1

Andere Einrichtungen / Additional establishments / Autres aménagements

Im EG Restaurant mit Bestuhlung im Freien, Zwischengeschoß und 1. OG 11 Personalzimmer mit Aufenthaltsraum, Teeküche usw., EG direkte Verbindung mit Ladenzentrum / In the ground floor restaurant with tables in the open air. Mezzanine and first floor, 11 rooms for personnel with recreation room and kitchenette, etc. Ground floor direct connection to shopping / Au rez-de-chaussée restaurant avec aménagement en plein air. Entresol et premier étage 11 chambres pour le personnel avec salle de séjour, cuisinette, etc. Rez-de-chaussée liaison directe avec le centre commercial

o = in Gesamtbebauung vorhanden / existing in development / existant dans le grand ensemble

Grünegg AG, Highrise Block
St.Gall, Switzerland

Hch. Graf, St. Gall

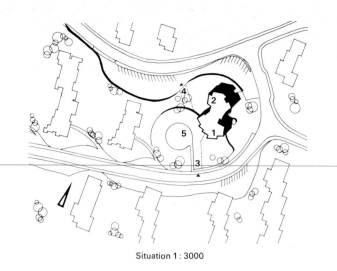

Situation 1 : 3000

Erdgeschoß / Ground floor / Rez-de-chaussée

Normalgeschoß / Typical floor / Etage type

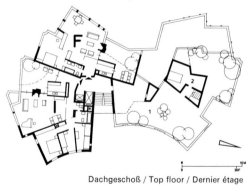

Dachgeschoß / Top floor / Dernier étage

Modellphoto / Model / Photo de maquette

3-Zimmer-Wohnung Typ E, 1 : 100 / 3-room flat type E / Appartement de 3 pièces type E

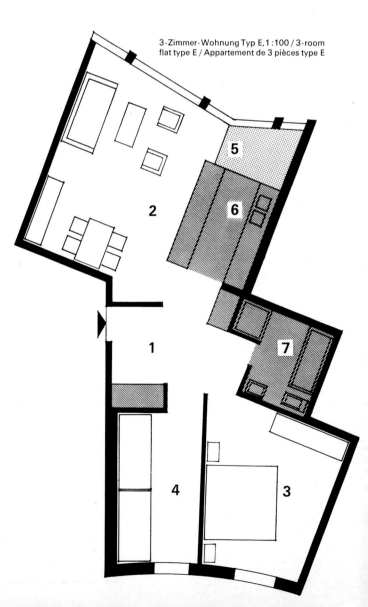

Wohnungstyp / Apartment type / Type de l'appartement		A	B	C	D	E	F	G	H	I
Zimmer pro Wohnung / Rooms per apartment / Chambres par appartement		1	1	2	2½	3	2½	4½	4½	4½
Anzahl Wohnungen / Number of apartments / Nombre d'appartements		9	9	9	9	9	1	9	9	1
Aufenthaltsfläche einschließlich Korridore / Living area including corridors / Zone de séjour avec corridors	m²	23.6	21.7	47.2	59.8	58.6	65.6	68.7	77.7	98.5
Nebenraumfläche / Auxiliary rooms / Pièces auxiliaires	m²	6.1	5.8	9.6	12.9	8.8	13	15.5	13.9	15.5
Fläche der Wohnung ohne Mauern und Treppenhaus / Area of apartment without walls and stairwell / Surface de l'appartement sans murs ni escaliers	m²	29.7	27.5	56.8	72.7	67.4	78.6	84.2	91.6	114

Aufenthaltsfläche der Wohnung / Living area / Zone de séjour m²

	A	B	C	D	E	F	G	H	I
Wohnschlafzimmer / Living and bedroom / Chambre à coucher et de séjour	20.2	17.9							
Wohnraum / Living room / Séjour							17.6	28	
Wohn- und Eßraum / Living and dining room / Séjour et salle à manger			21.1	33.4	23.4	45			42.1
Eßraum, Halle / Dining room, hall / Salle à manger, hall							14.8	7	
Elternschlafzimmer/Parents' room/Chambre des parents			17.8	18.2	15.9	14.6	16.7	18.8	18.8
Kinderzimmer / Children's room / Chambre d'enfant				9.3			8.8	11	11
Kinderzimmer / Children's room / Chambre d'enfant							10.8	10.6	10.6
Andere Räume / Additional rooms / Chambres supplémentaires									
Interne Verkehrsfläche, Korridore / Internal circulation area, corridors / Circulation interne, corridors	3.4	3.8	8.3	8.2	10	6		10.3	16
Balkon / Balcony / Balcon									
Loggia		4.2	5.1	7.2	3.5	25	4.8	3.7	24.3

Nebenraumfläche der Wohnung / Auxiliary rooms / Pièces auxiliaires m²

	A	B	C	D	E	F	G	H	I
Küche / Kitchen / Cuisine			4.4	6.4	5	5.8	6.2	5.7	6.7
Kochnische / Kitchenette / Cuisinette	1.5	1.1							
WC							2	1.8	3.1	3.1
Bad, Dusche / Bath, shower / Bain, douche	3.6	3.8	4.3	4.1	3.1	3.9	4.7	4.1	4.1
Dusche, 2. Bad / Shower, 2nd bath / Douche, 2e bain									
Einbauschränke / Built-in closets / Placards	1	0.9	0.9	2.4	0.7	1.3	2.8	1	1.6
Abstellraum in der Wohnung / Storage area in apartment / Débarras dans l'appartement									

Allgemeines / General information / Information générale

Baujahr / Year of construction / Année de construction	1967/68
Bauhöhe / Height of building / Hauteur du bâtiment	32 m
Geschoßzahl / Number of stories / Nombre d'étages	11
Anzahl Wohnungen / Number of apartments / Nombre d'appartements	65
Einzelhochhaus / Single highrise building / Maison-tour isolée	ja
Teil einer Gesamtbebauung / Part of a development / Partie d'un grand ensemble	ja
Frei finanzierter Wohnungsbau / Private housing / Construction de logements à financement libre	nein
Sozialer Wohnungsbau / Public housing / Construction de logements à caractère social	ja

Umgebung / Surroundings / Environs

Gesamtfläche des Areals / Total area / Superficie totale de l'aire	6 045 m²
Überbaute Fläche (einschließlich Garagen) / Built-upon area (including garages) / Emprise au sol (y compris les garages)	2 200 m²
Grünflächen / Garden area / Zones vertes	4 000 m²
Spielplatz / Playground / Place de jeu	360 m²
Parkplatzfläche / Parking area / Surface des places de stationnement	200 m²
Parkplätze / Parking / Places de stationnement	15
Garagen / Garages / Garages	100
Garagenfläche / Garage area / Surface des garages	3 200 m²

Verschiedene Nutzräume / Utility rooms / Chambres de service

Abstellräume / Storage / Débarras	250 m²
Keller / Cellar / Caves	330 m²
Velo- und Kinderwagenraum / Bicycles, baby carriages / Bicyclettes, Poussettes	120 m²

Aufsicht / Controlled area / Zone contrôlée

Eingangspartie / Entrance area / Entrée	85 m²
Hauswart (Sicht auf Eingang) / Janitor / Concierge	nein

Kinderaufenthalt und Freizeit / Children's recreation and hobby area / Jeux et loisirs

Kindergarten / Nursery / Jardin d'enfants	nein
Spielzimmer / Playroom / Salle de jeu	
Bastelraum / Hobby room / Atelier de bricolage	25 m²
Gedeckter Spielplatz / Covered play area / Place de jeu couverte	nein
Terrassen / Terraces / Terrasses	145 m²

Vertikalverbindungen / Vertical circulation / Circulation verticale

Haupttreppe / Main stairway / Escalier principal	2
Nottreppe / Emergency stairway / Escalier de secours	
Personenlift / Elevator / Ascenseur	2
Warenlift / Freight lift / Monte-charge	1

Andere Einrichtungen / Additional establishments / Autres aménagements

Im EG Restaurant 150 m² und Läden / On the ground floor, restaurant of 180 sq.yd and shops / Au rez-de-chaussée restaurant 150 m² et magasins

Situation 1 : 3000:
1 Hochhaus / Highrise block / Maison-tour
2 Restaurant
3 Einfahrt / Drive entrance / Entrée
4 Ausfahrt / Drive exit / Sortie
5 Kinderspielplatz / Playground / Terrains de jeu

Erdgeschoß / Ground floor / Rez-de-chaussée:
1 Eingangshalle / Entrance / Hall d'entrée
2 Briefkästen / Letterboxes / Boîtes à lettres
3 Restaurant
4 Küche / Kitchen / Cuisine
5 Laden / Shop / Magasin

Dachgeschoß / Top floor / Dernier étage:
1 Dachterrasse / Roof-garden / Terrasse sur le toit
2 Lüftung, Lift / Ventilation, lift / Aération, ascenseur

3-Zimmer-Wohnung Typ E, 1:100 / 3-room flat type E / Appartement de 3 pièces type E:
1 Eingang, Garderobe / Entrance, cloaks / Entrée, garde-robe
2 Wohn-Eßraum / Living-dining room / Séjour, salle à manger
3 Elternschlafzimmer / Parents' bedroom / Chambre à coucher des parents
4 Kinderzimmer / Children / Chambre des enfants
5 Loggia / Covered balcony / Loggia
6 Küche / Kitchen / Cuisine
7 Bad / Bath / Bains

Tabelle der Durchschnittswerte
Graphic Synopsis of average floor areas
Tableau récapitulatif des valeurs moyennes

5.5-6.7 Minimum-Maximum
6.1 2 Durchschnittswerte und Beispiele / Average values and examples / Moyennes et exemples

	1 Zimmer Room Pièce	**2** Zimmer Rooms Pièces	**3** Zimmer Rooms Pièces	**4** Zimmer Rooms Pièces	**5** Zimmer Rooms Pièces
Beispiele / Examples / Exemples	7	17	21	14	9
Wohnraum / Living room / Séjour		17.4–21.3 **19.2** 4	18.0–22.6 **19.7** 3	9.7–28.0 **18.0** 5	19.6–48.0 **29.1** 4
Eßraum, Halle / Dining room, hall / Salle à manger, hall	5.5–6.7 **6.1** 2	4.7–16.8 **9.0** 4	5.5–16.8 **10.4** 3	6.4–26.1 **14.1** 5	11.2–17.7 **14.7** 4
Wohn- und Eßraum / Living and dining room / Séjour et salle à manger	17.8–26.5 **21.7** 7	15.0–33.4 **21.5** 13	15.2–42.4 **24.8** 18	20.1–42.9 **29.9** 9	21.8–42.9 **28.5** 5
Elternschlafzimmer / Parents' room / Chambre des parents		10.5–21.3 **14.7** 16	10.0–21.3 **15.2** 21	12.0–28.0 **16.5** 14	14.4–18.9 **15.9** 9
Kinderzimmer / Children's room / Chambre d'enfant			7.5–17.2 **11.5** 21	9.4–19.6 **13.1** 14	8.9–16.3 **12.8** 9
Kinderzimmer / Children's room / Chambre d'enfant				9.7–12.4 **10.6** 9	8.0–14.4 **11.0** 8
Interne Verkehrsfläche, Korridore / Internal circulation area, corridors / Circulation interne, corridors	1.8–5.0 **33.0** 5	2.1–9.4 **5.6** 15	1.9–16.9 **9.5** 21	2.8–17.2 **12.5** 14	4.8–18.0 **13.6** 9
Balkon / Balcony / Balcon		4.2–16.5 **9.0** 5	4.2–29.2 **15.7** 7	6.0–34.3 **22.0** 7	9.4–34.0 **23.9** 6
Loggia	3.0–5.5 **4.3** 2	3.0–14.6 **7.2** 8	3.5–17.7 **7.4** 12	7.5–34.3 **7.1** 6	11.4–19.0 **14.6** 4
Küche / Kitchen / Cuisine	3.8–6.6 **3.3** 3	4.0–6.5 **5.7** 15	4.8–12.7 **7.4** 22	5.5–13.0 **8.1** 14	5.6–12.2 **8.1** 9
Bad, Dusche / Bath, shower / Bain, douche	3.6–4.0 **3.8** 7	2.7–5.2 **3.8** 17	2.7–5.6 **3.8** 21	3.2–6.7 **4.4** 13	3.2–6.3 **4.2** 9
Einbauschränke / Built-in closets / Placards	1.0–1.1 **1.0** 3	0.4–2.5 **1.6** 10	0.7–4.7 **1.9** 17	0.3–3.8 **2.0** 11	0.3–3.7 **2.1** 8
Abstellraum in der Wohnung / Storage area in the apartment / Débarras dans l'appartement	2.0–3.0 **2.5** 2	1.0–2.5 **2.4** 6	1.4–4.0 **2.4** 9	1.4–3.8 **2.8** 8	2.2–6.4 **3.6** 4
Aufenthaltsfläche einschließlich Korridore / Living area including corridors / Zone de séjour avec corridors	22.8–30.3 **25.8** 7	31.8–59.8 **42.7** 17	40.5–81.4 **61.9** 21	55.4–105.2 **81.3** 14	81.4–120.5 **96.0** 9
Pro Zimmer / Per room / Par pièce		21.4	21.3	20.3	19.2
Nebenraumfläche / Auxiliary rooms / Pièces auxiliaires	5.2–12.6 **8.7** 7	5.0–15.4 **11.3** 17	8.8–22.6 **14.7** 21	10.9–24.5 **17.6** 14	13.5–23.9 **18.0** 9
Pro Zimmer / Per room / Par pièce		5.6	4.9	4.4	3.6
Fläche der Wohnung ohne Mauern und Treppenhaus / Area of the apartment without walls and stairwell / Surface de l'appartement sans murs ni escaliers	29.4–40.7 **34.5** 7	41.1–72.7 **54.0** 17	53.5–102.5 **76.6** 21	69.8–128.3 **98.9** 14	96.7–190.0 **114.0** 9
pro Zimmer / Per room / Par pièce		27.0	25.5	24.7	22.8

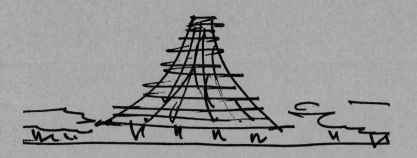

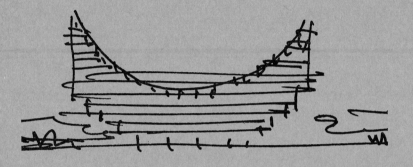

Thoughts on Future
Development

Otto Glaus

As highrise building is more expensive than traditional building, it would be reasonable to assume that, for financial reasons alone, such buildings might remain few and far between and that even in the future, they may remain an arbitrary demonstration of superfluous resources. This is a highly significant question for town-planners.

My query is this: may not highrise building, on the contrary, become an inevitable necessity in urban development? This assumption is based on a variety of reasons.

In 1830 the population of the world was estimated at one billion. Today's figure is three billion, for the year 2000 it is six billion, and that will increase to a minimum of twelve billion by

Funnel landscape

the year 2050. These figures, in the nature of all prognoses for the future, vary with every research programme, but I think it incumbent upon us to examine all possible developments. Little Switzerland, for instance, with five million inhabitants today, will have twenty million by 2070, that is in a hundred years' time. Zurich, its largest city, with a population of 450,000 today, will be a city of two to two and a half million. Many towns and villages will grow in similar proportion, although the greatest population mass will inhabit Switzerland's central regions.

The recently much-discussed linear city will stretch from Geneva across Lausanne, Berne and Zurich as far as St. Gallen and house approximately ten to fifteen million people. Conditions like these will arise in all industrial countries of the West, and indeed already exist to some extent in Germany, Holland, England and the United States.

Before the Second World War, several nations were anxious about the then-falling birthrate. Today, the threat of over-population is hanging over the entire world. The causes are sufficiently well-known. Neither conflict nor crisis can affect the position to any large extent. Whether the world population figure reaches the twelve or even the twenty billion mark fifty years sooner or later, we must not postpone our planning or research.

In the early nineteenth century, social thinking was left to a

Towerscape

few pioneers and idealists. Today, it is the concern of all mankind. Jean Fourastié calls our society 'la société de l'homme moyen riche'. The rest of the world is reaching this status more rapidly than anyone could have thought possible even a few years ago. The living standards of the socially well-placed citizen of the world is high, and becomes the standard by which we must plan.

Planners, architects, sociologists and politicians will soon have to ask themselves if they are in a position to build cities fit for men. In most of the European cities, there are from 270 to 325 square feet of housing space available for each citizen. In many Asiatic cities, this figure drops to 32 to 64 square feet. Soon there will be more urban building than there have ever existed before, producing conditions that will make

The old town flows into the country

international collaboration and the co-ordination of research imperative. Teilhard de Chardin says, in his *Vision of the Future,* that if mankind is not to perish, it must join together in a world-wide community and a universal culture.

The growing human avalanche will cover for the most part valuable arable land with a flood of housing. However, this need not be accepted as an inevitable fate if we plan correctly and in time. If we intend to preserve large agricultural areas, our cities must have clearly defined approaches and boundaries. We know that nature as well as the city is in peril. Today's problems are so complicated that well thought-out, co-ordinated and legally binding large-scale planning has become a necessity in most countries of the world. The continuous population increase, the requisitioning of the countryside by indus-

try and technology and the requirements of the millions who wish to live in cities could, in due course, produce the era of the megalopolis in all reality.

Modern society is in existence, but its adequate living space is far from assured. Jean Fourastié asks if 'l'homme riche' of today's democratic society will not be a very poor man in the future. Poor because of his subconsciously insatiable demands which must in the end create a vicious circle. We are witness to a paradox today: man has reached the pinnacle of affluence and personal freedom on the one hand, but on the other, his individual freedom is menaced by overcrowding and its consequences.

Sociologists predict even more personal freedom in ten to fifteen years to come, when the maximum time to be spent at

"L'homme moyen riche"

work will be thirty hours a week. How and where is the city-dweller to spend his leisure? What will the future definition of leisure be? What will be the consequences? These and similar questions occupy town-planners today.

Today's society is pluralist, therefore heterogenous, and this is the society for which we must plan. Even so, questionable calculations have been made according to which each individual, building his individual house, would still leave sufficient land-reserves available. Of all generations, ours cannot accept a statement where theory and practice lie so very far apart. All of us have witnessed the effect of this kind of building on our landscape and ourselves. We have experienced the loss of our countryside on the one hand and the boredom of our un-urban cities on the other.

When all is said and done, and if towns are not to flood and drown the country, if cities are to be truly cities, then in my opinion the answer lies in 'highrise towns'. By this I mean that highrise building must be put to use as a normal, highly valuable, integrated element in urban building. Highrise building allows us to achieve density when and where we wish. By mixing tall, medium-high and low buildings, slabs and towers, as well as the other highrise shapes that are beginning to make their appearance everywhere, new and truly urban housing-estates and centres will be created. Highrise building as an integral part of town-planning provides the much-needed opportunity for the large-scale creation of open space, while keeping down the collective cost. Owing to their concentration, road and access construction as well as other service installations are considerably cheaper in highrise areas than in zones of ordinary, more expansive building. These are proven facts. The public exchequer stands to profit by this situation and the furthering of this form of development is therefore directly in its interest.

Curiously, it is repeatedly suggested that town-dwellers would

The city-scape of the future

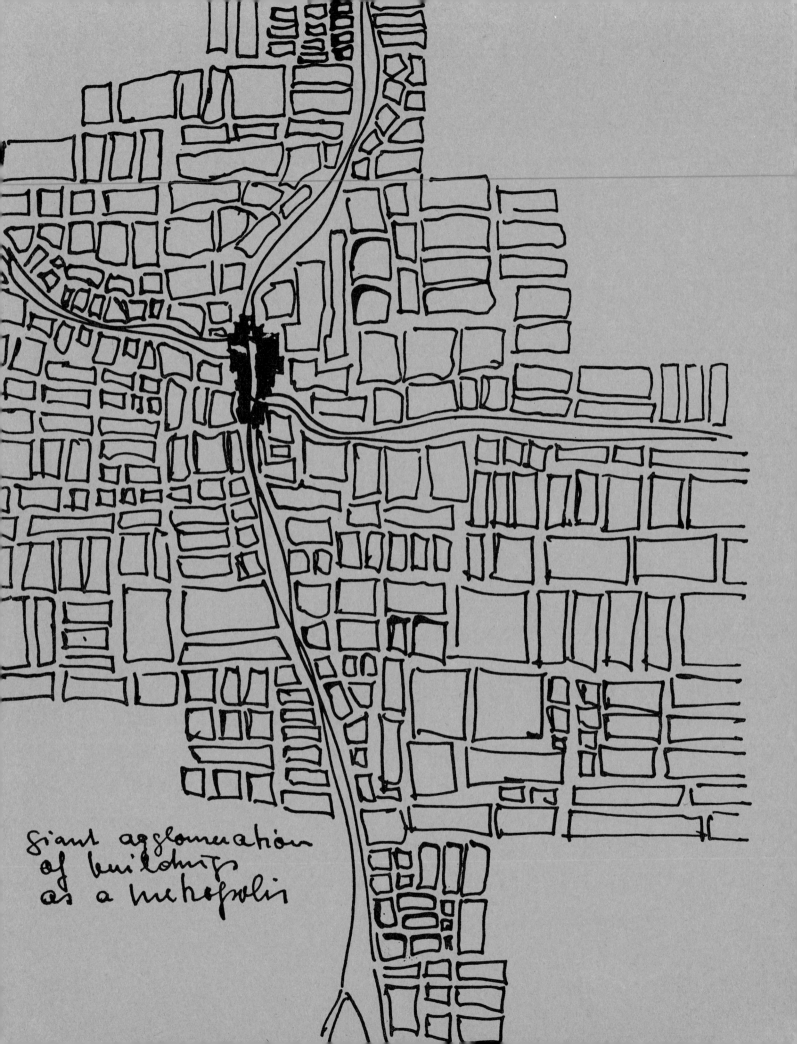

giant agglomeration
of buildings
as a metropolis

prefer to live in rural, rather than urban, surroundings. This statement is in itself rather paradoxical, as city people are by definition not country folk. To a large extent, though, to-day's city population has grown up in the country, and in our town-agglomerations the true 'urbanite' is often in the min-ority. True 'urbanites' are only those of the second or third gen-eration. We may, however, assume that neither our 'urbanites' nor our cities are the real thing. We should remember that with few exceptions our so-called modern cities are nothing but lumbering, giant agglomerations of buildings that have col-lected around a small city-core on which they feed. The orig-inal but truly urban cities were, until recently, sufficiently strong to fulfil their task, but now, slowly but surely, they are being smothered, split at the seams or otherwise invalidated.

Our new city giants consist of new areas attached to an old city-unit. Since these areas have now become multiple repro-ductions of the original, they in turn, formless and sprawling as they are, produce a new kind of urbanity with which we have to come to terms. There is no historical parallel that might serve for guidance.

Very probably, our future cities will have to be entities consist-ing of various independent units that will, by their over all order, form a viable organism. We need, however, not only self-contained cities, but largely independent city-districts, each with its own characteristic, appropriately modern atmosphere. What makes ancient or medieval cities so very attractive? Not only the romance that we read into them, but also the extra-ordinary conviction of their urban character and the real, though often discordant interplay of all the different urban features. Cities have never been purely rational creations, but have been imaginative also and, above all, monumental. There is little sign of the monumental in urban design today. Monu-mentality is proof of creative daring. Cities demand such daring. If we may assume that there is still today plenty of talent and

"mandala" of a
high-rise city

imagination about, then it must be the reign of the functional which stands in the way of our cities. However, it is not simply the much-discussed human scale that is missing from our town-agglomerations; there is no proper relationship of any kind at all. No relation between town centres and residential districts; residential districts and individual residents; the individual and his surroundings and above all to the urban entity. Highrise districts offer better facilities for the forming of human relationships, major or minor, than any other urban form. Their size and the distance between buildings alone guarantee pri-

vacy, yet no other form of housing is so well-equipped to create opportunities for easy human contact by providing public rooms, playing fields, clubs, shops, etc. Families as well as individuals are drawn into a larger whole. The proper highrise district helps the small craftsman and tradesman as well as all the other service industries. The diverse needs of a pluralist society demand these services close at hand, just as other societies have done before. No urban society can be fully viable without them.

Spatial relationship between buildings can be achieved by highrise building more successfully than with any other building type, by staggering, building less or more densely, etc. It is a great mistake to think of highrise districts as a collection of giant skyscrapers and mammoth buildings. Gigantism has nothing to do with highrise building, indeed it is the very thing to be avoided. If, up to now, higrise buildings have been deplorably ill-related, the fault lies largely with the authorities who allowed this to happen. More must be demanded of architects and private enterprise. It is a question of design. Business interests must not be allowed a free hand, nor architecture left

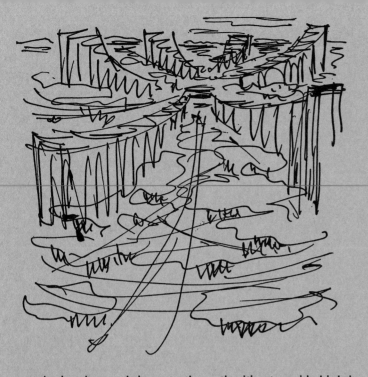

Star town

to take its chance. It is up to the authorities to guide highrise building in the proper spirit, and lead it onto the right lines.

It is surely a mistake to assume that the modern city-dweller has no use for the city or highrise building. Why then do people not remain in the country? Industry would only be too delighted to move out of towns. The contrary is true. The city-dweller wants the true city. Only we will have to build it for him. The magic and magnetism of the city has remained fundamentally the same since antiquity. The human being looking to the city for social amenities and crowds as well as for personal freedom has not changed over the years. Only the demands that society makes have altered: 'la société de l'homme moyen riche' now demands convenience, air, light, open spaces and, above all, comfort. These are genuine demands. Nothing impossible is asked of urban design. The great difficulty lies solely in the sheer size.

About two thousand years ago there lived more than a million people in a minuscule area within the walls of Rome, crowded into narrow twelve-storey tenement buildings. Conditions were similar in Constantinople and other cities of the ancient world. They can still be found today in the desert cities of Hadramout and the Yemen. They signify that people are looking for two things: security and the chance to participate in the glory of the Forum. Security is now replaced by convenience, and feudal pomp by the modern democratic orgy of entertainment. Admittedly, society has altered in form and makes more varied demands. But only the city can cater for exactly that. The centripetal town, as we know, cannot properly fulfil this function.

When towns, according to their size, have been divided into separate city centres, each with its own function, then the individual will be able to enter into some relationship with the town centre. Private and public traffic could then be more or less dealt with; the massive investments in open-air and under-cover parking only ruin our most beautiful districts. This situation is slowly beginning to be recognized. But in my opinion,

Hill town

a complete ban on private traffic in our town centres cannot be regarded as a solution appropriate to our society and way of life. Town-planners, on the other hand, fear that any partitioning-off might devalue their town centres, although they are even now in danger of being choked. Had our gigantic suburbs been planned as urban units, we should be in a different position now. No problem will be solved by scattering highrise buildings among existing buildings as though by chance; nor is there proof that town centres can only be viable in a townscape of millions, when all those people stream towards so small an area, as is the case with every larger city.

Man's inborn desire to live among others and to be close to the source of events does not demand such an over-exaggerated massing of humanity in the town centres. None of us doubts the urban reality of the small country town and its centre. Yet normal weekdays are quiet there and in the evenings the streets are almost deserted. A town's true urbanity does not consist only of business activity, noise and constant bustle.

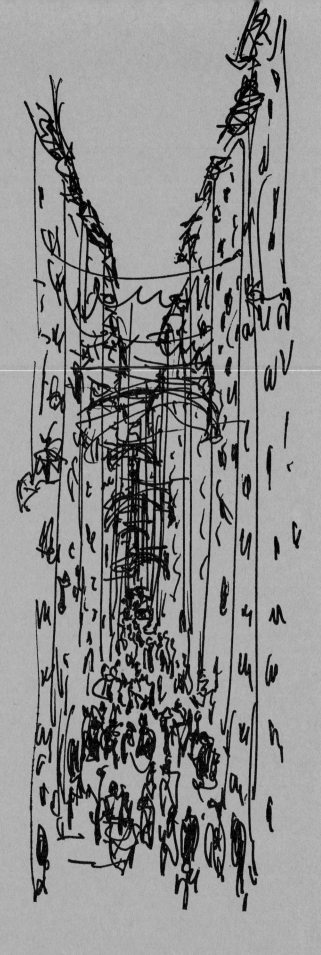

ancient
high-rise towns

The democratic metropolis

The urban entity has an ideological as well as a physical quality. City-dwellers should feel pride in their status and be able to love their towns. They should live as closely as possible to active and attractive city centres and take part in the communal life. Highrise districts, parking facilities, pedestrian links to the centre and many other important amenities will restore these possibilities. Coming from the outside, the city-inhabitant should be able to drive his car right up to his home. To the town centre, however, and especially to work, he should be able to use private transport or even walk. Perhaps it would not be out of place to observe here that in a few decades' time, private transport in the town centres will most probably be in the shape of petrol-less automatic mini-vehicles. Routes for private traffic should in any case be kept clear for service and shopping trips, and for these purposes there must be parking facilities in the town centres. It will, however, never be possible to provide sufficient parking space or enough approach roads and fortunately this is now becoming common knowledge. This holds

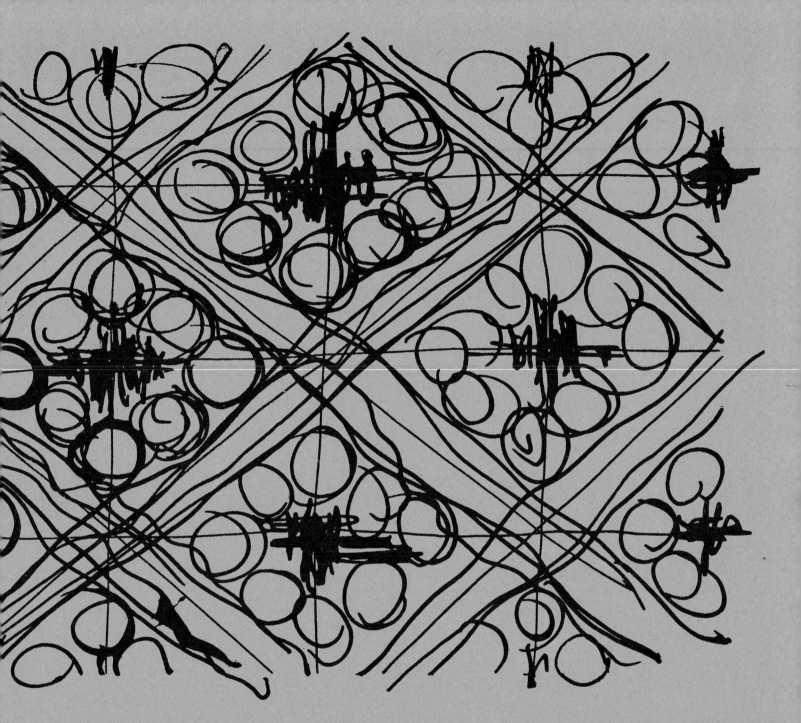

as good for small towns and even large villages as for major cities, although the larger the city the more apparent the effect. Motor-cars mean a great waste of space, whether traffic is moving or at a standstill. Moreover, they swallow vast sums of money in installation costs. Even drive-in supermarkets on the periphery solve neither traffic nor urban problems. In my opinion, it is not enough to calculate what number of cars can be accommodated in the city streets and squares, but necessary to find out the traffic-load any present or future urban fabric will be able to bear before this has come into existence. This means that it is vital to recognize the architectural boundaries within which active urban life is actually possible. Planners will then have to make early provision for appropriate district and town centres. Since we are still short of experience, I feel that local planning authorities will have to work out every possible variant to find out which system would best assure organic development on the right lines. I must, however, take this opportunity to say that I do not only mean the technical variants such as access, population and job densities, etc., which for so many years have been mistaken for town-planning. Creative thinking must come first if our modern technical aids are to be used to full advantage. Over the last century, it has too often taken second place, because the tasks have been so urgent and complex. The computer is no panacea, it is but the means to an end. This end is urban orderliness, and urban order must focus on the individual. He is what matters. And above order there must be a higher aim: the will to build fine cities for men, for only fine cities can be loved. Man has the right to cities that are comprehensible as well as beautiful; cities that will cherish him and where he can feel at home. What we need is order that stimulates. The well-known Berlin engineer Frei Otto says in this connection in an essay: 'stimulating orderliness is the surest remedy against waste.' Such order will always offer means for new and varied functions. These means must be explored in every possible way so that they will be ready for the future.